C000067754

Erosion

Erosion

The Psychopathology of Self-Criticism

GOLAN SHAHAR

OXFORD
UNIVERSITY PRESS

OXFORD
UNIVERSITY PRESS

Oxford University Press is a department of the University of
Oxford. It furthers the University's objective of excellence in research,
scholarship, and education by publishing worldwide.

Oxford   New York

Auckland   Cape Town   Dar es Salaam   Hong Kong   Karachi
Kuala Lumpur   Madrid   Melbourne   Mexico City   Nairobi
New Delhi   Shanghai   Taipei   Toronto

With offices in

Argentina   Austria   Brazil   Chile   Czech Republic   France   Greece
Guatemala   Hungary   Italy   Japan   Poland   Portugal   Singapore
South Korea   Switzerland   Thailand   Turkey   Ukraine   Vietnam

Oxford is a registered trademark of Oxford University Press
in the UK and certain other countries.

Published in the United States of America by
Oxford University Press
198 Madison Avenue, New York, NY 10016

© Oxford University Press 2015

All rights reserved. No part of this publication may be reproduced, stored in
a retrieval system, or transmitted, in any form or by any means, without the prior
permission in writing of Oxford University Press, or as expressly permitted by law,
by license, or under terms agreed with the appropriate reproduction rights organization.
Inquiries concerning reproduction outside the scope of the above should be sent to the
Rights Department, Oxford University Press, at the address above.

You must not circulate this work in any other form
and you must impose this same condition on any acquirer.

Cataloging-in-Publication data is on file at the Library of Congress
ISBN 978-0-19-992936-8

To RLM: SHFANIM!

In memory of Prof. Sidney J. Blatt—a giant in psychology and life

CONTENTS

Foreword   ix
  BY LARRY DAVIDSON
Preface   xi
Acknowledgments   xv

PART I   IN EFFECT

1. Self-criticism: The Culprit and its Modus Operandi   3

2. Eliminating Other Suspects   21

PART II   IN THEORY

3. Theories of Self-Criticism and their Discontents   41

4. **Authenticity and Self-Knowledge (ASK)**   57

5. Development, Families, and Social Systems: The Axis of Criticism **(ACRIM)**   81

PART III   IN PRACTICE

6. Credo: A Philosophy of Treatment   97

7. Specific Interventions and Guidelines   118

8. Final Thoughts and Future Directions   155

Notes   163
Glossary   169
References   171
About the Author and STREALTH   207
Index   209

FOREWORD

In keeping with what some contemporary psychological researchers might find an antiquated commitment to the scientist-practitioner model (it is, after all, over a half-century old), Shahar begins this elegant exploration of self-criticism with a story. I will follow suit. While I think of Shahar's many creative contributions to clinical science often, it is when I am facing real people dealing with real difficulties that I find his theoretical, empirical, and clinical work most useful and generative. Given the shift to checklists, protocols, and experimental manipulations that dominate the current scene, I can think of few researchers in the field of psychopathology whose work is as directly applicable to clinical situations as Shahar's. But back to the story.

I was recently a consultant to a case conference during which a psychiatric resident presented a patient she was having difficulty working with on an acute inpatient unit. The patient's behavior was "inappropriate" and off-putting; he appeared to respond to the female resident as if he were flirting with her in a bar rather than seeking care in a hospital. Hospitalized after a suicide attempt, the patient showed no signs of depression, seemed to have little appreciation for the gravity of his attempt, and was quickly categorized by the group as having a personality disorder. The presenting resident described considerable difficulty in trying to "connect" with the patient, and another resident, in a gesture of solidarity with his colleague, expressed the sentiment that, given what she had described, he was having a really hard time finding anything he could like about this man. Wanting to reinforce this moment of genuine self-disclosure, I thanked this resident for his honesty and suggested that his insight might be a useful clue to what the patient was trying to accomplish. Perhaps, I suggested, the degree to which the resident disliked the patient was only a pale reflection—a hint—of the degree to which the patient disliked himself. Perhaps he was, in this way, offering us an entrée into his experience of self-loathing and we were being challenged to find a way of dealing with his behaviors that would offer him a less destructive alternative. Thank you, Dr. Shahar.

This approach—which, within the context of the case conference, ignited a lively exploration of how a person might find him- or herself in such a situation, is based on the impressive body of theoretical, empirical, and clinical work—Shahar has carried out over the past two decades. I urge readers to refrain from being misled by the gratitude Shahar expresses to his mentors, colleagues, and students: his work is genuinely and profoundly original. His has been a truly creative (he would say inspired), thoughtful (he would say philosophically informed), and ground-breaking line of theorization and research that restores the field's almost forsaken respect for big ideas and the creed's acknowledgment of the basic sense of agency in people experiencing various forms of psychopathology. Not only is this important for understanding the nature and more pernicious, self-perpetuating effects of psychopathology (which make it so challenging to treat) but also and more important—at least to me—it restores to us the sense of compassion that brought us into this field to begin with.

Textbooks on psychopathology—along with many of the professors who teach them—run the risk of drawing caricatures of people experiencing various forms of mental illness, leading students to dislike, if not look down on, the very people they are being trained to help. Elevating the pathology over the person who is experiencing it can leave both the patient and the clinician feeling hopeless and helpless. Informed by an integrative array of perspectives and disciplines, Shahar's work is based on the deep conviction that there is always a suffering person underneath, behind, or alongside the illness. No matter how disabled this person may appear, there also remains at least a nascent sense of agency that can be elicited, encouraged, and engaged in the fight against the illness. In this way, Shahar carries on—and expands upon—a core emphasis of Sidney Blatt's work: The "agentic" nature of human beings. Having had the privilege of sharing Blatt's mentorship with Shahar and scores of others, I am confident that Blatt would be honored by the fact that this is book dedicated to his memory.

In addition to shedding new and extremely useful light on the central role of self-criticism in psychopathology, this book teaches two invaluable lessons. One, it is still possible—albeit arduous—to achieve the Boulder ideal of a scientist-practitioner, or, in Shahar's pointed rephrasing, a "practitioner-researcher." Two, it is possible to conceptualize/theorize, research, describe, educate people about, and treat various forms of psychopathology in a way that pays homage to the totality of the human situation and elicits compassion and empathy for the person experiencing it. For these two lessons, we all—clinical scientists, clinicians, patients, and family members—should be profoundly grateful.

Larry Davidson, PhD
Department of Psychiatry,
Yale University School of Medicine
New Haven, CT

PREFACE

To become a practitioner-researcher—this was my aspiration from the very moment I entered the field of psychology, more than 20 years ago. My desire was to be able to make a living by traveling from clinic to library to laboratory and back. "Psychology," was my thought as early as my first undergraduate year, "offers something very unique to people in distress: poetics of compassion that recognizes the predicaments into which people can fall—sharpened by razor-blade scientific reasoning capable of cutting across individual subtleties in order to decipher the morphology of suffering." Unbeknownst to me at the time, this awareness had been anticipated decades previously and implemented in the Boulder model—formulated in Boulder, Colorado, in 1949 (e.g., Baker & Ludy, 2000; Reisman, 1976). This approach has now become a well-established form of instruction (for an important modification, yet to be fully formulated, see Shoham et al., 2014).

It has taken me these 20-odd years—during which I received training in both Israel and the United States—to appreciate, like so many who have preceded me (e.g., Albee, 2000; Barrom, Shadish, & Montgomery, 1998; Belar, 2000; Davison, 1998; G. Frank, 1984; Mittelstaedt & Tasca, 1988; Nathan, 2000; O'Sullivan & Quevillon, 1992; Parker & Detterman, 1988; Shoham et al., 2014; Steenbarger, Smith, & Budman, 1996; Stricker, 2000; Zachar & Leong, 2000), the formidable challenges this practitioner-researcher model faces. Myriads of clinicians are hostile to science—a circumstance mirrored in the suspicion harbored by psychological scientists toward the "applied." A serious lack of clinical resources, opportunities, and scientific endeavors is aggravated by a singular focus on grants and publications within universities and other research institutes engaged in clinical training. Nor can proficiency in analyzing complex numeric data compensate for a lack of ability to immerse oneself in another person's suffering.

Some years ago, I asked a bright academic clinical psychologist colleague whether he has time to practice. Having made an important contribution to clinical psychological science at a very young age, he had not only dedicated himself as a graduate student to obtaining the best clinical training possible but also displayed great talent for assessment and psychotherapy. "You must be kidding," he responded. "With all the pressure to get grants, what I'm *really* trying to do is avoid getting fired."

As huge as the obstacles lying in the way of integrating clinical science and practice may be, they are not insurmountable. Now, perhaps more than ever before, a constant interface between the two attitudes appears to be developing. Exciting new discoveries in psychology, psychiatry, medical science, and neuroscience have begun to convince some in even the most resistant of circles—psychoanalysis, for example—that empirical findings must constitute a quintessential element of clinical acumen if this is to be beneficially applied (e.g., Fonagy, 2010; see regrettably, however, Blass & Carmeli, 2007; Hoffman, 2009). At the opposite pole, scientific clinical psychology circles are increasingly coming to the sobering realization that brief, manualized treatment for specific, largely noncomorbid disorders is far from providing a cogent answer to contemporary mental-illness maladies. Leading clinical scientists are thus calling for a more nuanced, ideographic approach that takes the individual's historical/narrative background into consideration (e.g., Haynes, Leisen, & Blaine, 1997; Kazdin, 2007).

This book welcomes the breath of fresh air embedded in bridging science and practice and seeks to give it space to spread its wings and expand. Specifically, I seek to convince everyone possible—practitioners, researchers, practitioner-researchers, patients, and other advocates of psychological treatment—that the most sophisticated integration of science and practice feasible is required for the study of self-criticism.

Self-criticism possesses numerous aspects. As a personality trait, it emerges in rigorous empirical research as a—perhaps the most—significant dimension of personal vulnerability to psychopathology and psychosomatics. As an existential stance, self-criticism constitutes one of the ways in which individuals define themselves in their own eyes and in relation to the social and inanimate world. Self-criticism can also be regarded as a social malady—the consequence of a culture redolent with evaluation, both positive and negative (G. Shahar, 2001).

Although much has been written on this subject, much still remains to be developed. I believe that, over the course of these 20 years and with the help of a great many people—mentors, collaborators, and students—I have made some pertinent discoveries concerning the character and function of self-criticism. This book is an attempt to share these with a wider audience.

The findings are presented in three parts. In Part I, entitled "In Effect," self-criticism plays the part of the perpetrator. Identifying it as the "culprit" in CHAPTER 1, herein I review the voluminous research that demonstrates the potentially instigative role self-criticism plays in a host of psychopathologies and adaptation disorders. This chapter also surveys the research, which suggests that self-critical vulnerability is active—that is, that self-critics create the very interpersonal conditions underlying their distress, ultimately consolidating self-critical vulnerability in the process.

In CHAPTER 2, "Eliminating Other Suspects," I examine several psychological traits and constructs that appear to resemble self-criticism: depression, personality disorders, neuroticism, self-esteem/self-efficacy, perfectionism, and rumination. I do so to demonstrate that these constructs are in fact distinct from the real culprit and that the latter's effect holds even when these factors are taken into account. The overall purpose is to convince the reader that self-criticism not only is a formidable dimension of vulnerability but also constitutes a uniquely formidable one.

In Part II, entitled "In Theory," I summarize extant theories of self-criticism and present my own. CHAPTER 3 is dedicated to the presentation of five theories—those proposed by Blatt, Beck, Bandura, Gilbert, and Rogers, respectively. These either explicitly account for self-criticism or touch upon it tangentially (but significantly). I present the key postulates of each and evaluate their strengths and weaknesses, focusing on key gaps between the theories and extant research. In the following two chapters, I describe my own theory of self-criticism. CHAPTER 4 addresses the **ASK** part of my theory. **A**uthenticity represents our unique set of talents, interests, and physiological-affective cognitive proclivities. **S**elf-**K**nowledge pertains to the extent to which we are aware of such authentic tendencies—an awareness contingent upon nurturing and flexible relationships with others. Iatrogenic, criticism-based parent-child exchanges prompted by a combination of parent and child characteristics lead children to become self-critical, thereby creating a wedge between **A** and **SK**. In CHAPTER 5, I describe how vicious interparental cycles increase the child/adolescent's self-criticism, subsequently spilling over to relationships with other family members, peers, teachers and other school personnel. I then draw on Urie Bronfenbrenner's ecological development theory to chart various spheres of social and societal influence that function synergistically to increase self-criticism over the life-span. The Axis of Criticism (**ACRIM**) that develops as a result construes self-criticism as a stable and destructive force in individuals' lives.

Part III, "In Practice," suggests ways in which clinical practitioners might deal with patient self-criticism. In CHAPTER 6, I present a general approach to psychotherapy. Developed over the last two decades, this is deeply inspired by the psychotherapy integration movement—in particular, by perspectives that address the ironic, self-defeating nature of human action. One of the most prominent of these is Wachtel's cyclical psychodynamic theory. CHAPTER 7 adduces specific psychotherapeutic interventions that offer the possibility of helping patients live with and—importantly—outside their self-critical inner voice. This chapter focuses on the treatment of self-critical adolescents and young adults. Finally, in CHAPTER 8, I discuss broad-based conclusions and implications for future theory, research, and practice related to self-criticism.

ACKNOWLEDGMENTS

The discoveries I share in this volume owe much to their communal and cumulative nature. Were it not for the outstanding tutelage of the late Prof. Sidney J. Blatt (Departments of Psychology and Psychiatry, Yale University), I would never have found myself in a position to "tell tales" regarding self-criticism. Prof. Blatt constituted a prominent figure within clinical psychological theory and research for over five decades, crafting exquisite theories relating to the personality development, psychopathology, and psychotherapy within which self-criticism plays such an important role (e.g., Blatt, 2004, 2008). I had the honor and privilege of working as a postdoctoral student under Prof. Blatt between 2000 and 2002—a course of study that changed my life in every possible aspect. Although I ultimately set forth on my own path, I was accompanied not only by his blessing but also by a full awareness of my intellectual and personal debt to him. Prof. David C. Zuroff, Blatt's principal collaborator and a leading personality psychologist in his own right, exercised a similarly decisive impact on my training and thinking on all issues relating to personality, psychopathology, and research methodology.

Prof. Larry Davidson—my second postdoctoral mentor and later my faculty advisor during my tenure as assistant professor of psychiatry at Yale School of Medicine—has served as a profound source of inspiration over the years, teaching me a great deal about continental philosophy, psychosis, and qualitative research. Distinguished Professor Paul Wachtel—one of Blatt's doctoral students and among the founding fathers of the psychotherapy integration movement—has been an incalculable inspiration, in both theoretical and clinical terms. Regarding myself as a follower of his psychotherapeutic approach, I am in great debt to him for inaugurating me into the psychotherapy integration community.

Close colleagues—including Profs. Chris Henrich (Georgia State University), Eva Gilboa-Schechtman (Bar-Ilan University), and Nachshon Meiran and Galia Avidan (Ben-Gurion University)—have also helped me drive my self-criticism research further, introducing me to new theoretical perspectives and research methodologies. Other colleagues—Drs. Benni Feldman, Liat Tikotsky, Chana

Ullman, and Sharon Ziv-Beiman—kindly read the manuscript and made invaluable comments.

My doctoral and postdoctoral students at the Stress, Self, and Health Research Lab (STREALTH) are an ever-present source of inspiration, challenging me—and themselves—to examine the role that the self-concept in general and self-criticism in particular play within myriad health and societal issues. I would like to acknowledge my debt to those who contributed directly to this book. Moran Schiller collaborated in the writing of Chapters 1 and 2. Completing her PhD at STREALTH, Ms. Schiller is also currently midway through her clinical psychology internship. She investigates the complex relationships between stress, psychological symptoms, and the self-concept in emerging adulthood.

Dr. Liat Izhakey contributed to CHAPTER 2. Dr. Itzhakey recently completed her PhD at STREALTH and is about to complete her clinical psychology internship. She is currently pursuing postdoctoral training at the School for Trauma at Tel Aviv University. She studies severe personality pathology and nonsuicidal self-injury.

Dr. Ofer Rahamim and Tal Peleg-Sagy collaborated in the writing of CHAPTER 3. Studying the role of personality pathology in executive control, Dr. Rahamim obtained his PhD from STREALTH and the Executive Control Lab of the Department of Psychology at Ben Gurion University (under the supervision of Prof. Nachshon Meiran). He is currently midway through his clinical psychology internship. Ms. Peleg-Sagy completed her PhD at STREALTH and is midway through her clinical psychology internship. A certified sex therapist, she studies the well-being of female physicians and the psychosocial underpinnings of sexual disorders.

Dr. Michal Tanzer contributed to Chapters 4, 5, and 8. Dr. Tanzer completed her PhD conjointly at STREALTH and the Vision Lab of the Department of Psychology at BGU (under the supervision of Prof. Galia Avidan, PhD [director]). She is currently midway through her clinical psychology internship. She studies the role of personality and psychopathology in face perception from an integrated neuroscientific and psychological perspective.

Guina Cohen collaborated in the writing of Chapters 5 and 6. Ms. Cohen is completing her PhD at STREALTH, also being in the middle of her clinical psychological internship. She studies the links between personal goals and mental representations of self and others in young adulthood.

Dr. Dana Lassri contributed to CHAPTER 6. Dr. Lassri gained her PhD at STREALTH, also having completed her clinical-psychology internship. She studies the short- and long-term implications of childhood maltreatment. A recent recipient of a Haruv Institute postdoctoral fellowship, she currently serves as a postdoctoral fellow in the Department of Psychology at University College London and the Anna Freud Center.

Gal Noyman-Veksler and Dr. Sheera Lerman collaborated in the writing of CHAPTER 7. Ms. Noyman-Veksler is currently midway through her PhD studies at STREALTH also interning in clinical psychology. She studies the role of personal resilience in chronic illness and obstetrics and gynecology. Dr. Lerman completed doctoral and postdoctoral training at STREALTH, also working as a licensed rehabilitation psychologist and chronic pain investigator. A recent recipient of a Rothschild/Yad Hanadic postdoctoral fellowship, she is on her way to a second round of postdoctoral training at Johns Hopkins School of Medicine.

Julia Elad-Strenger contributed to CHAPTER 8. Ms. Elad-Strenger is completing her PhD at STREALTH also serving as a political, vocational, and organizational psychologist. She studies political stress, political radicalization, and the psychological underpinnings of attitudes toward human rights.

I hope that the experience of participating in this book will assist my graduate students in formulating their own theories, developing their own programs of research, and, eventually, writing their own books.

A word regarding my "rivals" is also in order. Many—if not all—scientists secretly wish to develop a new field of research or line of inquiry. This rarely happens, in fact—and is decidedly not true in the case of self-criticism research. Several key research groups are currently making a critical contribution to the study of the dimensions of personality/psychopathology. To name just a few: Prof. Patrick Luyten and his colleagues in Belgium, Prof. Paul Gilbert (United Kingdom), Profs. David Dunkley and Myriam Mongrain (Canada) (inspired by their mentor, David Zuroff), Profs. Murray Enns and Brian Cox (Canada), Prof. Edward Chang (United States), and many others. Although our theoretical interpretations of the findings—and possibly position regarding clinical practice—may differ, our empirical findings concur. I am particularly grateful for their work for two reasons. First, the compatibility between their findings and mine affirms that the overall picture emerging with respect to self-criticism is indeed a solid one. Second, reviewing their theoretical and clinical position is an enriching and vitalizing task, inspiring me to seek to carve out my own particular niche.

This is also the place to thank Liat Keren, my linguistic editor, for her intelligent and meticulous work on preparing the manuscript and Sarah Harrington from Oxford University Press for confidently guiding me through the process of writing my first scientific book.

Last—but far from least—my heartfelt thanks and appreciation go to all my patients, who educated me patiently and provided me with the stamina and wherewithal to write this book.

PART I

IN EFFECT

Self-criticism: The Culprit and its Modus Operandi

He comes with what he considers as an affliction; we examine how he lives.

—Bonime, 1965, p. 48

"Tachles, I'm all fucked up."

I am staring at Rina, trying to figure out whether she is joking.[1] She isn't. A stunningly attractive, poignantly sharp law student, she has come to me for help with panic attacks and recurrent major depression, coupled with what she describes as a chronic, unremitting self-hatred. She is plagued by a gnawing inner voice that insists she is worth nothing, will never amount to anything, and is unlovable. Believing herself to be a lost case, she assumes therapy doesn't have a hope in hell of helping.

At my request, she gives this voice a name—Danny, after one of the men she dated, who treated her unkindly. We have been surviving Danny for over a year now. Although some of the overt symptoms of panic and depression have begun to abate, Danny hangs around, his presence remaining evidence in particular of the "normal" issues Rina and I tackle that haunt many young-adult students—academic and romantic challenges. For my part, I enjoy working with Rina. When not depressed, she sparkles with energy and zest, her nuanced, self-reflecting sense of humor bringing warmth—even a sense of intimacy—to our sessions.

Although Rina craves love, virtually all her romantic encounters precipitately spiral into sex followed by rejection, leaving her feeling exploited, humiliated, and abandoned. One of her most recent dates had seemed to deviate from this pattern, however. Rina met Eran in a debate club and they hit it off immediately. Rina describes him as kind, sensitive, and gentle. He is also smart—a quality she unjustly disowns but cherishes in men. Being careful not to sleep with Eran immediately, as was her customary practice, when she finally did so, it felt natural, forming a satisfying experience all around.

After several weeks of dating, Eran professed his love for her, to which she responded in kind. Things went rapidly downhill after that, Rina asserting that she had suddenly become bored with Eran and picking fights with him—one of which escalated into a breakup she initiated. It was this crisis that landed her in my office declaring that she is "all fucked up."

Virtually irrespective of training and persuasion, we in the psychotherapeutic profession take language very seriously. Not only is it spoken by patients but it also speaks "on their behalf" (Gadamer, 1989). Over the years, attentiveness to our patients' choice of words and the endeavor to link them with their manifest struggles become second nature. As I listen to Rina, trying to work with her to figure out the dynamics of this relationship and its breakup, I am also wondering about her choice of words. She is "all fucked up," she says—overtly signifying her sense of deficiency. As in English, the Hebrew phrase "all fucked up" carries a strong sexual connotation. This suggests that she feels sexually humiliated—perhaps even violated—by the relationship. This is somewhat of an enigma, Eran—unlike the previous one-night stands she has engaged in—appearing to have treated her in anything but a denigrating fashion.

And the *tachles*? This Yiddish word parallels the Hebrew *tachlit,* "purpose," used within Israeli pragmatics—its social/political context—to express a core truth, the "gist" of something. What Rina might be telling me via this self-critical utterance is that she feels fundamentally—in her core sense of self—(sexually) deficient. Perhaps, "bottom line" she feels herself responsible for—that is, having purposefully created—the unhappy ending of this affair. Moreover, the "purpose" suggests that Rina's behavior is goal directed. Is it possible that her terminating the relationship was done in the service of demonstrating deficiency? If so, why?

Tachles, I am ahead of my own self here. This utterance is presented as a way of conveying the essence—the "brass tacks" (*tachles*)—of my thesis: as painful as it may be, self-criticism serves—deliberately, albeit inadvertently—as a way of responding to the social environment. The adverse effect self-critics seek to evoke in their environment is thus the result of a goal-directed action. Here, I am already adducing the argument prior to defining the constituent notions upon which it is based. Figure 1.1 schematizes this thesis, using Rina as a case model.

As gleaned from Figure 1.1, I believe that Rina's self-criticism—construed as an enduring personality trait—was activated by Eran's profession of love complemented by her reciprocal response. The dual declaration prompted a self-critical act—an active generation of life-stress within the context of a close, romantic relationship. This was done purposefully, if unwittingly. The breakup, in turn, induces a depressed mood, which propels Rina to infer her deficiency. Having brought about the breakup by picking a fight with Eran, she is "all fucked up." Self-criticism comes full circle.

"But," I hear a suspicious reader objecting, "you promised to bridge science and practice. Where is the bridge?" Although clinical illustrations are quintessential

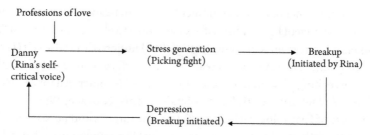

Figure 1.1 Rina's self-critical vicious cycle

to the understanding of clinical phenomena, without empirical support they are empty—if not dangerous. I am confident that the literature contains sufficient empirical support to substantiate the kind of vicious cycle depicted in Figure 1.1—and I will get to it in time. Before I do so, though, let me ask you to indulge me and adopt my personal definition of self-criticism:

Self-criticism is an intense and persistent relationship with the self characterized by (1) an uncompromising demand for high standards in performance and (2) an expression of hostility and derogation toward the self when these high standards are—inevitably—not met.

This definition is predicated, first and foremost, upon the notion that the "self" is not monolithic but consists of numerous interacting aspects. This postulate—prevalent not only in academic psychology (Linville, 1987) but also in clinical theory (e.g., Bromberg, 1996; Lysaker & Hermans, 2007)—can be traced back to the sociological-philosophical writings of Cooley (1902) and Mead (1934), which emanated from the symbolic interaction school of thought. Herein, the various facets of self-concept are presumed to be engaged in dialogue. Self-criticism—an essentially pathological form of dialogue—entails a relationship between at least two, and usually more, self-aspects, the critical agent being an active self-aspect that attacks the other(s).

I emphasize the nature of self-criticism as a form of *relationship with the self* in order to distinguish it from a "spectatorial" approach. The latter is a reflective, evaluative stance that argues that self-criticism is a set of beliefs (cognitions) about the self or an evaluation of the merits and flaws of the self (for a poignant criticism of this approach, see Coyne, 1994). I deem ongoing, structural self-aspects as ways of relating to our outmost "significant other"—our self. Under these circumstances, the passion and investment that characterize relationships in general—and close relationships in particular—manifest themselves in a person's relationship with his or her "self." This is clearly evident in the case of self-criticism and its vicissitudes.

I must distinguish the kind of self-criticism that features in psychopathology research from what I label "wannabe" self-criticism, the latter usually finding positive—or at least, respectable—expression in lay language. The latter form,

I argue, pertains either to transient moments of "self-bashing"—not taken very seriously even by the agent him- or herself—or attempts to elicit reassurance or "fish for compliments," consistent with Winnicott's (1965) notion of the false self (*Utterance:* "I suck." *Response:* "No way! You're great!"). It also surfaces in research about the role reassurance seeking plays in depression (Joiner, 1994; Joiner, Alfano, & Metalsky, 1992; Joiner & Metalsky, 2001; Joiner, Metalsky, Katz, & Beach, 1999).

In the case of (pathological) self-criticism, the intense and persistent relationship of agents with their self is characterized by (1) an uncompromising demand for high standards in performance and (2) an expression of hostility and derogation toward the self when these are inevitably not met. The first characteristic pertains to the agent's tendency to constantly raise the bar and never be satisfied with his or her accomplishments. Embedded in this tendency is a punitive stance toward the self that raises its voice in the wake of the self's invariable failure.

The importance of the joint action of the twin characteristics cannot be overemphasized. The first is not necessarily pathological—provided that it does not call upon the collaboration of the second. An attitude that says, "I constantly strive to improve, but when it doesn't work out I remind myself that I did my best" is essentially a benevolent attitude. (In CHAPTER 2, I return to the issue of personal strivings and self-criticism within the context of research into perfectionism. In CHAPTER 3, I invoke Paul Gilbert's theory of self-criticism, which links self-criticism with a lack of self-compassion). Once a self-castigating stance is superimposed upon the constant raising of the bar, I have laid an ambush for myself. Having pushed myself into failure, I slam myself for falling short.

"My" self-criticism definition is faithfully captured by standard research questionnaires designed to measure this psychological construct. The one most extensively used is the Depressive Experiences Questionnaire (DEQ; Blatt, D'Afflitti, & Quinlan, 1976). Tapping personality vulnerability to unipolar depression, the DEQ contains a pool of items describing experiences the symptoms frequently reported by depressed individuals. The 66 items selected were factor analyzed, leading to a solution consistent with Blatt's now seminal theory of personality development and psychopathology (e.g., Blatt, 2004, 2008; Luyten & Blatt, 2013). The first factor pertains to strong dependency needs, fear of object loss, and vulnerability to anaclitic depression. This is traditionally labeled "dependency." The second factor targets vulnerability to introjective—or self-critical—depression, consisting of items reflecting overriding guilt, chronic low self-worth, and active self-bashing. This is labeled "self-criticism." A third—rather unexpected—factor assessed self-confidence and inner strength, being entitled "efficacy."[2]

The Stress, Self, and Health Research Lab and I identified six DEQ items that veraciously encapsulate the essence of the self-criticism concept (e.g., "I often find that I do not live up to my standards or ideals"; "I tend to not be content with what I have"; "I find it hard to accept my weaknesses"; see Appendix A in

Rudich, Lerman, Wexler, Gurevitch, & G. Shahar, 2008). In numerous publications, we have demonstrated that a composite score based on these six items yields effects equal in magnitude to the entire 66-item scale. Other measures of self-criticism—such as the Dysfunctional Attitudes Scale (DAS; Weissman & Beck, 1978) and the Personal Style Inventory (PSI; Robins et al., 1994)—encompass the same elements, although arguably in a somewhat less precise manner (see Blatt, 2004; Dunkley, Zuroff, & Blankstein, 2003; G. Shahar, 2001, 2006a; and CHAPTER 6). Table 1.1 presents the six DEQ items we found to give the same effects as the full questionnaire.

Having defined self-criticism and explicated the way in which I believe it should be measured, I will now adduce the empirical evidence supporting its role in psychopathology. The best approach in this respect derives from an epidemiology/public health approach. This method is particularly useful due to its broad-based, statistically-robust features and informative constitution regarding two burning

Table 1.1 **The Depressive Experiences Questionnaire Self-Criticism Six-Item Scale (DEQ-SC6)**

Listed in the table are a number of statements concerning personal characteristics and traits. Read each item and decide whether you agree or disagree and to what extent. If you strongly agree, circle 7; if you strongly disagree, circle 1. Circle the midpoint (4) if you are neutral or undecided.

	Strongly Disagree						*Strongly Agree*
I often find that I don't live up to my own standards or ideals. (Item #7 in the original DEQ)	1	2	3	4	5	6	7
There is a considerable gap between how I am now and how I would like to be. (Item #13 in the original DEQ)	1	2	3	4	5	6	7
I tend not to be content with what I have. (Item #17 in the original DEQ)	1	2	3	4	5	6	7
I find it hard to accept my weaknesses. (Item #53 in the original DEQ)	1	2	3	4	5	6	7
I tend to be very self-critical. (Item #64 in the original DEQ)	1	2	3	4	5	6	7
I often compare myself with standards or goals. (Item #66 in the original DEQ)	1	2	3	4	5	6	7

questions: (1) Where does suffering concentrate? and (2) What are its potential causes?

According to a very influential recent review (Kazdin & Blase, 2011), the lifetime prevalence of mental disorder—broadly defined—as assessed by various estimates ranges between 12% and 47.4%. These are staggering numbers that carry a horrific price tag. Substance use alone costs the world $500 billion. Mental illness kills: suicidality—its most serious outcome—constitutes the third leading cause of death among the young (ages 15 to 24; Centers for Disease Control and Prevention, National Center for Injury Prevention and Control, 2010; Goldsmith, Pellmar, Kleinman, & Bunny, 2002). To further complicate matters, mental ailments are virtually inseparable from physical illness. This is true even if we maintain that no physical/biological aspects underpin mental illness—a consensually untenable assumption. This circumstance reflects the fact that the rate of common mental disorders—such as depression and anxiety—is extremely high among the physically ill, including patients in primary care (Coyne, Thompson, Klingman, & Nease, 2000) and the chronically ill (G. Shahar, Lassri, & Luyten, 2014).

This latter point deserves elaboration. Chronic illnesses constitute a growing proportion of the total global disease burden (Welch, Czerwinski, Ghimire, & Bertsimas, 2009). Over the past 50 years, they have steadily overtaken acute medical conditions as the primary cause of disability and use of health services in the United States, affecting 45% of the population and accounting for 78% of health expenditure (Anderson & Horvath, 2004; Holman & Lorig, 2004). Chronic illness is predicted to become ever more prevalent as populations age across developed countries and effective treatment is found for acute conditions. It is estimated that by 2020, chronic illness will account for 60% of the global disease burden (Welch et al., 2009). Not surprisingly, unipolar depression lies high on the chronic illness chart, the documented prevalence ranging between 9.3% and 23% (Moussavi et al., 2007).

Mental disorder forming a formidable foe, its accurate diagnosis constitutes a redoubtable challenge. Although this issue lies beyond the scope of these pages, one of the most pressing questions we face is: what causes it? This is, of course, the $64 million question—but one that science must answer. In my opinion, it has succeeded—at least in part—to date. Genetics indubitably plays an important role in the onset and course of most—if not all—mental disorders (e.g., Caspi et al., 2003). (I will discuss genetics and self-criticism in CHAPTER 4.) Compelling evidence also implicates external stress—acute or chronic, traumatic, major or relatively minor—in the onset and maintenance of mental disorder (Brown & Harris, 1978, 1989; Monroe & Reid, 2009). Although at times regarded with suspicion (e.g., Coyne & Whiffen, 1995), personality is also now increasingly being recognized as a putative cause of physical and mental health and illness (e.g., Jokela et al., 2013; B. W. Roberts, Kuncel, Shiner, Caspi, & Goldberg, 2007) and of depression in particular (Zuroff, Mongrain, & Santor, 2004a, 2004b).

I hope that Table 1.2 will convince you to consider the causal role of self-criticism in mental disorders—broadly defined—with the seriousness it deserves. The table is illustrative rather than exhaustive—not surprising in light of the explosion of self-criticism research. Together with additional research, the studies indicate that self-criticism predicts elevated unipolar depression (e.g., Priel & G. Shahar, 2000), hypomanic symptoms (Eisner, Johnson, & Carver, 2008), suicidality (R. O'Connor & Noyce, 2008), general anxiety (G. Shahar & Priel, 2003), social anxiety (G. Shahar & Gilboa-Shechtman, 2007), eating disorder symptoms (Fennig et al., 2008), substance abuse (Blatt, 1991), violent behavior (Leadbeater, Kuperminc, Blatt, & Herzog, 1999), chronic pain symptoms (Lerman, Rudich, Brill, & G. Shahar, under review), and poor academic achievement (G. Shahar, Henrich et al., 2006).

Table 1.2 **The Role of Self-Criticism in Mental Disorders, Clinical Problems, and Developmental Difficulties**

Bipolar Spectrum	*Suicidality*	*Depression*
Francis-Raniere, Alloy, and Abramson (2006)	Fazaa and Page (2003); R. O'Connor and Noyce (2008)	Blatt (1995, 1998, 2004); Blatt and Zuroff (1992); G. Shahar (2001, 2006a); Priel and G. Shahar (2000)
Psychosomatics	*Eating Disorders*	*Anxiety*
Lerman, G. Shahar, and Rudich (2012; pain); Lerman, Rudich, Brill, and G. Shahar (under review; pain); Luyten et al. (2011)	Dunkley and Grilo (2007; binge eating disorder); Fennig et al. (2008; anorexia nervosa)	Cox, Flett, and Stein (2004; social anxiety); Cox, MacPherson, Enns, and McWilliams (2004; PTSD); G. Shahar and Gilboa-Shechtman (2007; social anxiety)
Developmental/Interpersonal Problems	*Violence*	*Substance Use*
Zuroff and Duncan (1999); Mongrain, Vettese, Shuster, and Kendal (1998); Bareket-Bojmel and G. Shahar (2011); Lassri and G. Shahar (2012); G. Shahar, Henrich, Winokur, Blatt, Kuperminc, & Leadbeatter (2006; academic)	G. Shahar and Henrich (in preparation)	Blatt (1991; heroin); G. Shahar, Bar-Hamburger, and Meyer (in preparation; binge drinking)

In saying "self-criticism predicts," we must be careful to clarify what we mean. As we (hopefully) learned in undergraduate school, "correlation" is not equivalent to "causation" (see Kenny, 1979; Pearl, 2000). If a putative study rests upon a cross-sectional design in which all the variables—for example, self-criticism and depression—are assessed at the same time, all this gives us is a correlation between them. The correlation might describe a causal effect of psychopathology (e.g., depression) on self-criticism—in which case, self-criticism is a consequence of mental disorder. Although this might be a very interesting consequence, it is no more than that. It cannot justify any concerted effort toward assessing, treating, or preventing self-criticism.

"Causality" being an abstract notion or hypothetical construct (Pearl, 2000), scientists use elimination to approximate it. In other words, we hypothesize a cause for Y—conventionally labeled X. We then establish an X–Y association without which X cannot cause Y. Next, we have to eliminate the possibility that Y causes X. Logicians call this the *modus tollens* procedure. If Y, then X. If there is no X in the presence of Y, Y cannot be the cause.

One way to eliminate the possibility that depression causes self-criticism would be to create depression—that is, manipulate it in the laboratory—and then observe whether our participants' self-criticism manifested itself on a greater level. We cannot do this, of course, either conceptually or ethically—ethically, because it is immoral to subject participants to such a painful condition and conceptually because even if we were to "compromise" in inducing a depressed mood in the laboratory (asking the participants to recall a time when they were depressed or give them sad music to listen to), whether or not this was particularly pronounced in self-critics is really inconsequential. The difference between recalling a depressed time or listening to sad music and experiencing real, clinical depression is that between night and day. This discrepancy questions the ecological validity of laboratory experiments in which psychopathology is induced.

This is probably the reason that the science of vulnerability in general and personality vulnerability in particular is seldom—or at least not primarily—conducted within the laboratory. The field of personality vulnerability to psychopathology is characterized by ecological/ethological research methods similar to those typical of such disciplines as epidemiology and economics. Put simply, causality is modeled by assessing people in their natural environment, preferably over time (Davis, 1985).[3]

If we assess participants for self-criticism via the six items presented in Table 1.1, for example, and ascertain that they are not suffering from depression at that point in time, we can then follow up on them for, say, 6 months and diagnose their depression at the second assessment period. If elevated levels of self-criticism during the first period (Time 1) predict an increased likelihood of initially nondepressed participants becoming depressed, we have made progress toward establishing causal inference because we can rule out the possibility that their depression at the subsequent measurement (Time 2) caused their initial self-criticism. (Patience: I will get to the issue of third factors—or confounds—in short order.)

"Well," a reader in the back row may object, "this assumes that depression is categorical—an all-or-nothing phenomenon. Maybe it is; maybe it isn't. The jury is still out on that issue. But if depression is not categorical—if it is continuous, namely, a matter of degree—your findings are highly biased toward extreme cases of depression."

True. So let's assume that depression is a continuous variable. We will replace the former participants with new ones. At Time 1, we will administer a measure of self-criticism and a standard measure of depressive symptoms—say, the Beck Depression Inventory II (BDI-II; Beck, Steer, & Brown, 1996) or the Center for Epidemiological Studies Depression Scale (CESD; Radloff, 1977). Six months later, we will administer the BDI-II or CESD again to the same participants. At this point, we can examine the extent to which self-criticism at Time 1 predicts a change in continuous depression during the Time 1–Time 2 period. If it does, then—like the previous hypothetical study—we have taken a step forward by ruling out the possibility that this change in depression caused self-criticism, the self-criticism having been established as *preceding* the depression. This constitutes the logic of causal order in naturalistic designs as formulated by sociologist and methodologist James Davis (1985).

Do such studies in fact exist? They do, indeed—in abundance. For example, Leadbeater et al. (1999) found that self-criticism predicted an increase in externalizing symptoms—delinquency, aggression, and substance abuse—among early-adolescent boys over a 1-year follow-up. My doctoral research, conducted on mid/late-adolescent Israeli boys and girls, yielded similar results: Self-criticism assessed during the first week of school predicted an increase in emotional distress (i.e., depression and anxiety) over a 4-month interval (G. Shahar & Priel, 2003; see also Priel & G. Shahar, 2000). Dunkley, Sanislow, Grilo, and McGlashan (2009) found that in a clinical sample composed of participants with diverse diagnoses—eating, anxiety, substance abuse, and personality disorders—self-criticism predicted an increase in depressive symptoms over a 4-year interval. R. O'Connor and Noyce (2008) reported that among adult students and participants from the general population, self-criticism predicted an increase in suicidal ideation over a 3-month period—an effect mediated by ruminative thinking (see also CHAPTER 2). Finally, in perhaps the most sophisticated study conducted to date, Hawley, Moon-Ho, Zuroff, and Blatt (2006) made use of a state-of-science statistical procedure designed to establish the direction of the relationship between two or more variables—a procedure known as the latent difference scores method (currently labeled latent change scores [Ferrer & McArdle, 2010]). Analyzing data from the Treatment for Depression Collaborative Research Program (TDCRP) sponsored by the National Institute of Mental Health (NIMH), Hawley et al. (2006) demonstrated that across four treatments for depression, self-criticism predicted an increase in depression but not vice versa. (I will discuss the NIMH TDCRP project at length later.)

"But," it might be argued, "such a description of research findings based on a *main effect* approach is far too simplistic. It ignores the fact that one's vulnerability only comes to the fore in adverse situations." Accurate as both of these statements may be, research into the role of depressive vulnerability in general—and self-criticism in particular—has nonetheless been at the forefront of what is known as the "stress-diathesis model." This construes psychopathology as an outcome of life-stress superimposed on internal vulnerability (e.g., Monroe & Simons, 1991).

What is "internal vulnerability"? A relatively recent convergence of psychodynamic and cognitive theories of depression has drawn attention to two personality configurations that serve as dimensions of depressive vulnerability—the anaclitic-dependent/sociotropic and the introjective-self-critical/autonomous (Blatt, 2004; Blatt, G. Shahar, & Zuroff, 2001; Blatt & Zuroff, 1992). According to Blatt—the pioneer of this conceptualization (e.g., Blatt, 1974, 1995; Blatt & Shichman, 1983)—the anaclitic dimension is predicated upon the need to secure close and nurturing interpersonal relationships. When it spirals into extremity (see CHAPTER 3), this dimension manifests itself in pathological dependency. The introjective dimension reflects the need to establish a consolidated, positive, differentiated yet integrated self-identity. In its extreme form, this takes the form of an overemphasis on achievement and success, excessive guilt, and—most pivotally—self-criticism.

Both cognitive and psychodynamic theories of depressive vulnerability acknowledge that the link between vulnerability and depression is not direct but activated—or "moderated" in methodological terminology—by specific, personality-congruent life-events. According to the congruency hypothesis (Hammen, Marks, Mayol, & DeMayo, 1985; Zuroff & Mongrain, 1987), individuals with extreme dependency tendencies experience depressive symptoms only when their pivotal concerns (e.g., maintaining close and protective interpersonal relations) are threatened by stressful interpersonal events (e.g., rejection, confrontation, abandonment, or loss). Those with extremely high self-criticism or autonomy levels experience depressive symptoms only when their principal concerns (e.g., achievement) are threatened by failure-related events (e.g., exam failure or being laid off). The congruency hypothesis is presented in Figure 1.2.

At first glance, the congruency hypothesis is very robust. Not only is it clear and empirically testable but it also lends itself to straightforward clinical applications. The latter qualities very likely account for the considerable empirical research it has yielded (for a review, see Blatt & Zuroff, 1992; Coyne & Whiffen, 1995; Nietzel & Harris, 1990; Robins, 1995). The results of these studies, however, have largely been disappointing. Although most have demonstrated the

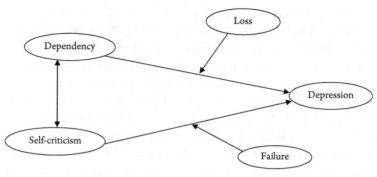

Figure 1.2 Congruency hypothesis

specific vulnerability of dependent individuals to interpersonal events (e.g., Priel & G. Shahar, 2000; G. Shahar, Joiner, Zuroff, & Blatt, 2004), an equivalently specific vulnerability to failure-related stress *but not interpersonal stress* has rarely been indicated among self-critical individuals (for reviews, see Blatt & Zuroff, 1992; Coyne & Whiffen, 1995). Findings have in fact highlighted an interaction of self-criticism with both interpersonal and achievement-related stress. This suggests, once again, that the vulnerability implicated in this personality construct is general and broad rather than specific and narrow in scope.

In addition to this empirical quagmire, the congruency hypothesis also suffers from two major conceptual problems. First, I often think of it as pertaining to personality *resilience* rather than vulnerability. We all encounter an endless flow of life-events, daily and over the course of our lives. If a person is only vulnerable to a specific set of events—say Set A—he or she is invulnerable to all other events (e.g., Sets B, C, D, etc.). Put differently, such a person may be said to be invulnerable to (resilient in the face of) many sets of events. Second, it assumes that—whether "dependent" or "self-critical"—individuals are largely passive in relation to life-events, reacting to rather than generating them. The latter problem may well have been partly responsible for leading researchers to seek an alternative view of personality vulnerability to depression and related psychopathology.

As far as I am aware, the first person to suggest that both dependency/sociotropy and self-criticism/autonomy generate rather than react to life-stress was David Zuroff (1992). His postulate is highly consistent with a group of novel theoretical perspectives in behavioral science that may be cautiously classified under the label "action theory" (G. Shahar, 2006a). These theories share a common emphasis on the impact individuals exert on their social environment—epitomized in Bandura's well-known principle of reciprocal determinism (Bandura, 1978; see CHAPTER 3). In line with this principle—which states that person and context co-create one another—developmental psychologists repeatedly indicate that children and adolescents impact their development by shaping their social context (Brandstädter, 1998; Lerner, 1982).

A similar theme has been adduced within social psychology. Prominent investigators such as Buss (1987) and Swann (1983, 1990; Swann & Read, 1981; Swann, Rentfrow, & Guinn, 2003) have demonstrated that individuals actively elicit responses from others, this in turn shaping their own personality. In psychopathology research, key theorists and investigators such as Coyne (1976), Depue and Monroe (1986), Hammen (1991, 2006), Joiner (1994, 2000; Joiner et al., 1999; Pettit & Joiner, 2006), and others have shown that individuals—particularly depressed patients or people vulnerable to depression—actively generate interpersonal circumstances that subsequently maintain their depressive state.

Interestingly, these conceptualizations and findings were developed, discussed, and applied to dissociation from a highly compatible theory produced within the field of psychotherapy integration—Wachtel's cyclical psychodynamic model (P. L. Wachtel, 1977, 1994, 1997). Emerging from a joint interpersonal psychoanalytic and behavioral perspective, this theory describes a vicious cycle whereby individuals externalize their (unconscious) conflicts in the interpersonal arena, thereby bringing about the very circumstances they dread. (I will elaborate on cyclical psychodynamics and my own version of it in CHAPTER 6.)

These ideas have begun to permeate the field of personality vulnerability to depression. Researchers around the world—most prominently in Canada, Israel, and Belgium—are devoting their efforts to exploring the effect of dependency and self-criticism upon the social environment. The pattern that has emerged from this program of research is as alarming as it is straightforward. Self-criticism repeatedly generates negative life-events and conflict within close relationships. It also "degenerates" (i.e., fails to generate) protective interpersonal factors, such as social support (Dunkley, Sanislow et al., 2006; Mongrain, 1998; Priel & G. Shahar, 2000) and positive life-events (G. Shahar & Priel, 2003). This, in turn, aggravates emotional distress, a pattern summarized in Figure 1.3.

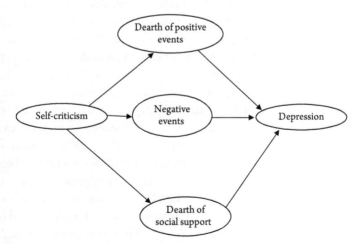

Figure 1.3 Impact of self-criticism upon the social environment

But what about dependency? Action theory-informed research has also revealed the presence of a complex pattern regarding this trait. Dependency appears to generate both risk factors, such as negative life-events, and protective factors, such as positive life-events and social support (Mongrain, 1998; Priel & G. Shahar, 2000; G. Shahar, 2008; G. Shahar & Priel, 2003). Coupled with the model that indicates that dependency only interacts with loss-related events to predict psychopathology, these studies suggest that dependency entails both risk and resilience. These findings have led Bornstein (1998a) and myself (G. Shahar, 2001, 2008; G. Shahar, Elad-Strenger, & Henrich, 2012; G. Shahar & Priel, 2003) to revisit the traditional assumption (Abraham, 1924) that dependency is "infantile" and pathological.

Particularly dramatic evidence for the active nature of self-critical vulnerability has emerged from analyses conducted by Blatt, Zuroff and colleagues, in whose productive partnership I was also subsequently privileged to participate. These analyses rested on data collected as part of the NIMH-sponsored TDCRP (Elkin, 1994). The TDCRP was a randomized clinical trial in which three active treatments for major depression were compared—cognitive-behavioral therapy, interpersonal therapy, and treatment with imipramine (a tricyclic antidepressant) plus clinical management and administration of an inactive placebo plus clinical management. Although the initial analyses of the TDCRP data indicated very few outcome differences among the three active treatment groups (Elkin, 1994), Blatt, Quinlan, Pilkonis, and Shea (1995) found a robust effect of personality and outcome. Participants with elevated pretreatment self-criticism (labeled by the authors as "perfectionism") were less likely to exhibit symptomatic improvement at termination than their less self-critical counterparts. (For reviews of this outstanding research program, see Blatt, 2004; Blatt & Zuroff, 2005.) As noted earlier, in subsequent analyses (Hawley et al., 2006), this group later conclusively established that self-criticism predicted depression—but not vice versa—in the TDCRP data.

Blatt, Zuroff, and their colleagues then set out to identify the mechanisms via which pretreatment personality exerts an adverse effect on outcome. Their initial findings (Zuroff et al., 2000) suggested that the adverse effect of self-criticism was partially accounted for—"mediated" in methodological terms—by patients' difficulty in contributing constructively to the therapeutic alliance. Even after taking the therapeutic alliance into account, however, a residual effect of self-criticism on outcome remained unaccounted for.

Applying the action theory approach that had proved so successful in elucidating the active nature of self-critical vulnerability, our team set out to test an action model of the iatrogenic effect of self-criticism on treatment outcome. Our reasoning was that the "missing link" in this effect is patients' relationships with other people in their lives. Irrespective of treatment, other studies had already demonstrated the effect of social relationships outside of treatment on the outcome of pharmacological and psychotherapeutic treatment of depression (Moos, 1990; Vallejo, Gasto, Catalan, Bulbena, & Menchon, 1991). As Zlotnick, Shea, Pilkonis, Elkin, and Ryan (1996) demonstrated, for example, social relations—measured by both the number of relationship domains rated by the patients as satisfying and the number of people with whom the patient had close and satisfying relations (i.e., the number of confidants)—were related to low depressive symptoms during the TDCRP follow-up period.

Our study (G. Shahar, Blatt, Zuroff, Krupnick, & Sotsky, 2004) did, in fact, indicate that, in addition to its adverse effect on the therapeutic alliance, self-criticism also negatively affects social relationships outside treatment. Specifically, we showed that pretreatment self-criticism predicted a deterioration in satisfaction with social relationships over the course of treatment—this in turn predicting symptom aggravation. When this indirect effect of self-criticism on outcome via the social context was added to the previously demonstrated effect of self-criticism on the therapeutic alliance (Zuroff et al., 2000), the two interpersonal mechanisms fully accounted for the adverse effect of pretreatment self-criticism on treatment outcome. In other words, this research reveals that self-critical depressed patients actively sabotage their recovery by impeding social relations *both inside and outside treatment.*

Self-criticism not only derails treatment of depression but also appears to directly impact chronic physical pain. A complex research collaboration between my lab and the specialty pain clinics of Soroka General Hospital in Beersheba, Israel, has led to a series of studies addressing the links between self-criticism, sensory and affective pain (sensory pain referring to the actual pain sensation, affective pain to the cognitive-affective evaluation of pain—e.g., pain as attacking, punishing, etc.), emotional distress (depression and anxiety), and other pain-related cognitive and interpersonal variables. One of our focuses lay on the patient-physician relationship. While this is paramount for virtually all medical conditions, it is especially important in the diagnosis and treatment of chronic pain. Chronic pain nearly always being vague, frequently evading pinpointing to anatomical findings, patients frequently feel ashamed of experiencing it ("Is it all in my head?"). Chronic-pain patients thus need their doctors to be particularly kind, patient, sensitive, and informative. In fact, the success of the medical treatment is at risk if their doctors do not exhibit these qualities (Diesfeld, 2008; Frantsve & Kerns, 2007).

An important element of the patient-physician relationship is the optimism/pessimism with which physicians regard their patients' prognosis (Wylie, Hungin, & Neely, 2002). Our group (Rudich et al., 2008) approached chronic pain patients in the waiting room before their first visit to a specialty pain clinic and asked them to fill out a full range of self-report measures relating to pain level, depression, self-criticism, and other variables. After they had met with their designated pain physician—who was not privy to their responses to the questionnaires administered before their appointment—we asked the physician to rate the percentage likelihood of their prognosis, in terms of both pain and functioning, on a 0 to 100 scale. The two ratings being very strongly correlated ($r = .80$), they were combined into a single measure. We then predicted the physicians' prognosis from the patients' questionnaires and chart information. The only statistically significant predictor was self-criticism: elevated levels of patient self-criticism predicted a more pessimistic physician prognosis. In a follow-up study on a subsample of these patients (Rudich, Lerman, Gurevich, & G. Shahar, 2010), we found that pessimistic prognosis in fact prospectively predicted an increase in patient depression and the affective component of pain.

Whether this constitutes a self-fulfilling prophecy—namely, the care received by self-critical patients is suboptimal—or the physician's psychological acumen enables him or her to identify patients who will not improve without necessarily knowing that these are self-critical patients remains an unknown. Coupled with our findings and those from studies in Belgium evincing that self-criticism prospectively predicts an increase in sensory and affective pain, pain-related depression, and chronic fatigue symptoms (Kempe et al., 2011; Lerman, G. Shahar, & Rudich, 2012; Lerman et al., under review; Luyten et al., 2011), these findings nonetheless indicate, yet again, that self-criticism constitutes a serious vulnerability factor, the mechanism underlying this vulnerability being interpersonal.

How exactly do self-critical individuals create a pathogenic social environment? Independent research by David Dunkley in Canada and my group in the United States and Israel has proposed two potential scenarios—maladaptive coping and impaired motivation. This process is summarized in Figure 1.4.

In a series of publications, Dunkley and colleagues have shown that "self-critical perfectionism"—a complex construct composed of both self-criticism (as measured by Blatt's DEQ) and perfectionism (measured by other scales)—predicts various forms of "maladaptive coping strategies." The latter include emotionally venting without approaching the problem and trying to solve it. Maladaptive coping strategies predict "hassles" or negative daily events (Dunkley & Blankstein, 2000; Dunkley et al., 2003). Research by both Dunkley and colleagues (e.g., Dunkley &

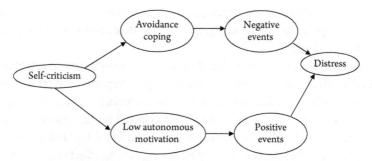

Figure 1.4 Process whereby self-critics create a pathogenic social environment

Kyparissis, 2008; Dunkley, Zuroff, & Blankstein, 2006) and myself (G. Shahar, 2006b) however, suggests that self-critical perfectionism is actually self-criticism. I will elaborate on this fact in CHAPTER 2.

G. Shahar, Henrich, Blatt, Ryan, and Little (2003) investigated 900 American adolescents to assess their personality traits, including self-criticism, level of depression, experiences of negative and positive life-events, and motivational style. The latter formed the focal variable, being constructed according to Deci and Ryan's self-determination theory (SDT; Deci & Ryan, 1985). SDT divides motivation into two broad categories—autonomous and controlled. Autonomous (sometimes also known as "intrinsic") motivations emanate from one's "true self," thus representing authentic wishes and goals. Controlled motivations stem from the pressure—external or internalized—brought to bear by other people. Extensive research has revealed that autonomous motivations are highly predictive of well-being. Controlled motivations appear to be more complex, showing no clear-cut associations with either well-being or psychopathology.

In this study, G. Shahar, Henrich, and their colleagues assessed American adolescents' autonomous and controlled motivations by asking the participants to state the reason behind their behavior in both the academic and social domains. Items assessing autonomous motivations pertain to doing things because adolescents want to—because they bring them pleasure. Items assessing controlled motivations relate to things done because they are important or because they are expected by others. The findings indicate that self-criticism predicted low levels of autonomous motivation, in turn predicting low levels of positive life-events. This effect of self-criticism on autonomous motivation was replicated in two longitudinal studies of young Israeli adults (G. Shahar, Kalnitzki, Shulman, & Blatt, 2006; Shulman, Kalnitzki, & G. Shahar, 2009).

The pattern that emerges from these studies suggests that self-critics tend not to experience positive events because they shy away from doing things they really want to do. In a variation of Immanuel Kant's categorical imperative, this idea states: "If I am a self-critic and I feel like doing something, I won't do it." G. Shahar, Henrich, and their colleagues locate this pattern within what they define as the "absence principle" in developmental psychopathology. This states that the *absence* of protective processes (e.g., autonomous motivation leading to experience of positive life-events) may be more deleterious than the *presence* of risk-related processes.

If you recall the emphasis I placed earlier on research having established the prospective effect that self-criticism exerts on psychopathology, let me now confuse you slightly—though not for long—by adducing studies attesting to the *inverse* relationship. This research has been inspired by the scarring hypothesis formulated by Lewinsohn, Steinmetz, Larson, and Franklin (1981). These investigators proposed that depression may leave long-lasting effects on the personality self-concept—similar to the scarring effect of a wound on skin tissue. Despite its

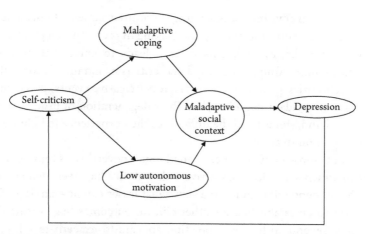

Figure 1.5 The self-critical cascade

intriguing nature and clinical appeal, empirical support for the scarring hypothesis has been highly inconsistent (for reviews, see G. Shahar & Henrich, 2010; Sowislo & Orth, 2013). Subsequent research has shown, however, that when research focuses on participants' self-representations as the putative outcome of depression, scarring effects become evident. Thus, for example, G. Shahar, Blatt, Zuroff, Kuperminc, and Leadbeater (2004) found a reciprocal longitudinal relation between self-criticism and depressive symptoms in early-adolescent girls, but not boys. Specifically, baseline levels of self-criticism in female participants predicted an increase in depressive symptoms over a 1-year period, baseline levels of depressive symptoms predicting an increase in self-criticism over the same time period. These findings have recently been replicated in a sample of Israeli adolescents followed up over 4 years (G. Shahar & Henrich, 2013), as well as in Israeli undergraduates in the third decade of their lives (Schiller, Hammen, & G. Shahar, in preparation).

As shown in Figure 1.5, when these effects of depression on self-criticism are added to the findings reviewed previously, a *self-critical cascade* emerges: self-critical individuals actively create the interpersonal conditions—negative events, lack of positive events, and an absence of social support—that lead to depression. This, in turn, increases levels of self-criticism, thereby raising depressive risk.

Chapter Summary

Rina's episodic romantic breakup—generated by her self-criticism that reinforced her vulnerability—is explained by the empirical research and exemplifies my pivotal argument, that self-critical vulnerability operates as a cascade or vicious cycle. Haunted by harsh and punitive inner dialogues, individuals adversely impact their social environments, leading these environments to become replete with risks (e.g., negative life-events) and lacking in protective factors (e.g., social support, positive life-events). This in turn leads to emotional distress (e.g., depression), culminating in increased self-criticism. Extant research also suggests that self-critics' generation of risk factors (negative events) is accounted for by their use of avoidant coping styles. Their degeneration of protective factors, on the other hand, stems from the difficulties they experience in being governed by autonomous motivation.

Important "loose ends" or unexamined issues nevertheless remain. First, the context in which self-criticism's active vulnerability has been demonstrated is largely that of depression and—to a somewhat lesser extent—anxiety. This pattern has yet to be established for other clinical outcomes (e.g., eating disorder symptoms). Second, although depression appears to exacerbate self-criticism, these findings pertain primarily to adolescents. It is thus possible that the full cascade described in Figure 1.5 is principally valid for adolescents. When individuals reach adulthood, self-criticism may induce depression—via interpersonal mechanisms—but scarring might no longer be operative (but see Schiller, Hammen, & G. Shahar, in preparation). We are dependent upon further research to determine whether or not this is the case.

What we do know is that an abundance of empirical evidence—even more dramatic evidence being presented in the following chapter—already exists showing that self-criticism is extremely detrimental, devastating the interpersonal environment of self-critical individuals on a virtually daily basis. Consistent with the words of Bonime cited at the beginning of the chapter, self-criticism thus appears to be an affliction manifested as a way of life.

2

Eliminating Other Suspects

How often have I said to you that when you have eliminated the impossible, whatever remains, however improbable, must be the truth?
—Sherlock Holmes in Conan-Doyle, 1890, p. 111

In the previous chapter, I claimed that self-criticism constitutes a serious dimension of vulnerability to various forms of psychopathology. This argument is complemented by the contention that the vulnerability associated with self-criticism is active—that is, it creates the interpersonal conditions that lead to psychopathology, ultimately prompting an increase in self-criticism (i.e., the self-critical cascade). Yet even if I have convinced you that the two aforementioned claims are based on compelling findings, the data I have presented are not sufficient. One possibility has not been addressed in CHAPTER 1: what if self-criticism is a culprit in disguise? In other words, what if what "we"—those of us chasing after self-criticism in our labs and clinics—have mistaken another noxious agent for what we measure and identify as self-criticism?

This methodological issue has a name—the construct validity of the cause (D. T. Campbell & Stanley, 1963; see also Kazdin, 1992).[1] Specifically, let us assume two variables, X and Y. Say we have convincingly shown that X causes Y. Are we sure we know what X is? The only way to solve this problem is by resorting to our old logical friend—*modus tollens*—in order to eliminate other possible suspects hiding under self-criticism's skirt tails. We must show—empirically—that it is self-criticism (as we define and measure it), rather than other suspects, that serves as a dimension of vulnerability to psychopathology. The following constitute potential suspects: (1) depressive symptom spectrum, (2) personality disorders, (3) neuroticism, (4) low self-esteem, (5) perfectionism, and (6) rumination.

Related to the aim of the present chapter is the possibility that factors such as the ones mentioned previously might *amplify* the adverse effect of self-criticism on clinical outcome (e.g., G. Shahar, Blatt, Zuroff, & Pilkonis, 2003). I will examine this possibility here as well.

Self-Criticism is Simply a Symptom of Depression

A quick glance at the two central manuals classifying mental disorders—the *Diagnostic and Statistical Manual for Mental Disorders* (DSM; American Psychiatric Association, 2013) and the *International Classification of Diseases* (ICD-10; World Health Organization, 1992)—demonstrates that self-criticism is a reasonable suspect as a proxy for depression. For instance, one of the symptoms of a major depressive episode in DSM-5 is "worthlessness or guilt." In the extensively employed Beck Depression Inventory-II (BDI-II; Beck, Steer, & Brown, 1996), many of the items capture self-criticism—including a specific self-criticism item and items tapping guilt, a sense of failure, and so forth.

It might thus be argued that, rather than being a cause of depression, self-criticism lies at its core. Although statistically significant correlations between depression and self-criticism certainly exist, however, they are not prohibitively strong. Ranging between $r = .30$ and $r = .70$, they very rarely exceed 50% of shared variance (Coyne & Whiffen, 1995; Nietzel & Harris, 1990). In other words, 50% of the variance is unshared. Surely you would expect a consistent correlation between self-criticism and depression? As my mentor and friend David Zuroff once said to me, "I am yet to see a happy self-critic."

When we consider depressive symptoms/syndromes as a possible confound or alternative explanation of the effect of self-criticism on clinical and developmental outcomes, an interesting pattern emerges. Specifically, in those studies in which self-criticism is pitted against depression in predicting outcomes, often the adverse effect of self-criticism remains statistically significant while the effect of depression vanishes. Let me illustrate this with two research examples from my own work.

In CHAPTER 1, I described at length our study (G. Shahar, Henrich, Blatt, Ryan, & Little, 2003) seeking to integrate Blatt's theory of personality vulnerability with Deci and Ryan's (1985) self-determination theory (SDT). My intention in CHAPTER 1 was to illuminate the causal chain linking self-criticism, lower levels of autonomous motivation, and positive life-events. This was emphasized to shed some light on the motivational mechanisms through which self-criticism creates an improvised social environment (vis-à-vis the "absence principle"—see CHAPTER 1). In this chapter, I address another aspect of the results of this study—namely, the relative effect of self-criticism and depressive symptoms on adolescent motivational systems.

We measured adolescent depressive symptoms via the extensively used Child Depression Inventory (CDI; Kovacs, 1992), a self-report measure assessing child and adolescent depression that essentially constitutes an extension of the BDI. Kovacs (1992) introduced several additional items that tap areas of school, aggression, and other social/peer relations relevant to children and adolescents. We tested our theoretical model positing that self-criticism and other personality factors (e.g., dependency and efficacy) impact motivations, in turn predicting life-events. In doing so, we controlled for the potentially competing effect of CDI depressive symptoms. "Controlling for" means that whenever we predicted motivations by personality factors we also predicted them by depression. Personality and depression were thus compelled to compete in terms of their unique effects on motivation.

The results were illuminating. First, the correlation between self-criticism and CDI depression was $r = .60$, entailing only 36% of shared variance. This indicates the relative independence of the two constructs—that is, self-criticism ≠ depression. Second, both self-criticism and depression predicted negative life-events, the magnitude of the effects being virtually identical (standardized coefficients = .24 and .25 respectively). Finally, and most importantly, self-criticism—but not depressive symptoms—predicted positive events, and the magnitude of this effect of self-criticism was appreciable (standardized coefficient = −.34). Thus, although both self-criticism and depression generated stress (negative events) in this study, only self-criticism adversely impacted positive life-events.

What about motivation? The results of a statistical model examining the effect of self-criticism and depressive symptoms on autonomous and controlled motivation were even more intriguing. While depressive symptoms predicted neither motivations, self-criticism predicted both. As indicated in CHAPTER 1, self-criticism predicted low levels of autonomous motivation, the magnitude of the effect reaching levels seldom observed in our field—a standardized coefficient of −.62. As noted in CHAPTER 1, autonomous motivation then predicted positive events, fully accounting for the effect of self-criticism on this type of event. Although controlled motivation did not predict negative events, thus not accounting for the effect of self-criticism on these events, it was self-criticism, *but not depressive symptoms,* that predicted controlled motivation. The magnitude of this effect was mild, but statistically significant (standardized coefficient = .13, $p < .01$).

Was this landslide triumph of self-criticism over depression in terms of predicting motivation and events random? Apparently not. Examining the associations between self-criticism and motivations in a sample of young Israeli adults participating in a preparatory academic program, we (G. Shahar, Kalnitzki, Shulman, & Blatt, 2006) again found that self-criticism predicted elevated levels of controlled motivation and low levels of autonomous motivation. Psychopathology—assessed via the extensively employed Brief Symptoms Inventory (BSI; Derogatis & Spencer, 1982)—failed to predict motivation levels. We also examined amotivation, an SDT term used to denote apathy and confusion that is associated with psychopathology and maladjustment (Ryan & Deci, 2000). Congratulations, you guessed correctly—self-criticism predicted amotivation while BSI psychopathology did not.

In G. Shahar, Kalnitzki et al. (2006), we also examined the effect of personality and psychopathology on young adults' goal construal—that is, the extent to which they perceive they are making progress toward attaining their goals and their future expectations regarding goal attainment. Here, too, self-criticism, but not BSI psychopathology, predicted these variables in expected ways: low levels of goal progress and future expectation of attaining goals. When the same group was examined again a year later (Shulman, Kalnitzki, & G. Shahar, 2009), the new findings replicated and extended those of G. Shahar, Kalnizki et al. (2006). Notably, baseline levels of self-criticism also predicted lower levels of academic success in this sample. As I mulled over this pattern of self-criticism—but not depression or related psychopathology—predicting life-events and motivations, I realized that it had been evinced in my doctoral studies (Priel & G. Shahar, 2000; G. Shahar & Priel, 2003) and occurs elsewhere (Dunkley, Sanislow, Grilo, & McGlashan, 2006, 2009).

The implications of this pattern for public mental health are intriguing. Over the past two decades, the devastating price of depression in adolescence and young adulthood (E. P. Greenberg et al., 2003; Lynch & Clarke, 2006) has reached the point where adolescent depression has been deemed a major public health problem (Hyman, 2001). Vast budgets are thus being allocated to programs designed to screen for, prevent, and treat depression among the young (see Stice, Shaw, Bohon, Marti, & Rohde, 2009; S. B. Williams, O'Connor, Eder, & Whitlock, 2009). What if, however, in focusing on depression we are overlooking an equally real and perhaps even more ominous problem—namely, young people's sense of self, particularly their self-criticism? The study noted earlier (G. Shahar et al., 2003) suggests that, even if we successfully neutralize depression in adolescents and young adults—a very unlikely prospect—the calamitous effect of self-criticism will remain because it is independent of depression. Frequently, it has an even stronger effect than the latter!

From a clinical point of view, this lacuna is particularly glaring with respect to young-adult amotivation. While my reading of the literature suggests that amotivation is mentioned only in passing partly due to its complicated nature, my experience as a practitioner has taught me that the problem is painfully real—particularly among extremely talented young adults. Let me illustrate this clinically.

Adam was 25 when he was referred to treatment with me for what his parents believed to be depression. As part of routinely administered measures of depression and related psychopathology at various stages of treatment, I learned at intake that his level of depression was not in fact very severe; he scored 17 on the BDI. Ultimately, Adam was diagnosed with dysthymic disorder. Indeed, Adam's suffering emanated from the fact that he felt utterly, irrevocably stuck.

Adam was brilliant. He had a wide array of interests. He knew a lot about history, philosophy, and physics. Fascinated with Italian culture, he had taught himself Italian. He was keenly interested in nutrition, making a habit of performing an annual month-long body cleansing during which he only ate rice and drank water. He wrote prose and poetry, albeit sporadically, which I considered to be of high quality. Despite all this, he experienced himself as a lifelong dropout—a large portion of his life-trajectory providing a solid basis for this feeling.

Adam grew up in a rural area nurtured by very loving but highly permissive parents who set very few boundaries and created little structure in his life. Knowing that he would not be reprimanded or punished for not doing his homework, Adam brushed it off. Assured that his parents would not disapprove if he evaded mandatory army service, he did so. Eventually, he found himself at age 21 smarter than most of his peers but without a high school graduation certificate (known as *bagrut* in Israel—literally equivalent to "maturity") and, much worse, without direction. In an effort to create some structure and direction, he applied to a preparatory academic program, gained his *bagrut*, and was admitted to medical school. Finding the studies uninteresting, however, he dropped out after the first year. At this point he came to me for therapy.

Two salient themes characterized Adam's experience of himself and the world—his amotivation (or lack of desire to accomplish anything) and his self-criticism. Employing a Multiple Selves Analysis—a therapeutic intervention that relates to patients' perception of themselves as multifaceted (see Chapter 7)—I found that Adam easily identified his numerous "sides" (i.e., self-aspects). With respect to his amotivated self-aspect, he came up with what I thought a very revealing name, calling it *adipulator*—a pun on his name and the word "manipulator." I apprehended his amotivated side as representing a major identity-confusion. Adam himself understood it as a clever plot to evade responsibility, utilizing this "side" of himself to reproach himself. My clinical impression—mirroring the research noted earlier—was that, like so many other young adults, Adam's self-criticism was the *cause* of his amotivation, generating considerable turmoil within him.

A final qualification is in order concerning the comparable effects of self-criticism and depressive symptoms on other outcomes. It is quite possible that, rather than competing with one another, self-criticism and depression actually augment each other's adverse effects on development and health. Christopher Henrich and I with our colleagues detected just such a pattern among American early-adolescent boys, but not girls. Specifically, among early-adolescent boys, self-criticism prospectively predicted a decrease in grade point average over a 1-year interval, but only when baseline levels of depressive symptoms were high (G. Shahar, Henrich et al., 2006).

Self-Criticism as a Personality Disorder Aspect

In this book, self-criticism is construed as a pathological personality trait. The DSM and ICD generally refer to personality pathology under the rubric of "personality disorder"—a pervasive and long-lasting set of traits expressed via cognition, affect, interpersonal functioning, and impulse control.

As with depressive disorders, it is thus important to note that self-criticism is more than an aspect of a personality disorder. Specifically, it might be argued that the following personality disorders embed self-criticism: borderline personality disorder (BPD), narcissistic personality disorder (NPD), avoidant personality disorder (APD), and obsessive-compulsive personality disorder (OCPD). Depressive personality disorder (DPD), a somewhat controversial personality disorder identified in Appendix B of the DSM-IV-TR (American Psychiatric Association, 2005), is also worthy of further study (see later). The putative relationships between self-criticism and these personality disorders are explicated next.

BPD is characterized by an identity disturbance that expresses itself in a marked and persistent unstable self-image or sense of self. Clinically, this is exhibited in fluctuations between idealization and devaluation of self/others. The devaluated state is compatible with self-criticism, and so a positively directed association between BPD features and self-criticism might be expected.

NPD is a classic disorder of the self (Kohut & Wolf, 1978), pertaining to grandiosity and need for admiration. The grandiosity, arrogance, and entitlement reflected in virtually all the criteria of an NPD diagnosis are obviously inverse to the phenomenology of self-criticism. A negatively-directed association between NPD and self-criticism might thus be expected. Indeed, clinical theory and experience (e.g., P. Cramer, 1995; Reich, 1960) suggest that narcissism is a defensive response to experiences of worthlessness and active self-bashing.

APD pertains to ongoing social inhibition and subjective inadequacy in social situations. One of its features is its view of the self as socially inept, personally unappealing, and inferior to others. Here, too, we might thus anticipate a positively directed association with self-criticism.

OCPD is characterized by excessive perfectionism—known to be closely associated with self-criticism (see later). Associations between OCPD and self-criticism might therefore be expected.

DPD relates to a pervasive, personologic experience of depression, centering on inadequacy, worthlessness, and low self-esteem and a critical, blaming, and derogatory attitude toward the self. Both these criteria—the latter in particular—being highly compatible with self-criticism, they are indicative of a very strong, positively directed association between DPD and our putative trait. Importantly, DPD no longer appears in the DSM (American Psychiatric Association, 2013).

What empirically derived associations between self-criticism and these personality disorders have actually been demonstrated, however? Although little research into this topic has been conducted, those studies available evince only weak associations (Morse, Robins, & Gittes-Fox, 2002; Ryder, McBride, & Bagby, 2008). Two studies in particular are noteworthy in this context.

The extensive assessment protocol of the landmark Treatment for Depression Collaborative Research Program (TDCRP) study referred to in CHAPTER 1 also included a measure of personality-disorder features. The Personality Assessment Form (PAF) was scored by clinical evaluators at intake and termination and by therapists following the second treatment session and at termination. It consists of descriptive paragraphs emphasizing salient features of each of the 11 DSM-III Axis II personality disorders. Ratings of the extent to which the features described were characteristic of the patient's long-term personality functioning were determined for each disorder on a 6-point scale ranging from 1 ("Not at all") to 6 ("To an extreme degree"). Shea et al. (1990) found that patients in the TDCRP with any type of personality disorder evinced a significantly worse outcome in social functioning than patients without. Similarly, patients exhibiting the features of an odd-eccentric personality disorder cluster (composed of BPD, NPD, and histrionic and antisocial personal disorder) reported higher depressive symptoms at termination than patients with no personality disorder.

As part of my mentored collaboration with Blatt, Zuroff, and personality-disorders expert Paul Pilkonis, we sought to compare the relative role of self-criticism—which we labeled at that time "pretreatment perfectionism"—and personality-disorder features in treatment outcome (G. Shahar, Blatt, Zuroff, & Pilkonis, 2003). The findings indicated weak correlations ($rs = .03$ and $r = .23$) between patient pretreatment self-criticism and personality-disorder features, respectively. The only two correlations that reached standard statistical significance ($p < .05$) involved the depressive personality disorder ($r = .23, p = .004$) and the odd-eccentric cluster ($r = .17, p = .03$). Only the first correlation was statistically significant in the face of the Bonferroni correction method, which takes into account the number of statistical tests performed (i.e., $.05/4 = .0125$).

We then predicted patients' clinical status at termination, calculating a composite score from various symptoms and functioning scales (see Blatt, Zuroff, Quinlan, & Pilkonis, 1996) from baseline clinical status, pretreatment perfectionism (self-criticism), and various personality-disorder clusters and features. The statistically significant predictors were baseline clinical status ($\beta = .18, p < .05$), self-criticism ($\beta = .19, p < .05$), the odd-eccentric cluster ($\beta = .19, p < .05$), and depressive personality disorder features ($\beta = .26, p < .01$). Self-criticism thus evinced a unique effect of treatment outcome—independent of the effect of personality-disorder features.

If you recall, we found that the effect of self-criticism on treatment outcome was mediated (i.e., accounted for) by its adverse effect on two interpersonal domains: the therapeutic alliance and the social network (G. Shahar, Blatt, Zuroff, Krupnic, & Sotsky, 2004). In light of these findings, we sought to evaluate whether the effect of the personality-disorder features that significantly predicted treatment outcome was also obtained via these interpersonal domains. We (G. Shahar, Blatt, Zuroff, & Pilkonis, 2003) found that it was not. In other words, when therapeutic alliance and satisfaction with the social network were predicted from their baseline levels, pretreatment clinical status, the odd-eccentric and depressive-personality features (the two personality-disorder variables predicting treatment outcome), and pretreatment self-criticism—the only predictors were baseline levels of the interpersonal domain and pretreatment self-criticism ($\beta = .17$, $p < .05$; $\beta = .22$, $p < .01$ for the therapeutic alliance and social network, respectively). This study thus indicated that (1) pretreatment self-criticism does not overlap with personality-disorder features; (2) pretreatment self-criticism appears to influence treatment outcome independently of personality-disorder features; and (3) unlike the effect of personality-disorder features on treatment outcome, the effect of pretreatment self-criticism on outcome is clearly delineated as interpersonal.

One of the most interesting statistical trends detected in this study was an interaction between self-criticism and personality-disorder features in predicting treatment outcome ($p = .08$). Specifically, the effect of self-criticism on treatment outcome was particularly pronounced among patients with elevated levels of DPD and vice versa. Despite its intriguing pattern—reminiscent of the interactive effect of self-criticism and depressive symptoms on early-adolescent boys' academic achievement noted earlier (G. Shahar, Henrich et al., 2006)—we reported this trend with great caution, urging future replications. This led to a second study, which will be reported here.

The work of my former doctoral student Liat Itzhakey focuses on the role of personality in self-mutilation—also labeled nonsuicidal self-injury (NSSI). In one study, Itzhakey replicated and extended previous studies (Glassman, Weierich, Hooley, Deliberto, & Nock, 2007) attesting to the role of self-criticism in NSSI in in-patient adolescents suffering from eating disorders (Izhakey, G. Shahar, Stein, & Fennig, under review). Of primary interest here, however, is her study of NSSI in young adults. This two-wave study of Israeli undergraduates was conducted over a 4-month interval and included collection of data regarding personality disorders. Self-criticism was assessed using the Depressive Experiences Questionnaire (DEQ) and personality disorder features via the Personality Disorders Questionnaire-4 (PDQ-4; Hyler, 1994). The PDQ-4 consists of 99 self-administered true/false items yielding scores for 12 DSM-IV personality disorders and two validity scales—a "Too Good Questionnaire" and a "Suspect Questionnaire"—employed to identify underreporting and random responses. Scale scores are calculated by counting the number of "true" responses to items that correspond to the specific scale. The study also examined depressive symptoms via the BDI-II (Beck et al., 1996).

Zero-order correlations between all personality-disorder features and self-criticism were low to modest in magnitude (rs ranging between .12 and .57)—further confirming the independence of the two constructs. We then attempted to replicate the trend found in G. Shahar, Blatt, Zuroff, and Pilkonis (2003) by predicting Time 2 depressive symptoms from (1) Time 1 depressive symptoms, (2) Time 1 depressive-personality disorder features, (3) Time 1 self-criticism,

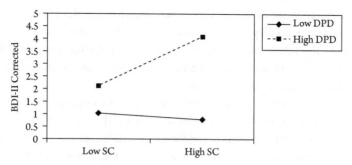

Figure 2.1 The prospective effect of self-criticism on depressive symptoms is augmented by baseline depressive personality-disorder (DPD) features*

Notes: The y-axis expresses Time 2 levels of Beck Depression Inventory-II (BDI-II) depressive symptoms corrected for Time 1 levels of BDI-II depressive symptoms. The x-axis expresses low versus high levels of self-criticism (SC). The solid and dashed lines represent low and high levels of DPD features.

* As noted, the DPD category no longer appears in the *Diagnostic and Statistical Manual of Mental Disorders*-V. The findings presented here suggest that this omission is unfortunate. Steven Huprich, a leading DPD researcher, has recently revitalized the construct via the malignant self-regard (MSR; Huprich & Nelson, 2014), which integrates features of narcissistic, depressive, self-defeating, and masochistic personality disorders. Although the MSR construct has straightforward relevance to self-criticism, only having surfaced in empirical research it awaits future research.

and (4) an interaction between depressive personality-disorder features and self-criticism. Due to the small sample size, the overwhelming stability of depressive symptoms in this population (the test-retest correlation = .72), and our clear expectations regarding the direction of the effect (per G. Shahar, Blatt, Zuroff, & Pilkonis, 2003), we employed a one-tailed test of significance.

As shown in Figure 2.1, a statistically significant interaction between depressive personality-disorder features and self-criticism emerged ($b = .64$, $SE = .38$, $\beta = .11$, $t = 1.67$, $p = .048$). Under high levels of depressive personality-disorder features (i.e., 1 standard deviation above the mean), self-criticism predicted an increase in depressive symptoms over time ($b = 1.14$, $SE = .62$, $\beta = .18$, $t = 1.82$, $p = .035$). Under low levels of depressive personality-disorder features (i.e., 1 standard deviation below the mean), virtually no relationship was found between self-criticism and changes in depressive symptoms over time ($b = -.14$, $SE = .64$, $\beta = -.02$, $t = -.22$, $p = .82$). This pattern seems to replicate G. Shahar, Blatt, Zuroff, and Pilkonis' (2003) findings regarding the trend toward a statistically significant interaction between self-criticism and DPD in the TDCRP study.

Self-Criticism is Merely Neuroticism

The Five Factor model of personality (Costa & McCrae, 1992; Goldberg, 1993)—also known as the Big Five model (McCrae & John, 1992)—has been the most influential perspective in personality psychology for decades (Wiggins, 1996). It stipulates five personality traits, identified using lexical methodologies assumed to constitute the pillars of human personality: neuroticism, extroversion, agreeableness, conscientiousness, and openness to experience. Of these five, neuroticism is most relevant to the present discussion.

Neuroticism pertains to a chronic tendency to experience distress (e.g., anxiety, depression, irritation, anger, etc.). Decades of research have implicated this personality trait as a noteworthy risk factor for psychopathology, principally depressive disorders (for a review, see Lahey, 2009). It may be argued, however, that the effect of neuroticism on depression is tautological: people who are constantly depressed (i.e., have high neuroticism) tend to develop depressive symptoms over time (for a similar claim, see Farmer et al., 2002). Alternatively, neuroticism may be regarded as capturing a key temperamental and psychophysiological dimension behind affect regulation and hence psychopathology. Irrespective of these issues, when neuroticism is taken into account statistically in predicting changes in depression over time, little change is left to predict.

Two questions need to be raised with respect to self-criticism and neuroticism. First, are the two traits distinguishable? Second, assuming that they are does self-criticism rise to the challenge of predicting psychopathology even when neuroticism is taken into account? Extant research answers a clear yes to both questions. Clara, Cox, and Enns (2003) examined the distinctiveness of self-criticism and neuroticism using confirmatory factor analysis (CFA). They tested a series of preconceived models depicting the relationship between variables. The a priori, theoretically-based nature of CFA renders it a superior method to other factor-analytic methods—such as exploratory factor analysis (EFA). Thus, whereas Bagby and Rector's (1998) EFA-based study found a considerable overlap between self-criticism and neuroticism, leading the authors to conclude that the two are putatively redundant, Clara, Cox, & Enns' (2003) CFA study indicates that the relationship between self-criticism and neuroticism is better described by a two-factor than by a single-factor model. Despite the strong correlations between them ($r = .78$ and $.82$ in two independent samples), this finding suggests that the constructs are distinct.

Clara et al. (2003) also reported that adding self-criticism to a model in which depressive symptoms are predicted by neuroticism improves the prediction of depression.[2] In fact, the vast majority of studies using both neuroticism and self-criticism as predictors of clinical and interpersonal outcomes replicate Clara et al.'s (2003) study, demonstrating that self-criticism exerts an independent, statistically significant, predictive power even in the presence of neuroticism (e.g., Bareket-Bojmel & G. Shahar, 2011; Cox, Enns, & Clara, 2004; Dunkley, Sanislow et al., 2006; Dunkley et al., 2009; Dunkley, Blankstein, & Flett, 1997; Enns, Cox, & Inayatulla, 2003; Johnson, 2003).

Is There a Difference Between Self-Criticism and Low Self-Esteem (and Low Generalized Self-Efficacy)?

While it stands to reason that self-critics—who are constantly monitoring themselves for flaws—will invariably have low self-esteem, theory and research in fact say otherwise. If you think about it, important differences exist between the mental stance of attacking the self and that of taking stock of one's worth—the latter act relating to one's self-esteem. Do some very accomplished individuals, clearly aware of their success and strength and constantly raising the bar for success, not deem their triumphs trivial? In a chillingly penetrating article inspired by media reports regarding the suicide of three highly gifted individuals, Sidney J. Blatt (1995) pointed to the possibility that self-criticism and self-esteem are not redundant (see also G. Shahar, 2001, to be discussed further in Chapter 5).

Self-esteem is one of the most extensively investigated personality and self-concept variables (e.g., Dubois & Tevendale, 1999; Harter, 1993; J. E. Roberts & Monroe, 1998; Rosenberg, 1965). It refers to people's representations of their typical, or general, global evaluation of self-worth (Kernis & Waschull, 1995). Low levels of this trait have repeatedly been demonstrated as associated with different psychopathologies (e.g., Abela, Fishman, Cohen, & Young, 2012; Abela & Skitch, 2007; Abela & Taylor, 2003; Orth, Robins, & Meier, 2009; Orth, Robins, & Roberts, 2008; for a review of the role of self-esteem in depression and anxiety, see Orth & Robins, 2014; Sowislo & Orth, 2013; but see Baumeister, Smart, & Boden, 1996; Dubois & Tevendale, 1999, regarding the debate over the causal status of self-esteem in psychopathology). In the context of self-criticism research, low self-esteem was initially construed as one of self-criticism's adverse outcomes (Zuroff, Moskowitz, Wielgus, Powers, & Franko, 1983). To the best of my knowledge, however, no longitudinal study is available to substantiate this supposition. The literature suggests that the associations between self-criticism and self-esteem range between -.44 and -.68, depending on the measurement (e.g., Abela, Webb, Wagner, Ho, & Adams, 2006; Dunkley & Grilo, 2007). This range is not consistent with redundancy.

As in the case of the link between self-criticism and depressive/personality-disorder symptoms, some studies attest to the possibility that self-criticism and low self-esteem interact in predicting outcomes. Investigating adults with a history of major depressive disorders, Abela et al. (2006) found that high self-criticism was associated with greater elevations in depressive symptoms following elevations in hassles among individuals with low but not high self-esteem. Abela and Taylor (2003) similarly evinced that self-criticism interacted with negative events to predict increases in depressive mood among third- and fourth-grade boys with low but not high self-esteem.

A series of brilliant studies in their own right are also relevant here, due to their explicit conflation of self-criticism and low self-esteem. Cox, Enns, and their colleagues analyzed data collected as part of the National Comorbidity Survey (NCS; Cox, Enns, & Clara, 2004; Cox, MacPherson, Enns, & McWilliams, 2004; Cox, McWilliams, Enns, & Clara, 2004; Pagura, Cox, Sareen, & Enns, 2006). The NCS's extensive assessment battery includes self-criticism items from the DEQ and (low) self-esteem items from the Rosenberg Self-Esteem Scale (Rosenberg, 1959). Combining these items together to form a self-criticism index, Cox, Enns et al. employed this index to predict a host of disorders while controlling for other personality and clinical factors. They first examined the relationship between child adversities (e.g., maternal antisocial behavior and neglect) and self-criticism among adults ($N = 5,877$; Pagura et al., 2006). Their findings indicate that individuals with elevated self-criticism are significantly more likely to report a variety of childhood adversities than those with low or moderate levels of self-criticism. In another analysis, they found that both neuroticism and self-criticism uniquely predicted symptoms of posttraumatic stress disorder ($N = 3,238$; Cox, MacPherson et al., 2004). In a further study, self-criticism—but not other personality factors—was associated with a lifetime prevalence of major depression ($N = 5,877$; Cox, McWilliams et al., 2004). Finally, they also reported that self-criticism and hopelessness uniquely predicted suicidal ideation and suicide attempts ($N = 5,877$; Cox, Enns et al., 2004). These impressive findings are particularly heartening to a self-criticism "fan" such as myself. However, because the measure used in these studies includes both items of self-criticism and self-esteem, it is not clear which of the two constructs drives these impressive effects on clinical outcome.

Another personality trait similar to—but distinct from—self-esteem is generalized self-efficacy. Developed by Albert Bandura, the self-efficacy construct pertains to the belief in one's capacity to exercise control over one's life (Bandura, 1977, 1997). Individuals with high self-efficacy approach difficult tasks with confidence in their own capabilities, visualize success scenarios, maintain a strong commitment to seeing tasks through (Bandura, 1997), and appear to be resilient in the face of traumatic events (Benight & Bandura, 2004; Luszczynska, Benight, & Cieslak, 2009). Although Bandura conceived self-efficacy as domain specific (Bandura, 1977), later studies construed it as a global construct pertaining to a motivational trait (Luszczynska, Gutiérrez-Dona, & Schwarzer, 2005; Luszczynska, Sarker, & Knoll, 2007; Schwarzer & Jerusalem, 1995; Shelton, 1990), positing that generalized self-efficacy may be adduced when the context is less specific or human behavior is widely ranged (Luszczynska et al., 2009). Both conceptualizations of self-efficacy—as a generalized trait or a dimension-based tendency—are pertinent to the understanding of social behavior. Generalized self-efficacy, for example, is associated with self-regulatory efficacy—in particular, empathic self-efficacy (Luszczynska et al., 2005). While empathic self-efficacy predicts pro-social behavior it is also predicted by this same behavior (Caprara, Alessandri, & Eisenberg, 2012).

As noted earlier, generalized self-efficacy is measurable by the DEQ (Blatt, D'Afflitti, & Quinlan, 1976). The six self-criticism items appearing in Table 1.1 have been extracted from this questionnaire. When the 66 items of this measure are factor analyzed, three factors emerge: dependency, self-criticism, and "efficacy." The latter is a rather unexpected factor assessing self-confidence and inner strength, corresponding to "general self-efficacy" (Kuperminc, Blatt, & Leadbeater, 1997). Analyzing the White Plains data, we (G. Shahar, Gallagher, Blatt, Kuperminc, & Leadbeater, 2004) found a number of fascinating interactions between self-criticism and DEQ efficacy. Specifically, under low—but not high—levels of DEQ efficacy, self-criticism interacted with dependency to prospectively predict an increase in depression and other internalizing symptoms (e.g., anxiety) over the 1-year follow-up. Among adolescent boys, self-criticism and DEQ efficacy interacted to prospectively predict externalizing symptoms (e.g., aggression and delinquency). The pattern of this interaction revealed that self-criticism predicts an increase in externalizing symptoms when DEQ efficacy is low but not high. Thus, in this sample efficacy buffered against the adverse effect of self-criticism on externalizing symptoms (see also Blatt & G. Shahar, 2004b).

What is the precise phenomenological meaning of "high self-criticism" and "low self-esteem" and/or "low self-efficacy"? Adam, the patient I described in Chapter is a good example of a self-critic with high self-esteem/generalized self-efficacy. Adam was smarter than most people—and knew it. He was also quite talented—and knew it. Although aware of the fact that, with respect to many life domains, he would gain what he sought if he put his mind to it, he did not know what he wanted. Nor was he clear about the benefits of putting any effort into finding out what ambitions, dreams, or pleasures he might have—that is, he was amotivated. Rather than stemming from the feeling that he was not "good enough" (low self-esteem) or that he could not perform (low self-efficacy), Adam's angst derived from his identity confusion. The fact that he was not living up to his own potential made him feel as though he was not *real* (see CHAPTERS 4 and 5). In Adam's case, his high self-esteem/self-efficacy was in fact a liability (risk) rather than an asset (a source of resilience). It prompted awareness of what he had within him and what he could accomplish but had failed to (for a review of the mixed blessing of self-esteem, see Baumeister, Smart, & Boden, 1996; for a review of the risk/resilience dialectic, see G. Shahar, Elad-Strenger, & Henrich, 2012).

Self-Criticism? Perfectionism? Self-Critical Perfectionism?

Around the mid-1980s and early 1990s, two groups of researchers—the Frost group (Frost, Heimberg, Holt, Mattia, & Neubauer, 1993; Frost & Henderson, 1991; Frost, Lahart, & Rosenblate, 1991; Frost & Marten, 1990; Frost, Marten, Lahart, & Rosenblate, 1990) and the Hewitt/Flett group (Hewitt & Flett, 1991a,

1991b, 1993, 2002; Hewitt, Flett, & Ediger, 1996)—impressed the personality psychology field with their findings regarding multidimensional perfectionism. The former group developed a multidimensional model of perfectionism consisting of different subscales, some associated with striving and high achievement (e.g., high personal standards and need for order and organization), others with a wide range of clinical disorders—especially depression (e.g., excessive concern about making mistakes and perception of high parental standards). The latter group developed a multidimensional model of perfectionism divided into three subtypes of perfectionism: (1) other-oriented perfectionism (i.e., demanding that others meet unrealistic standards), (2) self-oriented perfectionism (i.e., an active striving to be flawless), and (3) socially prescribed perfectionism (i.e., the belief that others hold exacting or even impossible expectations that one must fulfill in order to gain approval). Examination of the link between the two models revealed a strong association between the total score of Frost's measure and Hewitt and Flett's self-oriented and socially prescribed perfectionism (Blatt, 1995).

Most, if not all, perfectionism research is influenced by Hamachek's (1978) seminal treatise on the topic. This distinguishes between adaptive, or normal, and nonadaptive, or neurotic, perfectionism. A similar distinction is currently made between adaptive, personal-striving (or standards) perfectionism and maladaptive, excessive-evaluative-concerns perfectionism (for reviews, see Blatt, 1995; Egan, Wade, & Shafran, 2011).

The literature on perfectionism is significant for my present purposes for several reasons. First, the rigor and elegance of the empirical studies contained in the literature guarantee their publication in top-tier psychological forums (e.g., Dunkley, Blankstein, Masheb, & Grilo, 2006; Egan et al., 2011; Hewitt & Flett, 1991a, 1991b; Hewitt, Flett, Besser, Sherry, & McGee, 2003; Hewitt et al., 1996). Second, the extensive usage of the label "perfectionism" in lay language buttresses the alliance between psychological science and vernacular speech. Third, the research has led to significant clinical attention regarding the best way(s) to treat perfectionism (Antony & Swinson, 2009).

My own major caveat regarding perfectionism studies relates to the fact that mounting research evidence suggests that maladaptive perfectionism—also labeled excessive-evaluative-concerns perfectionism (e.g., Dunkley & Kyparissis, 2008; Dunkley, Zuroff, & Blankstein, 2006; G. Shahar, 2006b)—is actually self-criticism. Dunkley, Zuroff et al. (2006) assessed 163 undergraduates via questionnaires across a 7-day period with respect to their levels of self-criticism (DEQ; Blatt et al., 1976), perfectionism (Hewitt Multidimensional Perfectionism Scale [Hewitt & Flett, 1991a, 1991b]; Frost Multidimensional Perfectionism Scale [Frost, Benton, & Dowrick, 1990]), and maladjustment. Inquiring into the two constructs' predictability of maladjustment, the study's findings revealed self-criticism to be a strong predictor of a wide range of maladaptive functioning (e.g., avoidant coping, negative affect, etc.). In contrast, perfectionism subscales were not uniquely related to any maladaptive functioning variables.

Powers and colleagues have demonstrated the differential effects of self-criticism and self-oriented perfectionism (referred to as "positive perfectionism") on goal pursuit (Powers, Koestner, Zuroff, Milyavskaya, & Gorin, 2011). The participants in these studies were individuals pursuing important personal goals (e.g., weight management, academic or musical careers). Self-criticism was associated with diminished goal achievement. When controlling for self-criticism, a positive association emerged between self-oriented perfectionism and goal pursuit. In other words, high standards unrelated to a punitive stance toward the self may play a positive role in personal striving (Powers et al., 2011).[3]

Several prominent researchers have sought to circumvent the confusion between "maladaptive perfectionism" and "self-criticism" by using the term "self-critical perfectionism" (Dunkley & Blankstein, 2000; Dunkley, Zuroff, & Blankstein, 2003; Luyten et al., 2011). In the past, I myself was guilty of this practice—thus contributing to the confusion—in my research on the treatment of depression using TDCRP data (G. Shahar, Blatt et al., 2003; G. Shahar, Blatt, & Zuroff, 2007; G. Shahar, Gallagher et al., 2004). Over the years, however, I have become increasingly uncomfortable with both the interchangeable use of "perfectionism" and "self-criticism" and the term "self-critical perfectionism" for several reasons. First, I was stunned by research demonstrating that the active ingredient in self-critical/maladaptive perfectionism appears to be self-criticism—particularly as measured by the DEQ (Dunkley, Zuroff et al., 2006). Second, my clinical work has convinced me that the real culprit is, in fact, active self-bashing rather than the quest for perfection. Take Rina, for example, the patient I described in CHAPTER 1. Rina would routinely get excellent grades in her academic studies, usually around 90 (out of a maximum of 100). Unlike a true perfectionist, however, Rina was not perturbed by her marks. The problem was (1) they did not convince her that she was not "stupid" (nor would a grade of 100!) and (2) on those rare occasions when she received a lower mark (e.g., 70), this formed unequivocal proof of her stupidity (for other clinical illustrations distinguishing between perfectionism and self-criticism, see A. C. Kelly, Zuroff, & G. Shahar, 2014).

The Link Between Self-Criticism and Rumination

The pioneering, highly influential research of the late Susan Nolen-Hoeksema highlights the role of rumination in psychopathology. As defined by Nolen-Hoeksema (1991), rumination constitutes a tendency to repetitively focus on one's feelings and their meaning, causes, and consequences. Further studies have adduced evidence of two subtypes of rumination (Treynor, Gonzalez, &

Nolen-Hoeksema, 2003): (1) brooding, which consists of "a passive comparison of one's current situation with some unachieved standard" (Treynor et al., 2003, p. 256) and is considered to be a maladaptive form of rumination, and (2) reflective pondering, which relates to "a purposeful turning inward to engage in cognitive problem solving to alleviate one's depressive symptoms" (Treynor et al., 2003, p. 256) and represents an adaptive component of rumination. Brooding is positively related to negative mood and predicts depression over 1 year; reflective pondering is negatively related to negative mood and predicts a decrease in depression over 1 year (Treynor et al., 2003). In a series of longitudinal studies, Nolen-Hoeksema demonstrated that rumination predicts elevated levels of depressive symptoms (Nolen-Hoeksema & Davis, 1999; Nolen-Hoeksema, Larson, & Grayson, 1999; Nolen-Hoeksema & Morrow, 1991; Nolen-Hoeksema, Morrow, & Fredrickson, 1993; Nolen-Hoeksema, Parker, & Larson, 1994), episodes of depression (Just & Alloy, 1997; Nolen-Hoeksema, 2000), and the onset of depression and anxiety symptoms (Nolen-Hoeksema, 2000; Nolen-Hoeksema & Davis, 1999).

Recent literature has revealed innovative findings regarding the relationship between the ruminative response style and various psychopathologies across age groups—for example, bulimia, substance abuse, depression and anxiety comorbidity, and suicidal ideation (McLaughlin & Nolen-Hoeksema, 2011; Miranda & Nolen-Hoeksema, 2007; Nolen-Hoeksema, Stice, Wade, & Bohon, 2007). Thus, for example, a study conducted among a community sample of 1,134 adults measuring rumination (i.e., brooding and reflection), depression, and suicidal ideation at baseline level and after a 1-year follow-up found that both brooding and reflection predicted thoughts about suicide (Miranda & Nolen-Hoeksema, 2007).

The conceptual link between rumination and self-criticism is straightforward, both entailing self-focused attention. Self-criticism, however, pertains to a personality structure—that is, to the way the self is organized and the type of relationships characterizing this organization's elements. Rumination, in contrast, is a (highly maladaptive) cognitive process designed to cope with emotional distress. Although people obviously adopt a critical attitude toward themselves when ruminating over their failures and inadequacies, it is possible to be self-critical without ruminating. In my opinion, this is what happens when self-criticism is translated into externalizing symptoms and disorders, such as conduct disorder and substance use, rather than internalized (as in depression and anxiety). Externalizing symptoms are more prevalent among men, internalizing symptoms among women. The first to propose that rumination accounts (at least partially) for gender differences in depression was in fact Nolen-Hoeksema (1990). She posited that women are more depressed than men, ruminating when distressed, while men tend to act out, or away, their emotional suffering (see also Mongrain & Leather, 2006).

Empirically, the association between self-criticism and rumination is not prohibitively high (e.g., $r = .52$ [Spasojevic & Alloy, 2001]). In one study, self-criticism prospectively predicted the course and outcome of major depression while rumination did not (Kasch, Klein, & Lara, 2001). In others, rumination was demonstrated to mediate the effect of self-criticism on depression (Spasojevic & Alloy, 2001) and suicidality (R. O'Connor & Noyce, 2008). The empirical literature and my clinical experience alike suggest to me that the latter studies adequately describe what goes on in depression and anxiety: self-criticism prompts people to ruminate, in turn increasing their propensity toward becoming anxious, depressed, and suicidal.

Chapter Summary

The purpose of this chapter was to convince the reader that self-criticism is (1) distinct from a host of similar factors and (2) uniquely, robustly, and consistently predictive of psychopathology even when pitted against these factors in the course of statistical prediction. I hope I have achieved this goal, not only because it substantiates the raison d'être of this book, but also—and primarily—because it matters clinically. It is one thing to mitigate the adverse effects of, say, low self-esteem, perfectionism, or depressive personality features, and another to derail the pernicious impact of self-criticism. Hopefully, the difference will become clearer when we address the issue of treatment.

Two caveats are in order before we go any further. First, although substantial, the research reviewed in this chapter is not voluminous. Many more studies of the similarities and differences between self-criticism and other vulnerabilities are necessary. For example, do self-criticism, low self-esteem, low generalized self-efficacy, and perhaps other self-related traits indicate an overarching, latent, self-concept psychopathology? If so, what would be the unique effect of self-criticism on psychopathology over and above this overarching factor? Do causal relationships exist between self-criticism and such traits as neuroticism—as suggested by Coyne and Whiffen (1995) almost two decades ago? What are the implications of these speculative causal relationships for vulnerability to psychopathology?

The second caveat—which also serves as a great opportunity—pertains to the findings regarding the interactions between self-criticism and other personality factors in predicting psychopathology. Earlier, I reported on two such interactions, one involving depressive personality traits, the other involving generalized self-efficacy (G. Shahar, Blatt, Zuroff, & Pilkonis, 2003; G. Shahar, Gallagher et al., 2004). Hitherto undetected interactions with other dimensions might exist as well. These interactions are important not only for scientific reasons, illuminating the complexity of vulnerability to psychopathology, but also from a clinical practice perspective. Specifically, they signal individuals for whom elevated self-criticism might be particularly problematic—for example, people with depressive personality features. They also point to possible directions for mitigating self-criticism by enhancing other dimensions—generalized self-efficacy, for example.

PART II

IN THEORY

3

Theories of Self-Criticism and their Discontents

If I have seen further it is by standing on the shoulders of giants.
(Isaac Newton, letter to Robert Hooke,
February 5, 1675 [Newton, 1959, p. 416])

The beginnings of the scholarly discussion of self-criticism can be traced back to Plato (Chang, 2008), although one of the most important theoreticians of the trait was Freud, the founder of psychoanalysis. In *Mourning and Melancholy*, Freud notes that the distinguishing mental features of melancholia are deep dejection, loss of interest in the outside world and the capacity to love, the inhibition of all activity, and "a lowering of the self-regarding feelings to a degree that finds utterance in self-reproaches and self-reviling, and culminates in a delusional expectation of punishment" (1917, p. 244). However you regard the "old stoic" (Gay, 1988), Freud demonstrated himself to be a scientific prophet with respect to self-criticism, anticipating contemporary research that highlights the centrality of the trait.

Other psychoanalytic thinkers—as well as cognitive, behavioral, cognitive-behavioral, and humanistic-existential theorists (Chang, 2008)—have also had important things to say about self-criticism. A comprehensive treatment of all self-criticism theories is not feasible here. I will thus focus on those theories that have led to significant empirical research. Specifically, I will critically review the following:

1. Sidney Blatt et al.'s psychodynamic/cognitive-developmental theory.
2. Aaron Beck's cognitive theory of depression (and related psychopathology).
3. Albert Bandura's social cognitive (formerly social learning) theory.
4. Paul Gilbert et al.'s cognitive-evolutionary theory.
5. Carl Rogers' humanistic perspective on the self and its contemporary representations by Deci and Ryan's self-determination theory and Torrey Higgins's self-discrepancy theory.

After presenting and evaluating each theory, I will conclude by comparing and contrasting them in tabular form.

Blatt et al.'s Psychodynamic/ Cognitive-Developmental Theory

Just as many consider mathematics to be a thing of beauty, I regard psychological theories in the same light. In my eyes, Sidney J. Blatt's theory is not only wise but also wondrous. Space constraining me from undertaking a comprehensive overview of the theory, I refer the reader to his numerous writings (Blatt, 1974, 1998, 2004, 2008; Blatt, Auerbach, Zuroff, & G. Shahar, 2006; Blatt & Luyten, 2009; Blatt, G. Shahar, & Zuroff, 2001; Blatt & Zuroff, 1992; Luyten & Blatt, 2011, 2013). Herein, I will survey the principal points of his theory, adduce some of its shortcomings, and specify the ways in which I depart from it.

Blatt integrates psychoanalytic object relations theory (ORT) with Piagetian/ Wernerian cognitive-developmental theories. Like other strands of psychoanalysis, ORT promotes the idea of the psychodynamic unconscious, contending that individuals unwittingly push some wishes, urges, thoughts, and emotions that threaten the self into the "unconscious." Although it lies beyond accessible awareness, this material nonetheless exerts a formidable influence on conscious awareness, behavior, and mental health. Focusing on the relational nature of the psychodynamic unconscious, ORT posits that mental representations of self, others, and self-with-others organize and structure both conscious and unconscious mental content (G. Shahar, 2015).

Blatt (e.g., 1995) perceived significant parallels between ORT and the cognitive-developmental theories of Jean Piaget (1956) and Heinz Werner (1948, 1957). Just as ORT investigates the formation of mental representations of self and others in the context of early parent-child relations, cognitive developmentalists examine the way in which representations of inanimate objects develop. Like schemas of the latter—which become more complex and abstract over time—representations of self and others become increasingly elaborate, abstract, and complex. The development of "cognitive-affective" schemas—or representations—of interpersonal relationships ("object relations") is also based on the cognitive development of schemas. Object relations likewise emerge as a direct function of the growing complexity of the parent-child interaction during the first years of life (Blatt, 1995; Blatt & Lerner, 1983).

Blatt propounds that two fundamental personality configurations are formed during the first years of life—the anaclitic-relational and introjective-self-definitional (Blatt, 1974, 1998, 2008). Both are built upon clusters of cognitive-affective representations of self and others. The anaclitic configuration taps into the universal need to establish stable, secure, and supportive/nurturing interpersonal relationships;

the introjective configuration seeks the construction of a stable, coherent, and essentially positive sense of self (Angyal, 1951; Bakan, 1966; Helgeson, 1994). The two configurations are born out of the vicissitudes of parent-child relationships, interacting with the child's cognitive development, genetic makeup, and external stresses (Blatt & Homann, 1992; Blatt & Zuroff, 1992). The increased intimacy and complexity in parent-child relationships propel the parallel development of cognitive-affective schemas. The anaclitic configuration enables the child to experience him- or herself in various ways, thereby enhancing cognitive-affective schemas of the self and enriching the introjective-personality configuration. The latter development in turn facilitates the child's ability to relate to others, thus augmenting the anaclitic configuration. The two configurations are therefore mutually reinforcing.

Blatt and colleagues posited that both the anaclitic and introjective configurations are essential to intact psychological development and physical and mental health (Blatt, 2008; Blatt, Cornell, & Eshkol, 1993). Disruptions of the normal dialectic developmental process can produce varied and diverse forms of psychopathology (Blatt, 2008; Blatt & Shichman, 1983; G. Shahar, Blatt, & Ford, 2003). Some individuals become fixated on interpersonal relations, developing "anaclitic disorders" characterized by a preoccupation with issues of relatedness (borderline and dependent personality disorders, anaclitic-dependent depression, and hysterical disorders). Others become obsessed with self-definition, developing "introjective disorders" marked by preoccupation with issues of self-worth, separateness, and control (schizotypic or overideational borderline, paranoid, and obsessive-compulsive personality disorders; introjective-self-critical depression; and narcissism [Blatt, 2008]). Blatt's distinction between the anaclitic and introjective has further led to the division of personality disorders into two principal clusters—anaclitic (dependent, histrionic, and borderline) personality disorders and introjective (paranoid, schizoid, schizotypic, antisocial, narcissistic, avoidant, obsessive-compulsive, and self-defeating) disorders (Levy et al., 1994; Luyten & Blatt, 2011, 2013; Ouimette, Klein, Anderson, Riso, & Lizardi, 1994).

Interestingly, anaclitic and introjective patients appear to respond better to different treatment modalities—psychoanalysis; supportive-expressive psychotherapy; psychoanalytically oriented psychotherapy; and brief, manualized treatments for depression (cognitive-behavioral and interpersonal therapies; Blatt, 1992; Blatt et al., 2006; Blatt & Ford, 1994; Blatt & Zuroff, 2005). Anaclitic patients seem to benefit from face-to-face, supportive-expressive psychodynamic psychotherapy, introjective patients from classic psychoanalysis (Blatt, 1992; Blatt & G. Shahar, 2004a). In intensive, psychoanalytically-oriented residential treatment, the primary change exhibited by anaclitic patients is manifested in terms of interpersonal relations. In contrast, therapeutic change is displayed by introjective patients in terms of symptom intensity and cognitive functioning—i.e., in terms of how they function and are seen to be functioning (Blatt & Ford, 1994;

Blatt, Chevron, Quinlan, Schaffer, & Wein, 1988). Introjective patients also appear to react adversely to brief, manualized treatment for depression (Rector, Bagby, Segal, Joffe, & Levitt, 2000; see CHAPTER 1).

Evaluation

As is so frequently the case, the problematic aspect of Blatt's anaclitic/introjective configurations scheme derives from the disparity between theory and empirical findings. While theoretically both configurations display equal measures of vulnerability, in practice the introjective configuration—particularly when operationalized with measures of self-criticism—appears to implicate greater vulnerability (Coyne & Whiffen, 1995; Nietzel & Harris, 1990; G. Shahar, 2001). As noted in CHAPTER 1, the anaclitic configuration—especially when operationalized via trait dependency—constitutes a complex dimension that encapsulates both risk and resilience. Clinical experience and psychometric findings also suggest that measures of self-criticism regularly pertain as much to anaclitic-dependent needs as to those of self-definition (e.g., Bagby, Parker, Joffe, Schuller, & Gilchrist, 1998; Desmet, Coemans, Vanheule, & Meganck, 2008; Hong & Lee, 2001; Kwon, Campbell, & Williams, 2001; Layne, Porcerelli, & G. Shahar, 2006; G. Shahar, 2006b; G. Shahar, Soffer, & Gilboa-Shechtman, 2008).

Having wrestled with this worrying theory–research gap for over a decade (e.g., G. Shahar, 2001), I have been compelled to search for ways to explain the theory/practice discrepancy. In the following, I offer several possible suggestions:

1. It may stem from inadequate measurement of the anaclitic configuration. Blatt et al. have also identified two independent subscales within this—one pertaining to healthy relatedness, the other to maladaptive neediness (e.g., Blatt, Zohar, Quinlan, Luthar, & Hart, 1996; Blatt, Zohar, Quinlan, & Zuroff, 1995; Whiffen & Aube, 1999). Other studies, however, have failed to confirm the vulnerability status of maladaptive neediness (e.g., Bacchiochi, Bagby, Cristi, & Watson, 2003 vs. McBridge, Zuroff, Bacchiochi, & Bagby, 2006; G. Shahar, Blatt, & Ford, 2003; G. Shahar, 2006b). In some of the studies that do appear to provide support for the vulnerability of neediness, it primarily predicts psychopathology when interacting with self-criticism (e.g., Mongrain & Leather, 2006). The possibility that further psychometric research may well discover similar facets within the self-criticism factor cannot be ruled out (for an initial attempt, see R. Thompson & Zuroff, 2004).

2. The outcome variables used to examine the vulnerability status of the anaclitic/introjective configurations may be artificially tilted toward the introjective conceptualization. Contemporary worldwide medical classifications (and related measures) of psychopathology originated in the Western world, known for its promotion of individuality and self-reliance (Guisinger & Blatt,

1994; Luyten & Blatt, 2013). This cultural bias may be responsible—at least partially—for the link between self-criticism and psychopathology. Blatt and Zuroff (1992) have consequently suggested that the anaclitic configuration should be more strongly associated with physical symptoms—these (presumably) being relatively unaffected by the Western self-based conceptualization of psychopathology. Other scholars have proposed that self-criticism may actually be adaptive in collectivist societies—such as Japan, for example (see Hamamura & Heine, 2008; Kitayama & Uchida, 2003; Markus & Kitayama, 1991).

Here, too, the empirical facts are at odds with the theory. While dependency does appear to be affiliated with physical illness (Bornstein, 1995, 1998b), so does self-criticism (Tang, Zhou, Liao, & Zhu, 2011). Similarly, if the link between self-criticism and psychopathology is in fact culturally biased, it should be much weaker in non-Western cultures—and particularly collectivistic societies. This does not seem to be the case. As measured by the Depressive Experiences Questionnaire (DEQ), self-criticism strongly predicts psychopathology among Japanese, Chinese, and Arab-Bedouin people in Israel (Abu-Kaf & Priel, 2008; Cohen et al., 2013; Kuwabara, Sakado, Sakado, Sato, & Someya, 2004; Tang et al., 2013; Yao, Fang, Zhu, & Zuroff, 2009).

3. Self-criticism's vulnerability might be related to a conceptual issue that differs—partially or fully—from that linked with the anaclitic-introjective configuration. In other words, the effort to confirm/refute the anaclitic-introjective distinction might prompt more penetrating insights into the nature of self-critical vulnerability. This is my explanation of choice and has challenged me to develop my own theory of self-criticism.

Beck's Cognitive Theory of Depression and its Relevance for Understanding Self-Criticism

Aaron T. Beck is the founder of the cognitive school of psychotherapy and a prominent figure within psychopathology research. Although his work is not identified with attempts to understand self-criticism per se, three aspects of his writings are pertinent to the present discussion: (1) sociotropy and autonomy, (2) the cognitive triad, and (3) his recent theory of modes.

In 1983, Beck proposed that sociotropy and autonomy form two dimensions of vulnerability to depression, the former being related to heightened needs for care and approval from others, the latter to a strong need for independence and achievement (Beck, 1983; Hammen, Marks, Mayol, & DeMayo, 1985). The two dimensions are routinely measured by the Sociotropy-Autonomy Scale (SAS; Beck, Epstein, Harrison, & Emery, 1983) or the Personal Style Inventory (PSI; Robins et al., 1994). Sociotropy and autonomy correspond roughly to Blatt's anaclitic and introjective configurations (Blatt, 1974; Blatt et al., 2001; Blatt & Zuroff, 1992). Theorists have thus anticipated that sociotropy (as measured by either the SAS or PSI) will be correlated with DEQ dependency and SAS/PSI autonomy with DEQ self-criticism. This expectation has only been partially fulfilled. While DEQ dependency and SAS/PSI sociotropy converge, DEQ self-criticism and SAS/PSI autonomy appear to be unrelated and self-criticism is occasionally correlated with aspects of sociotropy (Bartelstone & Trull, 1995; Blaney & Kutcher, 1991; Rude & Burnham, 1993; G. Shahar, 2006b; see also Mongrain & Blackburn, 2006).

Beck's theory of the depressive cognitive triad (Beck, Rush, Shaw, & Emery, 1979) preceded his proposal of the sociotropy/autonomy dimensions and is more relevant to the discussion of self-criticism. Herein, he contends that depression emanates from negative cognitions attached to three domains: self ("I am a failure"), world ("Everyone and everything is against me"), and the future ("I will never be able to succeed"). Although Beck does not label these as "self-critical," such negative cognitions regarding the self are likely to incorporate this trait.

In response to mounting criticism (e.g., Haaga, Dyck, & Ernst, 1991), Beck reformulated this theory in terms of "modes"—clusters of closely-linked schemas and related affective, behavioral, and motivational processes (Beck, 1996; Beck & Haigh, 2014). This framework moves beyond an exclusively cognitive (i.e., informational processing) approach to a focus on personality and psychopathology, integrating various aspects of psychopathology into a unified theory (Alford & Beck, 1997; for applications of this theory, see Rudd, Joiner, & Rajab, 2001; G. Shahar, 2013a).

As a Beckian "mode," self-criticism can be conceptualized as a cluster of schemas composed of cognitive, affective, behavioral, motivational, and physiological features. In this context, its cognitive features include both negative views about the self and an active internal self-bashing and constant scrutiny of one's flaws. A self-critical mode might also be linked to such emotions as self-directed anger and contempt (Whelton & L. S. Greenberg, 2005) and to changes in plasma homovanillic acid during stress (Gruen, Silva, Ehrlich, Schweitzer, & Friedhoff, 1997).

Evaluation

Although Beck's sociotropy-autonomy theory appears to be of little relevance to the understanding of self-criticism, the cognitive triad—which includes a component that captures negative cognitions toward the self—arguably constitutes one of the earliest precursors of self-criticism conceptualization. Interestingly, it implies a close connection between negative cognitions regarding the self (possibly a proxy of self-criticism) and negative cognitions concerning the future (hopelessness). In CHAPTER 4, I hope to develop an alternative link between self and future via the notions of authenticity and goal-directed action.

Finally, Beck's modal reformulation of his cognitive theory holds considerable potential for elucidating the links between the cognitive, emotional, motivational, behavioral, and physiological aspects of self-criticism. Even in its more advanced form, however, the thesis does not account for the active influence of self-criticism upon the environment (see CHAPTER 1, Figure 1.4).

Bandura's Social Cognitive Theory

Albert Bandura is the founder of social cognitive theory, one of the most comprehensive and fruitful approaches in general psychology (e.g., Bandura, 1977, 1978, 1986, 1991a, 1991b, 2001). I will note two particularly pertinent features of this theory—"reciprocal determinism" and self-reproach.

According to Bandura, while behavior is influenced by the environment, "the environment is partly of a person's own making. By their action actions, people play a role in creating the social milieu and other circumstances that arise in their daily transactions" (1978, p. 345). Environments influence individuals via nature (e.g., climate, the occurrence of natural or man-made disasters), cultural codes, social structures, and family relationships. Individuals actively shape some aspects of their social environment through their behavior, in turn impacting their personality structure and well-being.

Although the notion of "reciprocal determinism" might sound trivial in today's world, when Bandura formulated the principle it gave psychology a way to escape the deterministic conundrum of Freudian psychoanalysis and Skinnerian behaviorism. Hereby, it paved the way for a dialogue between behaviorism and cognitive psychology (Bandura, 2001). As I noted in CHAPTER 1, the reciprocal-determinism principle has inspired virtually all the psychopathology theories that highlight the importance of active person-context transactions (Brandstädter, 1998; Lerner, 1982; Sameroff, 2009; G. Shahar, 2006a; Swann, 1983, 1990; P. L. Wachtel, 1994)—as well as the research attesting to the active vulnerability of self-criticism that culminates in the self-critical cascade (CHAPTER 1, Figures 1.4 and 1.5).

According to Bandura (1991), one of the principal mechanisms via which individuals shape their social environment is self-regulation. People use external rewards and sanctions—which they then internalize—to change their behavior in such a way as to ensure the desired outcome in the environment (cf. Chang, Chang, Sanna, & Kade, 2008). As Bussey and Bandura (1992) observe:

> After an internalized self-regulative mechanism is developed through the combined influence of modeling, tuition, evaluative feedback, and environmental structuring, children guide their conduct by sanctions they apply to themselves. They do things that give them self-satisfaction and a sense of self-worth. They refrain from behaving in ways that violate

their standards to avoid self-censure. The standards provide the guidance; the anticipatory self-sanctions the motivators. Self-sanctions thus
keep conduct in line with internal standards. (p. 1238)

Bandura's view of self-criticism (which equals self-reproach/self-censure) appears
to rest upon three philosophical foundations. Self-criticism contains an "epistemic" element because it enables individuals to know what standards they hold.
It embodies an "ethical" dimension because it helps individuals abide by these
standards and do the "right thing." It carries a "teleological" aspect because it is
utilized in the service of goal-directed action. As I will discuss in the following
chapter, my own theory of self-criticism embraces the epistemic component, is
silent regarding the ethical facet, and modifies the teleological element.

Evaluation

Contemporary psychopathology research cannot be understood without acknowledging the impact reciprocal determinism has exerted upon the discipline
(cf. Hammen, 2006; G. Shahar, 2006a). This fact is preeminently exemplified in the
research into self-criticism that identifies its active vulnerability and cascade-like
nature. Bandura's notion of self-criticism as a self-regulatory stance nonetheless
fails to do justice to the trait's pernicious nature. When viewed as a way of controlling behavior, it should be associated with stress minimization rather than stress
generation. I will make a similar point when discussing Gilbert's theory.

A Cognitive-Evolutionary Approach
to Self-Criticism: Paul Gilbert et al.

Taking a cognitive-evolutionary perspective toward psychopathology and psychotherapy, P. Gilbert et al. conceptualize self-criticism in terms of "social mentalities" (P. Gilbert, 1995, 2000, 2005a, 2005b, 2009; P. Gilbert & Bailey, 2000;
P. Gilbert & Procter, 2006; Sloman & Price, 1987; Sloman, Price, P. Gilbert, &
Gardner, 1994). Via the process of evolution, social challenges have formed many
of the mental mechanisms that enable us to engage in various types of relationships. P. Gilbert and colleagues identify these as "pairs of roles" (e.g., dominant/
subordinate, caregiver/care receiver) that regulate and direct our behavioral
responses, allowing us to obtain the biosocial resources crucial to our survival (P.
Gilbert, 1989, 2000, 2005a, 2005b).

Social mentalities are a combination of motivations, emotions, cognitive-
processing mechanisms, and behaviors (P. Gilbert, 2000). The two most pertinent to self-criticism are social rank (or competitive) mentality and caregiving.

The former represents an attempt to gain status in order to become attractive to others. Directing attentional efforts toward the evaluation of the rival's status, it seeks to determine whether competition is worthwhile and to govern aggressive behavior. Positive affect is regulated by dopamine and the biological reward system and is associated with one's own success and the other's loss/failure.

Akin to parents' grooming of their infants to increase their chances of survival, the caregiving mentality reflects the desire to diminish distress in others, also involving the inhibition of aggression and hostility. Suffering on the part of people close to us (e.g., our infants) prompts negative affect. Positive affect is generated in the context of affiliation, soothing, and safety—allegedly being regulated by oxytocin. Like Bandura's theory and the psychoanalytic notion of internalization (Schafer, 1968), social mentalities are not limited to interpersonal relationships but also characterize self-self relationships—that is, those adopted by people toward themselves (P. Gilbert, 2000; P. Gilbert & Irons, 2005). This view conceptualizes self-criticism in terms of an imbalance between our inner social ranking and caring mentalities, self-critical individuals overdeveloping dominant-subordinate self-to-self relationships (P. Gilbert et al., 2001; Sturman & Mongrain, 2005, 2008) and underdeveloping caring self-to-self relationships (P. Gilbert, Baldwin, Irons, Baccus, & Palmer, 2006).

According to P. Gilbert et al., two forms of self-criticism can be distinguished. The "inadequate self" focuses on mistakes in order to correct them; the "hated self" is preoccupied with hurting the self and feelings of disgust. A third self-related dimension—labeled "reassuring the self"—taps the activation of the self-caring mentality. These three self-aspects can be measured via the Forms of Self-Criticizing/Attacking and Self-Reassuring Scale (FSCRS; P. Gilbert, Clark, Hempel, Miles, & Irons, 2004). Research evinces that the inadequate and hated dimensions are inversely related to self-reassurance (P. Gilbert et al., 2004; P. Gilbert, Baldwin, Irons, et al., 2006; Irons, P. Gilbert, Baldwin, Baccus, & Palmer, 2006).

This theory has spawned a psychotherapeutic strategy for reducing self-criticism known as Compassionate Mind Training (CMT; cf. P. Gilbert, 2009; P. Gilbert & Irons, 2005; P. Gilbert & Procter, 2006). CMT employs a variety of cognitive, behavioral, and interpersonal strategies that seek to enhance caring self-to-self relationships (see CHAPTER 7). The initial reports relating to CMT and related therapeutic regimens are encouraging. In clinical patients, CMT is associated with a reduction of depression, anxiety, shame, inferiority, submissiveness, and self-criticism (P. Gilbert & Procter, 2006). It enables acne sufferers to experience less shame and skin concerns (A. C. Kelly, Zuroff, & Shapira, 2009) and helps smokers reduce their unhealthy habits (A. C. Kelly, Zuroff, Foa, & P. Gilbert, 2010). It appears to be particularly well suited to highly self-critical individuals (A. C. Kelly et al., 2009; A. C. Kelly et al., 2010).

Evaluation

The theory has several significant strengths. In and of itself, the introduction of evolutionary thinking into the field of personality vulnerability to psychopathology constitutes a major accomplishment (see Buss, 2005, for a general treatment of evolutionary psychology). The fact that David Zuroff—Blatt's chief collaborator—is an advocate of evolutionary psychology has led P. Gilbert and Zuroff to collaboratively develop this direction (cf. A. C. Kelly et al., 2010; Zuroff, Fournier, Patall, & Leybman, 2010).

Second, the distinction between social rank and caregiving corresponds to Blatt's introjective/anaclitic differentiation, thus demonstrating continuity with previous theories emphasizing this type of human personality duality (cf. Bakan, 1966; Helgeson, 1994; see also Sturman & Mongrain, 2005). P. Gilbert's construal of caregiving as a fundamentally healthy social mentality may in fact shed light on the unexpected pattern of results linking interpersonal dependency and psychological resilience noted earlier.

Third, the cognitive-evolutionary theory persuasively bridges clinical theory and neurocognitive science, thus promoting fruitful investigation into the role self-criticism plays in information processing (Longe, Maratos, P. Gilbert, Evans, Volker, Rockliff, & Rippon, 2006).

Fourth, by identifying the "inadequate" and "hated" dimensions of self-criticism, Gilbert reinforces the notion of self-concept multiplicity—an overarching theme in psychology (cf. Bromberg, 1996; Lysaker & Hermans, 2007; McConnell, 2011; Rafaeli-Mor & Steinberg, 2002). Although few and far between, other attempts at identifying various forms of self-criticism have been made (Regev, G. Shahar, & Lipsitz, 2012; R. Thompson & Zuroff, 2004).

Finally—and of profound significance—is the link Gilbert et al. make between self-criticism and CMT. Here, theory and therapy are seamlessly connected, the empirical results concerning the efficacy of CMT also being favorable.

So what is the "discontent" to which the chapter heading alludes? Despite my appreciation of the theory's strengths, I nonetheless believe that its account of self-criticism is incompatible with the self-critical cascade described in CHAPTER 1. The cascade entails the active creation of a negative social context by self-critics, in turn leading to further self-criticism. If self-critics are primarily submissive, however, we would expect them to *avoid* confrontation, rejection, and interpersonal loss and possess a steady and relatively high level of social support gained via inhibiting self-assertion. My own clinical experience is consistent with this caveat. Rina, to whom I referred in CHAPTER 1, for example, began picking fights with her boyfriend shortly after he told her he loved her, leading to their breakup. In Rina's case, her self-criticism was most pernicious when her significant other treated her well.[1]

I am thus skeptical of the notion that self-critics should be encouraged to be self-compassionate. My doubts are supported by findings from Gilbert et al.'s own studies, which evince an inverse correlation between self-criticism and self-concept compassion (cf. P. Gilbert, Baldwin et al., 2006; P. Gilbert, McEwan, Matos, & Rivis, 2011). If the association rests on causality—namely, self-criticism (X) reduces self-concept compassion (Y)—an attempt at bolstering Y is unlikely to succeed in changing X.

My expectation is that self-critical patients will be suspicious and reject interventions based on the fostering of self-compassion. Experiencing the world as critical rather than caring, they are unlikely to think that cultivating the latter quality is a worthwhile pursuit. My forecast would be that self-critics would snub not only the content of the intervention but also the therapist who offers it. In general, I believe that patients experience interventions offered by therapists through the lens of their own particularized mental representations of self and others ("object relations"). Self-critical individuals are known to hold highly negative representations of others—including parental figures (Mongrain, 1998; Whiffen, Parker, Wilhelm, Mitchell, & Malhi, 2003). I therefore imagine them doubting the therapist's competence, sincerity, and/or good faith (see Blatt, 1995; G. Shahar, 2001; CHAPTER 7).

"Wait a minute!" I hear my imaginary Gilbertian critic respond. "What about the evidence you yourself have cited regarding the empirical links between self-criticism and submissiveness and the favorable effect of compassion-based treatment on self-criticism?" While I respect this data, I insist on placing it within a larger scientific and clinical context. Although study findings are consistent with a zero-order correlation between self-criticism and submissiveness (cf. Sturman & Mongrain, 2005), they are invariably cross-sectional and uncontrolled for potentially confounding variables (e.g., hopelessness). They also have no bearing on the active and adverse effect of self-criticism on the social context. Likewise, although the findings regarding compassion-based treatment are encouraging (A. C. Kelly et al., 2009; A. C. Kelly et al., 2010), I would need to see how such treatment works with clinically depressed individuals in a randomized clinical trial before becoming convinced that compassion-based treatment is capable of preventing a seriously-depressed self-critical patient from derailing his or her interpersonal relations within and without treatment alike. TDCRP patients have exhibited precisely this capacity.

Rogers' Humanistic Perspective

The humanistic perspective highlights the role of experiential—primarily affective—self-related processes in psychological development, health, and psychopathology. One of its most prominent proponents was the late Carl Rogers (1951, 1959, 1961, 1963), whose theorization concerning the organismic experience, the self, and discrepancies between the real and ideal self is highly relevant to self-criticism.

Rogers argues that "The organism has one basic tendency and striving—to actualize, maintain, and enhance the experiencing organism" (1951, p. 487). The self-actualizing tendency pertains to individuals' effort to become "who they are," in Nietzsche's phraseology—to actualize their potential in all possible domains (Rogers, 1963).[2] According to Rogers, this formidable biopsychological force must be reconciled with the need for positive regard—love, care, and esteem from significant others.

As posited by Rogers, the focal developmental question is whether a child's self-actualizing tendency—his or her "organismic valuing"—is congruent with the positive regard he or she receives from adults, primarily his or her parents. Does a child receive positive regard—rather than neglect or negative regard—for authentic (i.e., organismic) gestures and expressions? In those fortunate instances in which organismic experience is rewarded by positive regard, children are likely to base their experiences, decisions, and actions on their authentic identity. This then enables intact development and psychological health, producing "fully functioning persons" (Rogers, 1961).

Rogers and others have directly influenced Deci and Ryan's self-determination theory (Deci & Ryan, 1985; Ryan & Deci, 2000a). SDT distinguishes between autonomous (intrinsic) and controlled (extrinsic) motivation (see CHAPTERS 1 and 2) by construing autonomous motivation as emanating from one's "authentic identity." Deci and Ryan and their colleagues have amassed an impressive body of empirical literature suggesting that autonomous motivation does in fact foster healthy development and functioning (for reviews, see Deci & Ryan, 2012a, 2012b; Deci, Ryan, & Guay, 2013).

Unfortunately, societal norms and parents' developmental pains frequently prevent parents from giving their children positive regard for their authentic behavior. The conditions of worth (i.e., the terms that must be met to gain approval of one's conduct) thus create a gulf between self-actualizing tendencies and the need for positive regard. This, in turn, causes the child to experience a divide between authentic experience and self-concept.

An example I frequently adduce when teaching Rogers is that of a soft, mellow Israeli boy. Such a type is the direct antithesis of the Israeli myth of the *sabra* or quintessential Jewish Israeli (Israelashvilli, 2013)—a male warrior/philosopher eager to defend his country (e.g., G. Shahar, 2013a). Parents of such a hypothetical child who identify with the *sabra* myth may well be reluctant to approve or regard their child's non-*sabra*-like character. Over time, he is likely to begin criticizing himself for expressing—or even experiencing—such unrewarded traits.

Particularly noxious is the gap that may develop between a child's organismic experience and his or her ideal self, which pertains to an individual's perception of what he or she desires to be(come). The ideal self is thus largely responsible for propelling us to grow, expand, develop, experiment, and achieve. To the extent that a person's ideal self is based on his or her organismic experience ("I enjoy playing the piano so I wish to become a pianist"), this person's sense of self will be congruent with his or her organismic valuing. Conversely, the sense of self held by a person whose ideal self is based on parental conditions of worth ("I need to be a good boy and study") will be incongruent with his or her organismic valuing. The latter state will lead to a lower self-image, ultimately leading to self-criticism. As Rogers himself recognized (1963), discrepancy between organismic experience and the self—particularly the ideal self—constitutes the hallmark of psychopathology.

The distinguished social psychologist Tory Higgins has upgraded this notion in his self-discrepancy theory (Higgins, 1987; Higgins, Roney, Crowe, & Hymes, 1994). Higgins argues that our experience of ourselves is governed by two "self-guides"—the "ideal self" and the "ought self." Whereas the "ideal self" refers to what we wish to become, the "ought self" relates to what we believe we should become. Both the ideal and ought selves are compared with the actual self—what we believe we actually are. Disparities ensuing from this comparison lead to negative affect. Specifically, an actual-ideal self-discrepancy that prompts dejection (a feeling of failure and shame) and an actual-ought self-discrepancy that leads to agitation (guilt and anxiety). Although no studies to date have examined the association between self-criticism and these two gaps, self-criticism is likely to be associated with both.

Evaluation

In my opinion, Rogers' humanistic theory adds a vital dimension to the understanding of self-criticism by adducing the notion of authenticity and the real (true) self. Authenticity is central to the theory I will develop in the following chapters.

Another noteworthy strength of Rogers' approach lies in its implication of parent-child relationships in the generation of self-criticism. This directly recalls Blatt's anaclitic and introjective psychopathologies (Blatt was, of course, Rogers' intern). According to Blatt—and empirical studies—harsh, judgmental, and punitive parents instill self-criticism in their children (Blatt, 1995; Koestner, Zuroff, & Powers, 1991).

Another very important strength I perceive in Rogers' perspective lies in its emphasis on self-concept multiplicity. In propounding that negative self-image stems from the discrepancy between a person's organismic experience and his or her ideal self, Rogers presumes that the self is constituted of numerous interacting facets.

Having developed his theory long before research identified self-criticism as a central dimension of vulnerability, Rogers cannot be blamed for neglecting key features of the trait—such as self-criticism's active vulnerability or the scarring effect of psychopathology on self-criticism, for instance. Only one aspect of the theory thus appears to me to be inherently weak—namely, the way in which a person recognizes authentic, organismic experience. Rogers assumes that knowledge

Table 3.1 **Summary of Leading Theories of Self-Criticism**

	Definition of Self-Criticism	*Strengths*	*Limitations*
Blatt et al.	A marker of the introjective personality configuration. A tendency to adopt a punitive self-stance when standards are not met. Internalized based on critical and harsh parent-child relationship.	Locates self-criticism in an overarching and coherent theory of personality, development, psychopathology, and psychotherapy. Has inspired decades-long, voluminous research on self-criticism with an extensively-used measure (Depressive Experiences Questionnaire).	Self-criticism confers much more vulnerability than dependency. Measures of self-criticism appear to belong to both introjective and anaclitic configurations. Does not account for the self-criticism cascade.
Beck et al.	One of the pillars of the cognitive triad, defined as negative cognitions toward the self. Alternatively, a "mode" or cluster of schemas linking cognitive, affective, motivational, behavioral, and physiological processes.	Historically, negative cognitions toward the self constitute a precursor of self-criticism. Links self and the future. The notion of modes purports to bridge various studies of self-criticism.	Being adevelopmental, it does not specify the origins of self-criticism. Does not account for the self-criticism cascade.
Bandura	Self-criticism pertains to self-reproach or self-censure—internal guides that regulate behavior in accordance with standards. These guides are adopted from external guides provided by others (parents).	Reciprocal determinism has inspired research into active person-context exchanges, which in turn led to identification of the self-critical cascade. Self-reproach is epistemic and teleological, enabling the recognition of standards and their pursuit.	Does not account for the self-critical cascade because it predicts that self-reproach will minimize—rather than generate—interpersonal strife.

P. Gilbert et al.	A submissive stance toward self and others resulting from an overdominant social-ranking mentality at the expense of a caregiving mentality. Results from an interaction between bioevolutionary tendencies and specific parent-child relationships that set the stage for a critical self-self relationship.	Introduced evolutionary biology and psychology into the field of personality and psychopathology Bridges clinical theory and cognitive research. Gave rise to a clearly delineated mode of (compassion-based) therapy. Initial empirical findings concerning the intervention are favorable.	Self-critical submissiveness is inconsistent with both clinical experience and empirical research, which evinces the trait's tendency toward creating interpersonal havoc. Self-criticism is likely to discourage compassion from others and self-compassion.
Rogers	Self-criticism results from a discrepancy between a person's organismic valuing (authenticity, true self) and experience of him- or herself. (Deci and Ryan's self-determination theory attests to the importance of pursuing organismic valuing.) This results from a disparity between organismic valuing and the need for positive regard from others, primarily parents. This gap is internalized throughout development. The discrepancy is particularly painful when it involves actual (organismic, true, authentic) experience and the ideal self (Higgins's self-discrepancy theory adds the actual/ought self discrepancy).	Introduces the novel dimension of authenticity. Is consistent with the notion of self-concept multiplicity.	It is unclear how self-knowledge (i.e., knowledge of the organismic valuing) is attained. The theory assumes that this happens naturally. The theory does not account for the self-critical cascade (although the self-critical cascade was identified long after the theory's development).

about one's nature is largely a natural process: to the extent that the human environment allows a child to "find him- or herself," organismic valuing will prevail. I find this an extremely naïve assumption. In the following chapter, I will in fact argue that self-knowledge is a hugely challenging task even under relatively simple and straightforward conditions—not to mention in our globalized, postmodern world (Strenger, 2011) (see CHAPTER 5). Without self-knowledge, authenticity cannot be identified, let alone enacted. This, I will posit, is where self-criticism comes in.

Chapter Summary

Table 3.1 summarizes all the theories reviewed in this chapter. For each theory, I supply the definition and origins it adduces for self-criticism and present its strengths and weaknesses. The table demonstrates the existence of two patterns. First, all the theories—with the exception of Beck's (originally) developmental approach—employ the notion of internalization, identifying critical and judgmental parent-child exchanges as a precursor of self-criticism. Second, none account for the self-critical cascade gleaned from the research reviewed in CHAPTER 1. Blatt's, Beck's, and Rogers' theories are agnostic toward this cascade (Rogers' theory, of course, originated long before the cascade was identified). Bandura's and Gilbert's theses contain implicit derivatives that predict the inverse of the results of empirical studies. Their theories thus lead to the hypothesis that self-criticism should minimize interpersonal strife—an assumption counterindicated by research.

The task that lies before me at this juncture is thus to build upon the consensus regarding the central role played by internalized harsh and judgmental parent-child relationships in self-criticism. At the same time, I must also construct a clear conceptualization that will explain the trait's active vulnerability and cascade. The following chapter is devoted to this endeavor.

4

Authenticity and Self-Knowledge (*ASK*)

Only the True Self can be creative and only the True Self can feel real.
(Winnicott, 1965, p. 147)

Each to each a looking glass/reflects the other that doth pass.
(Cooley, 1902, p. 152)

Having spent so much time in the lab and library in the previous chapters, I suggest we now head back to the clinic. After all, this is where some fresh insights might be found.

I recently described the case of an extremely self-critical young-adult (A. C. Kelly, Zuroff, & G. Shahar, 2014). Although Ilan was a highly intelligent and successful 20-year-old undergraduate student with a history of success, his experience of child neglect and marginalization by family and friends had led him to feel depressed his whole life. At intake, it became apparent that over the years his depression had been twofold: superimposed upon long periods of comparatively moderate depression were acute, severe, and—most importantly—suicidal depressive episodes. Such is the face of double depression—a serious, refractory condition (J. P. McCullough et al., 2000; Pettit & Joiner, 2006). Underlying Ilan's suffering was a clearly malignant self-criticism, reflected in his repeated self-derogatory dismissal of his talents and achievements. Despite his alarming symptomatology, however, he was determined to try treatment.

With Ilan, I based my integrative psychotherapeutic strategy (see CHAPTER 6) on cognitive-behavioral therapy for depression (Beck, Rush, & Shaw, & Emery 1979) with some slight modifications (see A. C. Kelly, Zuroff, & G. Shahar, 2014). Feeling that the first psychotherapy sessions were proceeding well, I was taken aback by Ilan's dejection and pessimism. He reported experiencing the sessions as ineffective, regarding me as a smug, know-it-all psychologist who cared little about him as a person. Surprised and hurt, I sought to inquire about the specifics of my intervention in the hope of identifying the infiltration of iatrogenic elements. None were apparent. I then made a mistake, proposing that perhaps I was not the right therapist for him and that he might consider seeking another. He immediately responded, "This is it? You're giving up on me that quickly?!" I then realized that my own self-criticism, surfacing in relation to my failure to help Ilan ("I am not helping him—perhaps I am not good enough") had been activated. I also surmised that embedded in Ilan's expressed skepticism regarding my helpfulness was a series of questions: Are you committed to caring for me? Can you survive my depression and suspiciousness? Do you have the wherewithal? Am I "treatable"?

The question "Who am I?" is predicated upon three principles. The first is metaphysical: an "I" exists as a stable core of myself that I need to get to know and rely on. The second is epistemological—there are ways to know this "I." The third is that the answer is elusive; otherwise, the question would be irrelevant. The emotional context within which the question is frequently posed—marked by anguish and urgency—further confirms that the task of self-knowledge is far from easy or certain.

These three principles represent my own theoretical approach to the problem of self-criticism. I construe self-criticism as a distorted and highly maladaptive form of self-knowledge. The present chapter is dedicated to elaborating this approach.

There is Such a Thing as a "True Self"

My take on the history of psychology is that, by the nineteenth century, it was well on the way to capturing the essence of human personality. This task was greatly facilitated by its endorsement of the notions of "authenticity" and the "true self." As presented in Table 4.1, an impressive array of very different theoreticians share this notion. The research emanating from their theories is presented in Table 4.2. Rather than being exhaustive, this information is provided in the service of convincing you that psychology has long paid serious attention to the notion of authenticity.

All of a sudden, however, something went wrong. The emergence of postmodern "philosophy" calling the very notion of ontogeny into question, the idea/existence of a true, authentic self was completely undercut (e.g., Gergen, 1991). Coupled with this trend, empirical psychology began to shift away from the classic version of the humanities toward an atomistic approach to the person. This focused on specialized research of isolated processes frequently employing sophisticated methodologies at the expense of an overarching description of the person (see Bevan, 1991; Dewsbury, 2000, 2009; Sternberg, 2005). Driven out of personality and clinical psychology from both sides, the "authentic self" is today principally confined—primarily under the auspices of Deci and Ryan's self-determination theory (see also Gillath, Sesko, Shaver, & Chun, 2010; Harter, 2002)—to developmental and social psychology.

Even the remedies proposed by the theoreticians and investigators noted in Tables 4.1 and 4.2 are not without confusion. A quick glance at the two tables

Table 4.1 **Theories of Authenticity**

Theoretician	Term and Definition	Role in Health
Allport (1955)	Self: The core of personality, transcending individual traits.	Developing an authentic, complex self is crucial for psychological health, enabling a sense of uniqueness and wholeness.
Bollas (1987)	Vitality, identity	When sacrificed, this leads to the development of "the normotic personality," which is governed by artificial norms, roles, and principles.
Horney (1950) See also Paris (1999)	Self-realization: A set of intrinsic potentialities based on our genetic makeup and in need of a supportive environment.	Protects against conflict and neurosis.
Jung (1971)	Self: The creative and authentic potential	Its expression is crucial for mental health.
Kohut (1971)	Nuclear self: An innate core of the self awaiting development in the context of the parent-child relationship.	Parental failures to serve as "selfobjects"—human "objects" in the service of the child's self—derail the development of the nuclear self, leading to "disorders of the self."
Laing (1969) See also M. G. Thompson (1994)	Self-deception	The source of psychopathology.
Maslow (1968) See also Kenrick, Griskevicius, Neuberg, & Schaller (2010)	Self-actualization: The highest form of human motivation.	The more we pursue it, the healthier we are. Its absence leads to "metapathologies"— painful experiences tied to a lack of meaning rather than to psychiatric conditions (e.g., senselessness).

(*continued*)

Table 4.1 **Continued**

Theoretician	Term and Definition	Role in Health
Rank (1968)	Will: An inner force dictating development, relationships, and health.	Must be respected by others in order to enable healthy development and therapeutic success.
Rogers (1951, 1959, 1961, 1963)	Organismic valuing: Our true, authentic, biologically based nature.	The more dominant it is in our unfolding experience, the more "fully functioning" we are.
Turner (1976)	Real self: Experiences people deem as parts of themselves. Institutional real-self experiences are consistent with social roles; impulse-based real-self experiences are unrelated to social roles.	In modernity, we have witnessed a trend toward impulse-based experience.
Winnicott (1965)	True self (vs. false self): An authentic experience enabling aliveness, spontaneity, and "feeling real." This fragile core of human personality is frequently defensively hidden by the False Self—representing the compliant and reactive aspect of our personality.	When the false self dominates the true self, a pathology of subjectivity is instituted, manifested in rigidity, overcompliance, and emotional numbness.

attests to the diverse and ambiguous ways in which "authenticity" and the "true self" are defined and operationalized. Some definitions appear tautological. Harter, for example, regards authenticity in terms of "Owning one's personal experiences, be they thoughts, emotions, needs, wants, preferences, or beliefs. . . . one acts in accord with the true self, expressing oneself in ways that are consistent with inner thoughts and feelings" (2002, p. 382; also cited in Gillath et al., 2010).

Not only does this definition account for authenticity in terms of the true self, these two terms customarily being used interchangeably, but it also fails to identify what is really "true" in a person's "inner thoughts and feelings." For example, I can "own" a desire to become a physician, only to find out—in the course

Table 4.2 **Research on Authenticity**

Researchers	Term and Definition	Role in Health
Bargh, McKenna, & Fitzsimons (2002)	True self: What people believe they really are.	Is expressed more readily over the Internet than in face-to-face interactions.
English & John (2013)	Inauthenticity: Lower levels of trait authenticity.	Mediates the effect of emotional suppression on poor social functioning.
Gillath et al. (2010)	State authenticity	Is increased following experimental manipulation (priming) that increases secure attachment.
Kolden, Klein, Wang, & Austin (2011)	Genuineness in therapeutic relationships.	Predicts improvement in psychotherapy.
Ryff (1989) See also Ryff & Singer (2008)	Virtues—what is special and unique about us. The authors draw on Aristotle's *Nichomacean Ethics* to explain the conditions necessary for *eudaimonia*—a life full of meaning (to be distinguished from happiness).	Components of our virtues (e.g., self-acceptance) ultimately lead to subjective well-being.
Sheldon, Ryan, Rawsthorne, & Illardi (1997)	True selfhood: Self-reported authenticity across different life domains	Elevated levels across various life domains predict psychological and physical well-being.
Wood, Linley, Maltby, Baliousis, & Joseph (2008)	Dispositional authenticity	Predicts high self-esteem and well-being.

of therapy—that this desire is not really mine but has been instilled in me by my parents.

I will thus take the risk of offering my own definition of the authentic self: *Self-authenticity pertains to a set of innate (biologically based) and immutable talents, interests, and physiological-cognitive-emotional proclivities that take shape via the transactions between an individual and his or her interpersonal, social, and cultural context. Self-authenticity is experienced via present-moment attention and future-oriented goal-directed action. An active pursuit of the authentic self leads to affirmation ("This is what I am"), curiosity ("This matters to me; I'd like to get in touch with it/figure it out/ do more of this"), and zest ("I have energy to do this"; "This makes me feel alive")—but not necessarily either tranquility or happiness.*

Let us break down this definition into its constitutive elements. My focus on talents, interests, and physiological-cognitive-emotional proclivities derives from the fact that they (1) are circumscribed and thus relatively clearly delineated; (2) emerge during early development; (3) are relatively easy to identify; and (4) are proximally related to our genetically-based, brain-wired biological endowment (Damasio, 2003; Fosha, 2013; Kandel, 1998; LeDoux, 2003; Northoff & Bermpohl, 2004; Northoff et al., 2006). By way of further elaborating on these physiological-cognitive-emotional proclivities, I am referring to:

- Individual differences in regulating physical pain and pleasure, pain-pleasure thresholds, bodily reactions to climate changes, inter- and intra-individual differences in circadian rhythms, and so forth (Adan et al., 2012; Geisser, Robinson, & Pickern, 1992; Higgins, 1997; McEwen, 1998; Solberg Nes, Roac, & Segerstromm, 2009).
- Particular cognitive styles capturing infant-turned-child attentional style; memory capacity; problem-solving modes; preferences for specific problems, riddles, and cognitive challenges; and so forth (Aminoff et al., 2012; Gruszka, Matthews, & Szymura, 2010; MacLeod, 1979; Witkin, 1950).
- Individual differences in emotional style—including thresholds for both negative and positive affect, emotional expressivity, and emotional complexity (Gross & John, 2003; Kring, Smith, & Neale, 1994; Larsen & Diener, 1987; Larsen & Ketelaar, 1991).

The majority of these characteristics are subsumed under the extensively-studied concept of "temperament" (Rothbart, 2011; Rothbart & Bates, 1998). While this relates to basic and innate physiological, cognitive, and affective styles, it does not necessarily include talents, interests, or problem-solving styles.

Parents of young children frequently take pride in the particular abilities their children exhibit, this sense growing exponentially the more children they have and the more the differences between them become evident. Thus, for example, our 12-year-old Lielle has been extremely quick, physically daring, and interpersonally engaging from birth, compensating with wit and charm for her disorganization and in love with animals since the first time she laid eyes on a large dog at the age of 1. Our 3-year-old, Matan, in contrast, is cautious, careful, and highly organized. His passion is for cars rather than animals. I submit that Lielle's and Matan's particular styles are stable and form the core of their authentic selves.

This does not mean that Lielle is destined to be a horse rider or veterinarian or that Matan will become a Formula 1 racing driver or engineer. Talents, interests, and physiological-cognitive-emotional proclivities assume their particular shape and form via person-context exchange. Different environments may pose diverse pressures, challenges, and problems for individuals with identical—or very similar—talents, interests, and physiological-cognitive-emotional proclivities. Children with identical talents, interests, and physiological-cognitive-emotional proclivities are also likely to interact differently with other caregivers or children, leading to widely varied expressions of their innate tendencies. Although I cannot summarize the field's findings here, behavioral genetics has long noted these striking variations (cf. Reiss, Plomin, Neiderhiser, & Hetherington, 2003). What is important to me at this stage is to be as clear as possible as to what constitutes the core of our being—and to marvel at the contingency and fragility of its developmental expression.

One way I find helpful in thinking about the interactions between core tendencies and social environment is to reflect upon the trajectory of young people. A while ago, a district attorney asked me to evaluate a 15-year-old boy who had murdered a peer. Not engaging in forensic psychology, I politely declined. From my brief conversation with the district attorney, however, I learned that the suspected murderer had no criminal record and was regarded as a "good"—albeit slightly tempestuous—boy. For hours afterward, I pondered how such a person could commit such an act.

These reflections took me to one of my favorite movies—*The Talented Mr. Ripley* (1999), starring Matt Damon. Based on a Patricia Highsmith novel, the plot takes place in the late 1950s in New York and Italy. The protagonist—Tom Ripley—is a young, lonely, homosexual man struggling to make a living. Hired by the wealthy Herbert Greenleaf to travel to Italy and convince Greenleaf's son, Dickie, to come back home to his ailing mother, Ripley instead befriends Dickie and his fiancée, Marge. As Ripley's feelings toward Dickie become stronger and more romantic, however, Dickie grows tired of Ripley. When the two go sailing in Dickie's boat, an argument erupts, culminating in Ripley hitting Dickie and inadvertently killing him. Ripley then proceeds to impersonate Dickie. While assuming Dickie's lavish lifestyle, however, Ripley finds himself having to commit numerous further crimes in order to conceal the first—including additional impersonations and two more murders.

As attested by an abundance of viewers, despite his abhorrent behavior Tom Ripley is a very likable character. Why are we so drawn to him? In my opinion, the enigma may be explained by the fact that the plot creates a wedge between Ripley's core being—which is intriguing but not inherently ominous—and his ultimately catastrophic actions.

Tom Ripley is a natural forger, impersonator, charmer, and persuader. Highly intelligent, he addresses himself to complex problems, to which he finds ingenious solutions in rapid-fire time. His outstanding visual-motor capacities enable him to duplicate documents, his powers of persuasion to assume any identity he likes. At the same time, the plot makes it very clear that he is a disadvantaged—perhaps even maltreated—young person who craves love and a sense of belonging. In fact, whereas his talents—forgery, impersonation, and persuasion—are masterful and elegant, his horrific crimes clearly derive from frustration and humiliation, undeniably causing him a great deal of anguish.

Wondering about the film, I imagine a scenario in which Tom Ripley is recruited by the CIA and provided with a stable, nurturing environment and a clear sense of mission and belonging. What a great spy he might have been! How heroic—rather than tragic—his life could have turned out to be!

This not being the case, and presumably born to an impoverished family wherein he had to apply his talents in the service of survival, Ripley's situation reminds me of Martin Heidegger's concept of "thrownness" (*Geworfenheit*). Herein, the founding father of existentialism refers to the fact that human beings are born into this world with no prior experience/knowledge or innate means for mastering the biological, historical, social, and cultural conditions into which they find themselves "thrown" and that govern their development (see also G. Shahar, 2010, footnote 2). When Ripley is hired by a rich gentleman to find the "prodigal son" and persuade him to come back home, one part of Ripley cannot refuse. Embarking on the mission, however, he uses his three formidable talents to actualize another core of his authentic being—to find love—rather than to fulfill the task at hand. Hereby, he seals his own fate.

In a seminal article entitled "Selection, Evocation, Manipulation" published in the highly prestigious *Journal of Personality and Social Psychology*, David Buss (1987) provides us with a chillingly clear framework for understanding Ripley's tragedy. In it, he challenges the research methodology preferred by social psychology—the analysis of variance (ANOVA) perspective of personality and the social context—whereby putative outcomes stem from a relatively static co-occurrence ("statistical interaction") of two factors:

> Individuals in everyday life are not randomly exposed to all possible situations. Individuals seek and avoid situations selectively. They elicit different responses from their social environment, sometimes unintentionally. Individuals also purposely alter, influence, change, exploit, and manipulate the environments they have selected to inhabit. These forms of interactions are not well captured by the ANOVA solution. (1987, p. 1215)

Ripley selects an environment consistent with his talents. Perhaps for the first time in his life, he evokes admiration and care, feeling visible and nurtured. In turn, he falls in love. When this love is threatened, he uses his manipulative powers to attempt to protect it. When these efforts are thwarted, calamity steps in.

Moving on to the next component of my definition of the authentic self, I posit that authenticity of the self is experienced via present-moment attention and future-oriented goal-directed action. Let me first discuss what happens in the present and then attend to the future.

The present is the only time in which our talents, interests, and physiological-cognitive-emotional proclivities are manifested in action—or, to use another Heideggerian key phrase—"in-the-world." A look at Tom Ripley's face as he practices imitating Dickie Greenleaf vividly illustrates this. He is "going-on-being" (Winnicott, 1960), fully functioning (Rogers, 1962), self-actualizing (Maslow, 1968), in a state of flow (Csikszentmihalyi, 1990), or mindfully immersed in present-moment awareness (Kabat-Zinn, 1990). The present is indeed an enormous gift—a temporal arena within which we may actualize our authentic potential.

With respect to the future—it appears to be here, and here to stay, at least in psychology. Recent conceptualizations and research in cognitive, developmental, personality, and clinical psychology alike propound it as the nexus of mental activity (for reviews, see Davidson & G. Shahar, 2007; D. Gilbert & Wilson, 2007; Seligman, Railton, Baumeister, & Sripada, 2013; G. Shahar, 2004, 2006a, 2010, 2011, 2013b; G. Shahar, Cross, & Henrich, 2004; G. Shahar & Davidson, 2009). The emergence of goal constructs in personality psychology (Austin & Vancouver, 1996)—characterized by terms such as "life tasks" (Cantor, 1990; Harlow & Cantor, 1994), "personal goals" (Brunstein, 1993), "personal strivings" (Emmons, 1986), "life planning" (Smith, 1999), "possible selves" (Markus & Nurius, 1986), and "personal projects" (Little, 1999)—provides concrete examples of this view. These constructs are highly compatible with Rychlak's (1977) teleological approach to psychological explanation. They are also consistent with findings from comparative psychology and neuroscience (e.g., Amati & Shallice, 2007) that attest to the unique role the prefrontal cortex—where the brain regions involved in planning and decision-making are located (e.g., Brodmann area 10; Koechlin & Hyafil, 2007; S. J. Gilbert, Spengler et al., 2006; Rushworth, Noonan, Boorman, Walton, & Behrens, 2011)—plays in human survival.

This empirical thrust was foreseen long ago by the interpersonal psychiatrist/psychoanalyst Harry Stack Sullivan:

> I am saying that, *circumstances not interfering*, man the person lives with his past, the present, and the neighboring future all clearly relevant in explaining his thought and action; and the near future is influential to a degree nowhere else remotely approached amongst the species of the living. (1953, p. 369 [original italics])[1]

My contention is that the talents, interests, and physiological-cognitive-emotional proclivities that represent our authentic self are in a constant process of being realized. From a phenomenological perspective, we are immersed in goals, plans, and projects that correspond to the shapes and forms we would like to assume in the short- and long-term future. In this sense, we are "becoming," "ahead of ourselves," or "locomotive." In David Cooper's words:

At any given point in an acorn's career, it is possible to give an exhaustive description of it in terms of the properties—color, molecular structure, and so forth—which belong to it at that moment. But no complete account can be given of a human being without reference to what he is in the process of becoming—without reference, that is, to the projects and intentions which he is on the way to realizing, and in terms of which sense is made of his present condition. As Heidegger puts it, the human being is always "ahead of himself," always *unterwegs* ("on the way"). (1990, p. 3)

Larry Davidson and I have made a similar point:

Human beings are not static entities that merely react to external forces, like billiard balls sitting on a pool table, but are locomotives that are constantly in motion. As a result, it is not sufficient in our science only to ask why people do what they do—a question we consider impossible to answer fully in the ways described—but it is also important to ask what the person is doing and what he or she is doing it for (i.e., with what intended aims). Through these questions we both preserve action as one pole of the relationship with environmental factors and introduce into our framework an orientation toward the future as well as the past. Our behavior not only stems from what came before it but is intended to bring about, or create, a future that does not yet exist. As captured with crystal clarity in one of Kant's (1929) antinomies, we experience ourselves both as being determined (somewhat) by our past while also deciding (somewhat) what we want to make of our future. (Davidson & G. Shahar, 2007, p. 221)[2]

In a series of theoretical articles, I have labeled the authentic self's forward-seeking as "projectuality" or "the attempt to become what I might." "Projectuality" contrasts with "eventuality"—the myriad stressors (acute or chronic) that prevent us from moving toward realizing our authentic self. Tom Ripley's projectuality is embodied in the fact that, when imitating the way in which Dickie Greenleaf speaks to his fiancée, he is not only honing his innate skills and talents but also forging a plan or course of action that will allow him to attain his desire—a sense of belonging and love. Fascinatingly, it is not Marge who serves as an eventuality. Ripley being attracted to Dickie and convinced that Dickie is in love with him, the real eventuality blocking Ripley's projectuality is Dickie—specifically, his insincerity, callousness, and dismissiveness of Ripley's place in his life.

But what about the past? Although my initial psychoanalytic persuasion might not be compatible with the focus on the present and future just discussed, I nonetheless draw upon the psychodynamic approach in appreciating the role our past plays in the formation of our "authentic self." Ultimately, however,

I choose a narrative-based version of the psychodynamic approach (Spence, 1982; Stolorow & Atwood, 1992) that eschews the hope of reconstructing one's past based on current unfolding—both within and without treatment—in favor of viewing past events as raw materials from which our life stories are "composed" (Hermans, 1996).

As I will argue in the following chapter, these "raw materials" are likely to have a profound impact on the way(s) in which we attempt to realize our authentic self in the present and project our talents, interests, and physiological-cognitive-emotional proclivities into the future. Thus, for example, a past history of maltreatment and deprivation—such as that I attributed to Tom Ripley—is likely to lead to a life story marred by cynicism and/or suspiciousness (for research evidence, see G. Shahar, Chinman, Sells, & Davidson, 2003). This, in turn, may lead to twisted attempts at realizing one's authentic self—ultimately "ending" in a cul-de-sac (as in Ripley's case; see also research on revictimization among victims of childhood sexual abuse, for instance, as reviewed by Marx, Heidt, & Gold, 2005). Despite acknowledging the significance of the past, however, I nonetheless align myself—together with an increasing number of voices within psychoanalysis (Safran, 1995; Strenger, 2002; Summers, 2003)—with the humanistic-existential-phenomenological school of thought that highlights the role of the present and future. I will return to this subject in CHAPTER 7.

This discussion of the role of the present, future, and past in the unfolding of the authentic self closely tallies with developmental science. The ability to reflect abstractly on the self—and to project the self into the future in particular—is clearly not a given but develops very slowly over the first decade of life. Dan McAdams (2013) has recently charted a self-based trajectory composed of three stages: self as actor, self as agent, and self as author. Self as actor pertains to the first 3 years of life, during which children learn to master their environment in order to regulate their selves. During this period, the self's contents consist primarily of social roles and skills. Self as agent comes to the fore between the ages of 7 and 9. A preliminary focus on the future then emerges alongside an emphasis on the present, the self's content consisting of goals, plans, and hopes designed to secure self-esteem. Self as author emerges around mid-adolescence, continuing through young adulthood (ages 15 to 25). In this stage, the self consists of one's life narrative, the past being on a par with the present and future and the principal developmental task being self-continuity. In line with McAdams's theory, I believe that, by the end of the third decade of life—when the majority of crucial life decisions are often made and the social environment is relatively fixed—the particular shape of the authentic self has largely been determined (Masten & Tellegen, 2012; but see other research on late blooming in adulthood in Masten & Wright, 2009).[3]

The final element in my definition of the authentic self is as follows: an active pursuit of the authentic self leads to affirmation ("This is what I am"), curiosity ("I'd like to get in touch with it/figure it out/do more of this"), and zest ("I have energy to do this"; "This makes me feel alive")—without necessarily entailing either tranquility or happiness. The major purpose of this component is to clarify what—and, even more importantly, what is not—yielded by pursuing an authentic self. Although my point is not original—Rogers and Maslow having already cautioned against the expectation that authenticity leads to either tranquility or happiness (Maslow, 1968; Rogers, 1963; see also Ryff & Singer, 2008)—it emphasizes that the pursuit of authenticity appears to be its own reinforcement.

As I am writing this book, I am not happy. I am tense and weary and have neglected my family. I am worried lest my written words do not adequately convey my ideas. I am apprehensive as to how readers are going to react to my arguments. I am concerned about the response of past mentors and current colleagues. I am pained by the fact that departments of psychology—and universities in general—are largely disinterested in faculty members publishing books. In Israel, where psychology is—correctly—regarded as an empirical science, university psychology budgets are based on peer-reviewed publications, number of graduate students, and, of course, obtaining competitive research grants. Colleagues are constantly asking me: "Why do you need a book?" My reply—"I don't need a book. I need to write one"—is an expression of my loyalty to my (presumed) talents and interests. My authentic self needs to contemplate large, integrative ideas; to move freely among different points of view; to narrate arguments; and, alas, to be polemic and opinionated. Thus, although I am tense, frequently exhausted, and sometimes burdened by this project, it also makes me feel real, going-on-being, fully functioning, and self-actualizing.

The Formidable Task of Knowing Myself

When I presented Rogers's theory in the previous chapter, I noted one of the major limitations from which it suffers—namely, the assumption that knowing one's organismic valuing (equal to the authentic self) is a relatively straightforward affair. The only thing required from the environment (parents) is empathy toward the developing child's organismic experience—that is, a positive and unconditional affirmation of it that allows the child to develop a positive, unconditional self-regard. Having argued that the task of knowing one's authentic self is much more laborious, I will now develop that argument further.[4]

The fact that we actually succeed in knowing ourselves at all is—to borrow a term from Ann Masten (2014)—"ordinary magic." The task of "knowing thyself" is not just hard; it is downright formidable, ridden with complications, and prone to going wrong. Here are some of the naturally-occurring obstacles:

1. Inherent complexity (multiple selves): Let me introduce a Neanderthal-like mental experiment and assume I have only two talents—running fast and throwing a spear. I barely keep up with all other tasks. Let us also presume

I have only two interests—male companionship and heterosexual relationships. Let us likewise contend that I have only two notable physiological features—I need a lot of sleep and am very sensitive to low temperatures (both true, in my case). My cognitive style is marked by seeking to grasp the bigger picture (the forest) at the expense of attending to details (the trees). Finally, I have only two emotional styles: I tend to dissociate from anxiety but am very sensitive to insults and humiliation.

My best-case scenario would be to hunt with the tribe exclusively during the summer months after a good, long night's sleep in the role of chaser after and spearer of the prey. I must rely on other hunters to guide me toward the game because I am not a detail person, and if I fail none of my fellow hunters can ridicule me. When I succeed, I must be rewarded by my comrades' friendship and my wife's admiration of my physique and prowess.

This is, of course, only one of 32 possible permutations of my talents, interests, and physiological-cognitive-emotional proclivities—and certainly far from the likeliest! The tribe would be forced to hunt in the winter as well and I would assuredly not always have the luxury of a good, long night's sleep before setting out. My fellow hunters would not necessarily assist me in honing in on the prey, probably at least some of the time voicing their frustration and disappointment in me when I failed. Rather than being rewarded by male friendship, I might be the target of envy. My wife, it need not be stated, simply might not be in the mood.

My point here is very simple: the authentic self is inherently, even mathematically, intricate. When this intrinsic complexity is combined with variable environmental conditions, it is plain that even figuring it out—let alone realizing it—constitutes an enormously challenging task.

This problematic is intimately tied to the issue of self-concept multiplicity. While personality, social, and clinical psychology recognized the polylithic nature of the self-concept early on (Guidano, 1987; Linville, 1987; Rafaeli-Mor & Steinberg, 2002; McConnell, 2011), the notion of the multiple self has recently been elevated to the status of an axiom (e.g., Klein, 2012). In clinical theory, if you are not addressing the multiple self, you might as well give up. The notion is advanced within (relational) psychoanalysis (Bromberg, 1996), social cognitive theory (Lysaker & Hermans, 2007), Young's schema therapy (e.g., Rafaeli, Bernstein, & Young, 2010), and even family-systems therapy (Satir, 1978; Wark, Thomas, & Peterson, 2001). Within postmodern thought, the existence of multiple selves forms a pillar of the argument against an ontological, "real" self (Gergen, 1991).

As far as I am concerned, however, the multiple self is primarily a testimony to the difficulty of gaining self-knowledge. It is an indication that (a) given human restrictions, knowing all self-states is impossible, but (b) knowing some is quite possible, and (c) even under dire conditions in which my authentic self is unknown, I may nonetheless discover aspects of it. In my scheme of things, self-concept multiplicity is thus a battle cry rather than bad news.

2. Eventuality (stress): The previous quote from Sullivan to the effect that, when circumstances do not interfere, humans are future oriented, was written in the context of explaining why an individual's need for satisfaction is thwarted. In other words, a child's anxiety—frequently prompted by maternal anxiety—shifts the emphasis of development from the need for satisfaction to the need for security. Superimposing Sullivan's theory upon Winnicott's concept of the true self, I (G. Shahar, 2011) have suggested that the need for satisfaction represents a pursuit of future-oriented authenticity. I labeled this "projectuality" and posited that such activity is blocked by external circumstances that threaten the child. I grouped these external circumstances under the label "eventuality." I then equated "eventuality" with life-stress, contending that—perhaps contrary to Sullivan's contention—circumstances *always* interfere. With stress being inexorable and ubiquitous, eventuality always threatens projectuality. That kids thrive in the face of this tension is yet another example of "ordinary magic" (Masten, 2014).

Let us now translate these ideas into the current definition of authenticity. Sheera Lerman and I (G. Shahar & Lerman, 2013) have conceptualized the idea as follows:

> Consider, for instance, the occurrence of chronic illness during adolescence, an important developmental period in which self and identity take shape. Imagine a 16-year-old teenager struggling to figure out her sexual identity within a social matrix of ongoing tension between herself and her parents and herself and her peers, compounded by mounting pressure to excel in school and prepare for college. Now imagine this teen struggling with an onset of diabetes, cystic fibrosis, juvenile rheumatic arthritis, or irritable bowel disease. . . . The demands these conditions will make on this hypothetical teen are formidable, and we can expect her physical and mental resources to be drained. This in turn will impede her ability to form—let alone pursue—coherent, self-related life goals. (p. 50)

Whether the stress is chronic, acute, relatively minor, major, or catastrophic, its presence interferes with the pursuit of an authentic self. What I am currently emphasizing is that one of the ways in which stress impedes authenticity is via its derailment of self-knowledge. The task of reflecting upon my current attempts at realization—let alone planning ahead for future attempts—is so cognitively daunting that it cannot be contemplated under the demands posed by life-stress.

I imagine the reader has already noted my fascination with Winnicott.[5] In his poetically poignant way of phrasing ideas, Winnicott (1960) used the term "impingements" to denote all the various environmental demands reality imposes—developmentally prematurely—upon the infant. The task of parents is to shield their offspring from these by acting as a "holding environment." When they fail in this role—as they invariably do from time to time—the infant is forced to attend to the impinging stress rather than simply "going-on-being" (equal here to "experiencing oneself"). Such experiences of the authentic self provide the data for a reflective self—whose objective is to attain as accurate a self-knowledge as possible.

3. The other ("mirroring"): In *No Exit*, Gaston utters one of Jean-Paul Sartre's (1944) most well-known dicta: "Hell is other people." A common interpretation of this adage is that living among other people is inevitable and that, despite our wish to control their view of us, they see us in the way they wish to.

From the point of view of *Authenticity and Self-Knowledge (ASK)*, our interpersonal nature not only mandates an evaluation by others but also demands that we learn about ourselves via the way in which others perceive us. This notion was first proposed during the early 1900s within the field of sociology (Cooley, 1902; Mead, 1934). In the context of symbolic interaction theory, Cooley coined the term the "looking glass self" (1902) to denote the way in which people's beliefs regarding how they are perceived by others influences their own self-concept (for supportive research, see Cook & Douglas, 1998; Yeung & Martin, 2003).

Returning to Winnicott, this brilliant thinker developed a similar "mirroring" theory that postulates that infants and young children's acquisition of a sense of self is enabled—at least partially—by looking at their mothers' faces: "What does the baby see when he or she looks at the mother's face? I suggest that, ordinarily, what the baby sees is himself or herself" (1971, p. 151). According to Winnicott, this happens only to the extent that the mother is "good enough"—that is, that she faithfully attends to her infant and sees him or her as he or she is rather than projecting her own moods, stresses, and hopes upon her child. If she fails in this task, the infant/child perceives a gap between his or her true experiences and the mother's face—an experience registered as an "impingement." Being forced to react to the mother rather than to simply be, the child ultimately develops a false rather than a true (authentic) self.

Interdisciplinary research on the recognition of emotional facial expression is particularly pertinent here. Emotional face perception provides salient social cues for understanding interpersonal communication and behavior (Russell, Bachorowski, & Fernández-Dols, 2003). The preference for looking at face-like stimuli emerges soon after birth (Johnson, Dziurawiec, Ellis & Morton, 1991), the first signs of the ability to recognize facial expression following within the first year of life (Walker-Andrews, 1997). Face processing thus constitutes a significant developmental and social step. Psychopathology is closely linked to the biased processing of emotional face stimuli (for reviews, see Bar-Haim, Lamy, Pergamin, Bakermans-Kranenburg, & Van IJzendoorn, 2007; Cisler & Koster, 2010; Clark, Chamberlain, & Sahakian, 2009; Mathews & MacLeod, 2005; Roiser, Elliott, & Sahakian, 2012; Yiend, 2010; for implications for psychotherapy, see Browning, Holmes, & Harmer, 2010; Hakamata et al., 2010).

The relationship between self-concept and interpersonal factors in the perception of emotional facial expressions has yet to be established, however. Focusing on these variables, Michal Tanzer, Galia Avidan, and I (Tanzer, Avidan, & G. Shahar, 2013; Tanzer, G. Shahar, & Avidan, 2013; Tanzer, G. Shahar, & Avidan, in preparation) have found that generalized self-efficacy is specifically associated with perception and memory of happy expressions (Tanzer, G. Shahar et al., 2013), perceived social support being negatively associated with recognizing angry emotional facial expression in both naturally-occurring situations (Tanzer, G. Shahar et al., in preparation) and experimentally-induced failure (Tanzer, Avidan et al., 2013). With specific respect to self-criticism, we are beginning to observe an effect of this factor on accurate recognition of angry facial expressions in adults, even after controlling for depressive symptoms ($b = .04$, SE $= .02$, $t = 2.40$, $\beta = .28$, $p = .02$) (Tanzer, G. Shahar et al., in preparation). People who are angry at themselves (self-critics) are likely to perceive others as being angry (at them?).

And Yet it Moves

Despite the aforementioned complications regarding self-knowledge, we do appear to know (parts of) ourselves—at least partially. Decades of psychological theory and research attest to the fact that when we do know ourselves this appears to lower our distress. Table 4.3 summarizes some of the theses and studies highlighting the importance of self-knowledge for psychological and physical health. These include classical theories, such as that of Erikson and Marcia on identity formation and George Kelly's theory on the person as scientist (Personal Construct Theory, G. A. Kelly, 1955). The table also highlights Swann's social-psychological self-verification theory (see also Wilson & Dunn, 2004) as a clear example of the need to know oneself. It also identifies self-concept clarity and sense of coherence as two major dimensions of resilience. Out of all this theoretical and empirical wealth, I will focus on the dimension of self-concept clarity and Swann's theory and research into self-verification.

Self-concept clarity (SCC; J. D. Campbell, 1990; J. D. Campbell et al., 1996) is defined as "the extent to which the contents of an individual's self-concept (e.g., perceived personal attributes) are clearly and confidently defined, internally consistent, and temporally stable" (J. D. Campbell et al., 1996, p. 142). SCC is negatively

Table 4.3 **Theory and Research on Self-Knowledge**

Theory/Research	Term and Definition	Role in Health
Erikson's Identity Theory (Erikson, 1959) See also Marcia (1966)	Identity pertains to a clearly delineated sense of self, supposedly accomplished during adolescence.	Identity diffusion—the inability to secure a sense of self—is strongly tied to psychopathology.
George Kelly's Personality Theory (G. A. Kelly, 1955)	Constructs: Mental representations of reality—including the reality of the self—aimed at predicting events (including self-related events).	Flexibility and a complex organization of one's personal constructs lead to health, whereas rigidity and simplicity lead to failure to understand/ predict reality, ultimately leading to psychopathology.
Self-Concept Clarity (J. D. Campbell, 1990)	A clearly defined self-concept.	Predicts low levels of psychological symptoms.
Sense of Coherence (Antonovsky, 1979)	Confidence that life is structured, predictable, and explicable; that resources are available; and that demands are worthy of investment.	Buffers against life-stress and increases physical and psychological health.
Self-Verification (Swann, 1983)	People's tendency to search for information that verifies their self-concept.	People with low self-esteem will search for information consistent with their sense of deficiency.

associated with depression, neuroticism, and rumination and positively associated with self-esteem (Baumgardner, 1990; J. D. Campbell et al., 1990, 1996; Matto & Realo, 2001; Story, 2004). It accounts for the effect of social comparison on depression (Butzer & Kuiper, 2006), and—among women—protects against the effect of internalized social standards of attractiveness, thereby reducing vulnerability to eating disorders (Vartanian, 2009). While findings from our lab support the idea of high SCC as a protective factor (Noyman-Veksler, Weinberg, Fening, Davidson, & G. Shahar, 2013), they also imply that it can act as a double-edged sword, embedding both resilience and risk. Specifically, SCC predicts an increase in subsequent psychotic symptomatology among individuals suffering from schizophrenia (this effect was pronounced when life-stress was high: see Weinberg et al., 2012).

According to Swann's self-verification theory (Swann, 1983, 1987, 1990), people search for evidence that verifies their self-concept. This tendency influences information processing (Murray, Holmes, Dolderman, & Griffin, 2000; Snyder & Swann 1978)—including attention and memory (Swann & Read, 1981; Swann, Rentfrow, & Guinn, 2003) and social interaction (Swann, Pelham & Krull, 1989). The theory may shed additional light on the relationship between emotional face perception and self/social variables (Tanzer, G. Shahar et al., 2013, in preparation) and/or psychopathology (Cisler & Koster, 2010; Mathews & MacLeod, 2005; Yiend, 2010). Namely, individuals with elevated self-efficacy might perceive faces as happy in order to verify their positive beliefs about their abilities—reflected in others' appraisal (Cooley, 1902). Self-critics, on the other hand, might be particularly attuned to angry facial expressions as a way of confirming their perception of their own self as defective.

The Biological Basis of Self-Knowledge (and Self-Criticism)

Self-focused attention has been defined as "an awareness of self-referent, internally generated information that stands in contrast to an awareness of externally generated information derived through sensory receptors" (Ingram, 1990, p. 156). This form of attention has been conjectured as implicated in self-regulatory processes that help individuals pursue their goals and desires (Carver & Scheier, 1990). Specifically, when individuals detect a discrepancy between their current self and a salient standard, they engage in disparity-reducing behaviors until the divergence is resolved. If the gap is too vast and cannot be diminished however, the individual enters a self-regulatory cycle that only ends when he or she meets the standard or acknowledges that the mission is impossible (Mor & Winquist, 2002). Also highly consistent with my conceptualization of self-criticism is the suggestion that when people get "stuck" in the self-regulatory process their inability to meet their own standards may lead to depression or negative affect (Pyszczynski & Greenberg, 1986).

The past decade has witnessed a tremendous growth in research on the biological underpinnings of self-focused attention. I will review some of this progress now, with some attention to technical details.

Of particular importance to self-focused attention is the "serotonin transporter gene"—more accurately known as the serotonin 5-hydroxytryptamine-transporter-linked polymorphic region (5-HTTLPR). It possesses a short (S) and long (L) allele version. Higher concentrations of serotonin exist in the synaptic cleft carrying the S version than in that carrying the L version (Heils et al., 1996).[6] The 5-HTTLPR polymorphism—specifically, the carrier of the S allele—is associated with neuroticism (B. G. Greenberg et al., 2000; Lesch et al., 2005; Sen, Burmeister, & Ghosh, 2004), attentional bias (Beevers, Gibb, McGeary, & Miller, 2007), increased risk for depression, and suicide attempts in the face of stressful life-events (Caspi et al., 2003; Caspi, Hariri, Holmes, Uher, & Moffitt, 2010; Caspi & Moffitt, 2006; but see Risch et al., 2009). According to Hariri et al. (e.g., 2002, 2005), individuals carrying the S allele show elevated amygdala responses to fearful faces. This hyperactivation is due to a weaker coupling between the amygdala and the brain region known as the subgenual cingulate gyrus (Pezawas et al., 2005) than in the case of the L allele.[7]

Fox, Ridgwell, and Ashwin (2009) found that the homozygous for the L allele exhibits a bias toward stimuli with positive valence. They interpreted this phenomenon as a protective factor against stressful life-events.[8] Further evidence for the substantial role 5-HTTLPR plays in modulating attention comes from studies examining the interaction of genes and cultures (Chiao & Blizinsky, 2010; See also Kim et al., 2010). Previous studies had already suggested that Western cultures differ from East Asian cultures in perceptual and processing types (Han & Northoff, 2008). Westerners are more typically "analytic" in processing type—attentive to local elements and ascribing events to internal factors. East Asianers process information in a more holistic nature, attending to the entire contextual environment and ascribing social events to external factors (Nisbett, Peng, Choi, & Norenzayan, 2001). This divergence in processing type has been linked to variations in the putative gene and its interaction with culture (Kim et al., 2010). The S allele has likewise been reported as serving as a protective factor in members of collectivistic cultures—suggesting that biased attention toward negative-valence information may facilitate collectivistic norms. The same negative bias is linked to adverse circumstances in individualistic cultures (Chiao & Blizinsky, 2010).

Another genetic makeup of interest is the brain-derived neurotrophic factor (BDNF) gene Val66Me, shown to be related to depression. A recent study has demonstrated that rumination mediates the link between BDNF and depression (Hilt, Sander, Nolen-Hoeksema, & Simen, 2007). Having alluded earlier to the emerging possibility that rumination mediates the effect of self-criticism on suicidality (R. O'Connor & Noyce, 2008; see CHAPTER 2), a causal link between BDNF and self-criticism and hence rumination and depression appears plausible.

Alongside the identification of molecular genetics as the underlying mechanism of at least some self-related processes, neuroscience has also made strides in understanding the self-concept. Of greatest relevance to the present discussion are studies investigating the underlying neural mechanisms of self-knowledge. These have yielded consistent findings regarding the involvement of cortical and subcortical midline structures (see reviews by Lieberman, 2007; Northoff, 2007; Northoff et al., 2006).[9] For example, Rameson, Satpute, and Lieberman (2010) have identified the involvement of specific brain areas in the midline structure (the precuneus, medial prefrontal cortex, ventromedial prefrontal cortex, subgenual anterior cingulate, ventral striatum in the basal ganglia, and amygdala) in both implicit and explicit self-processing. Alternation in subcortical and cortical midline structures might account for the increased analytic self-focus observed in depressed patients (Northoff, 2007). Relatedly, individuals carrying a homozygous S allele 5-HTTLPR appear to exhibit more activity in the medial prefrontal cortex during negative self-focus than those carrying the L allele. This may underlie the risk for depression (Ma et al., 2013).

Employing functional magnetic resonance imaging (fMRI), Longe et al. (2010) asked individuals to imagine themselves failing or making mistakes and be self-critical or self-reassuring. Their findings indicated that areas associated with conflict processing, inhibition, and error monitoring (e.g., the lateral prefrontal cortex, dorsal anterior cingulate cortex, dorsal lateral prefrontal cortex [DLPFC]) were positively linked with self-criticism. Consistent with this study and also employing fMRI, Hooley and colleagues (Hooley, Gruber, Scott, Hiller, & Yurgelun-Todd, 2005; Hooley et al., 2009) found individuals who had completely recovered from unipolar depression exhibited lower activation in the DLPFC and higher activation in the amygdala region in response to maternal criticism than healthy controls. This intriguing finding implicates a psychosocial stressor—maternal criticism—as a vulnerability factor in individuals with remitted depression. Maternal criticism is highly relevant to the theory I will elaborate in the following chapter.

Self-Criticism as Driving a Wedge Between Authenticity and Self-Knowledge

The theory being developed here adduces authenticity and self-knowledge as two of the cornerstones of self-development. A healthy self is predicated on a sufficient amount of in-the-world engagement of interests, talents, and physiological-cognitive-emotional proclivities—synchronized with sufficient knowledge about these authentic properties.

That both *A* and *SK* are brought to bear via action in the world cannot be overemphasized. My approach being profoundly existential—based on a strongly pragmatic epistemology (see G. Shahar, 2010, 2011; G. Shahar & Davidson, 2009)—I maintain that authenticity cannot be merely envisioned or fantasized but must appear in our daily routine and inhabit our ongoing activities. Similarly—as is probably obvious from my previous comment—the only means we possess of attaining *SK* is participation in worldly endeavors. Of necessity, we must therefore be involved in relationships with others. In an earlier work (G. Shahar, 2010), I coined the term "Agents in Relations" (AIR) to replace the archaic, metaphorically unnecessary term "object relations." AIR is highly compatible with one of Sartre's wonderful dicta: "It is not in some hiding-place that we will discover ourselves; it is on the road, in the town, in the midst of the crowd, a thing amongst things, a human among humans" (1939).

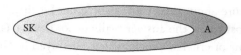

Figure 4.1 Authenticity (**A**) and Self-Knowledge (**SK**)

Figure 4.1 presents the synchronous relationships between **A** and **SK**. The figure includes two different shades of gray. Their intersection reflects the meeting of **A** and **SK**—captured in instances when I act in accordance with my nature and know that I do so. These are the moments in which I am in a state of flow, self-affirmation, going-on-being, and so forth. The more I know about my talents, interests, and proclivities, the more I am able to prioritize, delay gratification, and devise strategic future plans in order to realize them.

Even with my own superficial knowledge of the theory of and research into evolution, I believe that it makes perfect sense to deem these intersecting areas as human evolutionary prerequisites. Our species suffering from a very limited range of instinctual guidelines for self-preservation, we must exercise our advanced-brain capacities to analyze our environment—both physical and social—and anticipate the future in order to act (Amati & Shallice, 2007; D. Gilbert & Wilson, 2007; Seligman, Railton, Baumeister, & Sripada, 2013). Arguably, it is the very necessity of analyzing, planning, and deciding that gives rise to huge individual differences within the human species (e.g., Buss & Hawley, 2010; Guisinger & Blatt, 1994; Joseph & Shimberg, 2010; Tiskoff & Verrelli, 2003). It thus follows that, in order to survive as an individual among others, I must find my own nature and act in accordance with it (Strenger, 2011). For those readers not yet weary of my penchant for acronyms, here is another. My particularized model of adaptation (PMA) refers to those instances in which my authenticity and self-knowledge overlap.

It is precisely at this point that self-criticism steps in. In my view, self-criticism drives a wedge between an individual's authenticity and his or her accurate self-knowledge. Before I explain why, let me remind you that the self-criticism to which I am referring here is the harsh, punitive, derogatory, passionately cruel type I reviewed in the first two chapters.

Self-Criticism as a Distorted Form of Self-Knowledge

I argue that self-criticism constitutes a form of self-knowledge in which one self-aspect tells the other that it (the other aspect) is bad, deficient, inadequate, and so forth. The judgmental, derogatory, harsh tone of the self-talk inherent in self-criticism conveys the message that this self-knowledge is vitally important: "It is crucial that you understand that you are bad, deficient, inadequate, and so forth." This is profoundly wrong.

Why am I so sure about this? Can't people not be "bad," "deficient," and so forth? Well, in most cases, the answer really is no. Laying aside some relatively rare manifestations of cruelty—such as that portrayed in Golding's *Lord of the Flies*, for example—badness and deficiency are relative to specified standards. Bad in relationship to what? Deficient as opposed to what? Similarly, self-criticism's appeal lies in its generalized nature: you are generally bad, generally deficient. How many people do we know who are generally bad or deficient? Of these, how many were bad or deficient as children? Even when standards are invoked—"You bad boy, you stole a cookie from the jar!"—they are usually done so haphazardly and in an arbitrary fashion ("Why shouldn't I take a biscuit from the jar?"), with an intent to hurt rather than to inform or educate.

My point here is that the arbitrary, generalized, and comprehensive nature of self-criticism obscures the truth. What truth? The complex, multifaceted truth about our nature—that is, our talents, interests, and proclivities. If I am bad or deficient, that's it—end of discussion. No need to probe further.

A closely related aspect of this claim pertains to the fact that self-criticism automatically generates negative affect (e.g., shame, sadness, anger) and averts potential forms of positive affect that might be involved in benevolent self-scrutiny (e.g., pride or curiosity). As extensive psychological research has demonstrated, like physical pain negative affect is attention grabbing, locking attention inward (Barnett & Gotlib, 1988; Mor & Winquist, 2002; Persons & Miranda, 1992; Salovey, 1992; Segal & Ingram, 1994; Teasdale, 1983). The outcome is thus not only the feeling that "I am bad" but also a compulsion to remain focused on this feeling. This affective-cognitive stance thus consolidates distorted self-knowledge.

Self-Criticism as an Addictive Form of Self-Knowledge

Self-criticism is not only a distorted form of self-knowledge but also an addictive form. Why? Because self-critical self-talks are carried out with full conviction. When I am self-critical, I am not pondering the possibility that I might not really be a good person. I am saying to myself, resolutely, that I am bad. Likewise, I am not considering the possibility that I am not entirely wonderful but insisting that I am deficient.

In the context of the theoretical perspective developed earlier, self-clarity possesses tremendous appeal. When it evolves into a cohesive self-narrative, it is rewarding in and of itself. When I am self-critical, at least I know who I am. I am not confused about myself any more (recall Adam from CHAPTER 2 and the notion of painful amotivation). I have an identity. I am a (bad, deficient) person among persons. To relinquish this certainty is to fall back into confusion, a state that most individuals—assuredly our patients—find unbearable. As we will see in the next chapter, however, like other addictive behaviors this certainty is only temporary, authenticity not giving up easily. This leaves room for hope.

Self-Criticism as a Dangerous Divergence from Experimentation

Self-criticism being intense it is also arduous. We may liken it to a forceful prosecutor in a trial, against whom the best we can do is try and marshal some strength to defend ourselves, if only feebly (see CHAPTER 7). In the face of his or her punches, we have little energy and wherewithal to experiment.

By "experimenting," I mean launching action in-the-world that might enable me to benevolently examine my talents, interests, and proclivities. Children's play epitomizes this experimentation (as does adults', although this fact is frequently overlooked). Panksepp, the founder of affective neuroscience, argues that playfulness is a primary process—an intrinsic brain function with neuroanatomical and neurochemical substrates concentrated in subcortical regions (e.g., Siviy & Panksepp, 2011). Building on animal models of brain processes, he maintains that play promotes maturation of the frontal lobe regulatory functions. He thus posits that the decrease in rough-and-tumble play in Western society may be responsible for the current epidemic of childhood attention-deficit/hyperactivity disorder (Panksepp, 1998, 2007; Siviy & Panksepp, 2011). In his view, the establishment of "play sanctuaries" would encourage childhood play (Panksepp, 2007; Siviy & Panksepp, 2011), improve therapeutic outcomes (Panksepp & Watt, 2011), and contribute to the treatment of depression (Burgdorf, Panksepp, & Moskal, 2011).

Barbara Fredrickson's "broaden and build" theory of resilience is also relevant here. In a series of impressive studies, Fredrickson has demonstrated that positive affect enables people to withstand stressful situations. This is presumably because it helps them see the broad picture and thus build new strategies for reappraisal and coping (Fredrickson, 2001). Self-criticism producing negative affect and derailing the production of positive affect, it robs individuals of resources that inform them what they are good at (their talents), what matters to them (their interests), and how they regulate themselves (their proclivities).

Self-Criticism as a Noncalibrated Compass

Self-criticism leads us astray. In 2002—my first year as a faculty member in the Department of Psychiatry at Yale University's School of Medicine—I was given a marvelous opportunity: I was appointed by the Department of Psychology as an instructor for one of its Introduction to Psychology classes. Not only do I love teaching, always having viewed it as one of the strongest manifestations of my authentic self, but Intro to Psych had long been a class I had enjoyed teaching. Although the course went reasonably well, I had to make an enormous effort to excel—which threatened the time and energy I needed for my research and clinical work in the Department of Psychiatry. Moreover, I ran the class concurrently with a similar one given by Professor Peter Salovey, then chair of the Department of Psychology and a legendary lecturer and speaker (as of this writing, he is President of Yale). I thus had to contend with the fact that his class had hundreds of attendees and I only had 60.

Being in therapy at the time, I complained to my therapist that, while I loved the teaching, I was frustrated that everything at Yale had to be about excelling, everyone being constantly engaged in comparing themselves with others/being the best and seeking to improve. Somewhat bemused, my therapist replied: "You are absolutely right. But then there is this question of who brought himself to Yale?"

Obviously, I myself was responsible for this step—which I undertook for the right reasons and with a tremendously positive yield. I also applied for teaching the Intro to Psych class for good reasons—perceiving it as a "broadening and building" experience. My own self-criticism promptly interfered, however, seducing me away from my true destination—to be the teacher I could be—to focus on "being the best" (a decoy for preventing myself from ending up the worst). Rather than simply being, I compared myself with others, harshly evaluating myself—or, in Winnicott's terms, "reacting." Had I not been in therapy, I am convinced that my years at Yale would have turned into a time of anguish-filled distress rather than the self-realization and self-affirmation period it proved to be.

Thus, armed with the promise of clearly consolidated self-knowledge, self-criticism frequently acts as an elusive, poorly calibrated compass. Consistent with Buss's notion of environmental selection (Buss, 1987), self-criticism guides us toward evaluative, competitively harsh social environments in order to prove to ourselves that we are not as bad/deficient as we fear ourselves to be. When it has driven us into this state, it then proceeds to lure us into focusing on evaluation and competition rather than authenticity. Even when the putative social environment possesses features that are highly compatible with our authentic self, our self-critical voice deludes us into dismissing these and paying sole attention to harsh judgmental attitudes. It thus drives a wedge between our authenticity and self-knowledge.

Self-criticism also creates a rift between *A* and *SK* by eliciting the wrong sort of information from others regarding who we are. In order to elaborate on this process, we will need to consider the role of development, families, and social systems. This is the subject of the next chapter.

5

Development, Families, and Social Systems: The Axis of Criticism (*ACRIM*)

No man is an island, entire of itself.

(Donne, 1923)

Two of the central terms in the field of developmental psychopathology are "equi-finality" and "multifinality" (Cicchetti & Sroufe, 2000). Equifinality refers to the principle that a given end state can be reached by many potential means, multifi-nality to the principle that the same factors generate different clinical outcomes. In CHAPTER 1, I demonstrated how self-criticism contributes to a wide range of psychopathologies, illustrating multifinality. Here, I will discuss the diverse causal constellations that potentially prompt self-criticism—that is, equifinality.

I posit that, rather than being produced by a single causal chain, psycho-pathological self-criticism is engendered by an intricate combination of a child's heightened need for self-knowledge on the one hand and paternal criticism on the other hand. The first set of factors includes biogenetic propensities (see the conjecture regarding the role of "depressive genes" in self-focused attention in the previous chapter), as well as cultural emphases on expression and understand-ing of experiences. The second set—parental criticism—has already been shown to predict elevated levels of child self-criticism (Amitay, Mongrain, & Fazaa, 2008; Koestner, Zuroff, & Powers, 1991; Lassri & G. Shahar, 2012; McCranie & Bass, 1984; Pagura, Cox, Sareen, & Enns, 2006; Soenens, Vansteenkiste, & Luyten, 2010; Soffer, Gilboa-Shechtman, & G. Shahar, 2008). The most perni-cious forms of self-criticism—perhaps those manifested in the Treatment for Depression Collaborative Research Program—are obviously likely to stem from a co-occurrence of both sets of factors.

In the presence of highly toxic parental criticism, even children who are not very absorbed in self-knowledge may become highly self-critical. As Rogers

(1959) and Blatt (1995) have already noted, parents have the power to convince (almost) any child that he or she is deficient—a stance the child then proceeds to internalize (see Amitay, Mongrain, & Fazaa, 2008; Lassri & G. Shahar, 2012). Most clinicians would accept this as a straightforward and banal statement. What is seldom considered is the possibility of children developing self-criticism *in the absence* of parental disapproval.

It is important to ponder this possibility. Over the years I have encountered several such highly self-critical patients—children, adolescents, and young adults—whose families I know to be fundamentally nurturing and supportive. All patients have been intelligent, profound, inwardly directed, and highly sensitive to even mild forms of instruction, tending to perceive it as criticism. This clinical experience has led me to speculate that inward-directed attention and a strong yearning for self-understanding—perhaps coupled with "neuroticism"—may prompt children to develop a self-critical stance. The presence of stress in the family might augment this largely innate tendency for two reasons. Stress activates negative affect, which "locks" children and adolescents' attention inward (Miranda & Nolen-Hoeksema, 2007; Mor & Winquist, 2002; Persons & Miranda, 1992). Stress also bombards parents, thereby derailing their efforts to supervise their children and set limits and standards. Making it difficult for them to manage their child's emotional upheaval, it also contributes to the child's (accurate) experience of the parent as critical. The child in turn thus becomes self-critical.

Whatever the particular causal constellation that induces child self-criticism, I propound that over time it converges into a fixed pattern or "attractor" of sorts.[1] In criticism-based parent-child relationships, children are critical of themselves, thus evoking parental criticism (whether these parents are initially critical or not), in turn increasing their self-criticism. I submit that a principal—and rather ironic—reason for this type of relationship is the child's authenticity and its struggle to express itself.

According to Winnicott, the true self is hidden behind a false self, the latter protecting the former from "impingements" whose pain is too intolerable to bear. Despite my penchant for Winnicott, my theoretical position here is closer to that of Carl Rogers, who believed that authenticity cannot truly be oppressed (see I. Hirsch, 1994, for a similar view—essentially modifying Winnicott but without acknowledging Rogers). If you recall, I view authenticity as a crucial evolutionary thrust or Particularized Mode of Adaptation. I am proposing that, no matter how much the environment proscribes expressions of authenticity (i.e., an individual's talents, interests, and physiological-affective-cognitive proclivities), the authentic self will find ways to manifest itself in-the-world—primarily in relationships (per my Agents in Relations concept). The question is: *How well* can it do so? A central postulate of my present theory is that the authentic expressions of self-critical children are inevitably inept, misplaced, and noncoordinated. They thus ultimately evoke (further) parental criticism.

The reason for this lies in the fact that expressions of authenticity in self-critical children are frequently shadowed by anxiety. Children learn to distrust their authentic self (Rogers, 1963) because, receiving no clear sign that their genuine interests are approved of, they remain unsure of whether these are legitimate. They thus come to expect criticism if and when they pursue them (Blatt, 1995). This is precisely the pattern we found in our study linking self-criticism and self-determination theory. The higher the level of self-criticism the less one tends to engage in desired activities (G. Shahar, Henrich, Blatt, Ryan, & Little, 2003).

When expression of authenticity is perceived to entail a threat, it is likely to lead to failure. This, in turn, is likely to evoke criticism—even from essentially noncritical parents. This is especially true when parents are preoccupied with other concerns—such as economic or health-related stressors. Even mild forms of criticism may seem harsh to children who are already self-critical—that is, fearful of expressing their authenticity. Even if failure or success are irrelevant, anxious expressions of authenticity may be *miscommunicated*, leading to misunderstanding and rejection: "You want to go to a film with your friends again?! It's too expensive. You cost us too much money."

On some occasions, a self-critical child gathers enough courage to orchestrate a well-coordinated, highly-articulated expression of authenticity only to encounter a profoundly-critical parent for whom the child's innocent wishes are intolerably impertinent. A chilling example of such a circumstance occurs in the *Dead Poets Society* (1989). The film depicts the story of an English teacher named John Keating (played by the late Robin Williams) who employs unorthodox methods to teach poetry at a conservative elite prep school. Having discovered that Keating is an alumnus of the school and one of the founders of the now-defunct Dead Poets Society, one of his brightest students decides to try to revive the club, evoking fierce opposition from staff and parents alike. The authoritarian father of another one of the club's members strongly objects to the acting ambitions it stirs in his son. His son commits suicide when he feels he has failed to fulfill his (own) aspirations.

My theory posits a vicious, criticism-based parent-child relationship that ultimately consolidates the child's self-criticism. Vicious interpersonal cycles have pervaded clinical theory for decades (Shoham & Rohrbaugh, 1997; P. L. Wachtel, 1977, 1994, 1997; Watzlawick, Weakland, & Fish, 1974). Their existence has also been repeatedly confirmed in empirical research (e.g., Shoham, Butler, Rohrbaugh, & Trost, 2007)—including self-criticism studies (see Chapter 1). These cycles are labeled "ironic" because the individuals propagating them induce the very outcomes dreaded (Shoham & Rohrbaugh, 1997; P. L. Wachtel, 1997). The cycles involving self-critics are also imbued with both dread and hope (Mitchell, 1990). The dread comes from past failures at expressing ones' authenticity. The hope emanates from the realization that such an expression is mandatory for one's well-being.

If you recall, in the previous chapter I linked authenticity with future-oriented thought and goal-directed action. Therein, I proposed that people dedicate themselves not only to realizing their talents, interests, and proclivities in the present but also to projecting them into the future in an attempt to become what they might. Self-critical children and adolescents also seek to express their authenticity both in the present and in the future. Neil—one of the pupils in the *Dead Poets Society*—not only auditions for a part in the school play but also *wants to be an actor.* Although the future is, of course, unknown, children and adolescents are not necessarily aware of this fact. They thus look to their elders—primarily their parents—for clues (as in the famous song "Que Sera, Sera"). Neil does not simply want to be an actor: *he wants to be the kind of actor his father approves of and places his trust and hope in.* To a large extent, his acting is more than an expression of self-actualization. It is a *question*—an inquiry into the way Neil's parents perceive his true identity. I call this Inquisitive Action.

Despite Neil's attempt to express and articulate his Inquisitive Action as politely and clearly as possible, he receives the "wrong answer": "No, you cannot be an actor; you will be what I tell you to be." Successful "projectuality" being brutally denied him, Neil is forced into denying his own self. Life without hope of becoming what one might is frequently deemed not worth living. In other—less extreme—cases, self-critical children and adolescents continue to inquire despite being given the wrong answer. As to be expected from a vicious cycle, their very inquiry will invariably elicit wrong answers. Arguably, the only way to break out of this circularity is to find someone who acknowledges and affirms their authenticity.[2]

Self-critical children and adolescents are thus not likely to stop with their parents. They will direct their Inquisitive Actions toward siblings and other family members in their quest for someone who will allow them to be their authentic self. These attempts are charged with past criticism-based exchanges with parents that have consolidated the child/adolescent's self-critical faculties. They are therefore likely to be inept and awkward. While other family members—siblings, grandparents, aunts, or uncles—may step up to the plate, this happens infrequently.[3] In most cases, over time the child/adolescent finds him- or herself caught up in criticism-based relationships involving most—if not all—members of the family. In the event that he or she is taken to a psychiatrist/psychologist, he or she becomes the "identified patient" (Bateson, Jackson, Haley, & Weakland, 1956).

In the context of schizophrenia research, the great medical sociologist George Brown coined the term Expressed Emotion (EE; Brown, 1985; see Bhugra & McKenzie, 2003). Pertaining to critical, hostile, and overinvolved attitudes and behaviors directed by family members toward afflicted individuals, EE has subsequently been demonstrated as useful for understanding the role of family relationships in a wide variety of psychopathological conditions and physical illnesses. As suggested by Wearden, Tarrier, Barrowclough, Zastowny, and Rahill, "criticism is conventionally regarded as the principal scale" of the various EE dimensions and measurement scales (2000, p. 637). This has also been shown to be the case in children and adolescents (e.g., Asarnow, Tompson, Hamilton, Goldstein, & Guthrie, 1994).

The cogent vulnerability status of Critical Expressed Emotion (CEE) is reminiscent of the formidable vulnerability status of self-criticism summarized in CHAPTERS 1 and 2. I was thus very surprised to discover that very little empirical research has been conducted linking these two dimensions. I have only found two studies adducing a (tenuous) tie between CEE and self-criticism.[4] Herein, I am postulating that, within families, self-criticism and CEE create and sustain one another over time. The plot gets even thicker than this, however. Frustrated by the inability to exercise his or her authenticity within the family, the child/ adolescent increasingly turns toward other relationships—that is, with peers and school staff.

As is well known to all those interested in adolescent development, peer relationships—as important as they are throughout childhood—are paramount during early adolescence (ages 11 to 12 and onward; Buhrmester, 1990; Buhrmester & Furman, 1987; Furman & Buhrmester, 1985, 1992; Kuttler, La Greca, & Prinstein, 1999). Among psychoanalytic theorists, Harry Stack Sullivan (1953) has prominently identified "chumship" as a major facilitator of personality development. According to Sullivan, friendships have the power to compensate for what was missing in parent-child relationships. They may also soften blows inflicted within the framework of these relationships.

In the present context, however, I wish to argue that self-critical children/adolescents' relationships with peers are likely to *augment* the vicious cycle described earlier. This is because self-critics' inept, confused, potentially belligerent expressions of authenticity are likely to be transferred from family relationships to peer relationships, thereby generating further confrontation, rejection, and isolation. This presupposition is highly consistent with research attesting to ruptured relationships between self-critical adolescents and their peers (Fichman, Koestner, & Zuroff, 1994; Leadbeater, Kuperminc, Blatt, & Herzog, 1999; G. Shahar & Priel, 2003; Yu & Gample, 2009). Parents frequently regard their children's social adjustment as serving as an indication of "normality." I thus also suspect that they tend to view such peer quarrels as evidence of their child's failings. This, in turn, prompts them to be even more critical, thereby further solidifying the child's self-criticism.

It is easy to imagine similar processes occurring in the context of teacher-child relationships. These have been documented as being profoundly important not only with respect to academic achievement (McCormick, O'Connor, Cappela, & McClowry, 2013) but also with regard to students' mental health (Henrich, Brookmeyer, & G. Shahar, 2005; E. E. O'Connor, Dearing, & Collins, 2011). During times of stress, social support from school staff also appears to compensate for the lack of social support from friends or peers (e.g., DuBois, Felner, Brand, Adan, & Evans, 1992). Can parents or school staff neutralize the criticism-based vicious cycle characteristic of self-critical children and adolescents?

This is not an impossible scenario. Gifted and caring teachers and/or staff can provide children with a sense of visibility and affirmation that parents, siblings, and even peers are unable to supply. For this protective process to be success-ful, however, it must activate another—highly resilient—aspect of the child/ado-lescent's personality. The more self-criticism plays a prominent role in a child/adolescent's personality and behavior, the more likely he or she will be to relate to the teacher/staff member in the same way he or she relates to family members and peers. Self-criticism thus expands rejection beyond the family circle, in turn further consolidating it. Alarmed by their child's behavior in school, his or her parents might interpret these ruptures as further evidence of his or her failings, thus exacerbating the cycle.

My argument here is that children's and adolescents' self-criticism accumu-lates over time as a result of criticism-based interpersonal exchanges—first with parents, then with other family members, then with peers, and finally with teach-ers and school staff. The stronger the self-criticism, the greater the child's entrap-ment within a social ecology marked by confrontation, rejection, interpersonal loss, and criticism. To add insult to injury, drawing on Buss' (1987) idea of selec-tion I expect that, as children become adolescents and are entrusted with increas-ing levels of personal choice, they are likely to gravitate toward environments in which they will be forced to become competitive, self-judgmental, and self-critical in order to prove themselves to their (potentially critical) parents.

I group the various criticism-based cyclical interactions noted earlier under the label Axis of Criticism (**ACRIM**—or Axis of Criticism Model; see G. Shahar & Henrich, 2013, for a preliminary conceptualization). The importance of this label derives from its stress on the social ecology within which individual self-criticism resides. **ACRIM** drives home the message that the devastating effects of self-criticism stem from a net of social relationships that evolve over time and trap individuals—particularly children and adolescents—within their own vulnerability.

As implied by the previous discussion and depicted in Figure 5.1, social stress plays a major role in **ACRIM**. Specifically, when stressful events—injury or ill-ness, economic misfortune, exposure to victimization and crime—hit children and families, they activate criticism on the part of either or both. To illustrate, a parent who is laid off takes it out on the child, who later on ineptly expresses her reaction in school. This behavior infuriates the teacher, who lashes out against the child, much to the parents' dismay, and so on.

Notably, criticism from others is a stressful event in and of itself. It is thus likely to activate psychological vulnerability of all types. According to the stress-diathesis approach to psychopathology, criticism from others tends to

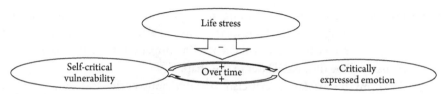

Figure 5.1 Stress as binding criticism-based relationships

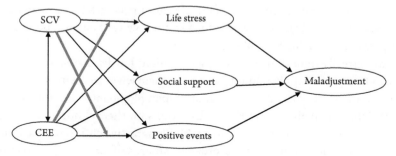

Figure 5.2 Interactive vulnerability of self-critical vulnerability (SCV) and critical expressed emotion (CEE)

Note: The thick lines represents moderating effects, whereby (1) SCV activates the stress-generating and support/positive-event degenerating effect of CEE and (2) CEE activates the stress-generating and support/positive-event degenerating effect of SCV.

strengthen the adverse effect of self-criticism on all forms of psychological symptoms and problem behavior. To continue the previous illustration, the laid-off parent lashes out at his or her self-critical adolescent daughter, who "takes it upon herself" and becomes depressed. Her consequent isolation from—or conflict with—her friends generates stress, derails her ability to engage in positive experiences (e.g., going to a film), and also degenerates social support. As illustrated in Figure 5.2, this snowballs into maladjustment.

The Broader Sociocultural Context

At this juncture, I would like to introduce into my discussion Urie Bronfenbrenner's ecological theory of human development (Bronfenbrenner, 1977, 1979, 1994). According to this theory, a child develops within five socio-environmental systems nested within one another. The "microsystem" pertains to groups and institutions that directly impact the child—epitomized by the family and including peers, neighborhoods, schools, and religious institutions. The "mesosystem" pertains to the links between various microsystems—a child's experiences at home that are related to experiences at school, for example. The "exosystem" impacts the child from outside his or her own world: A parent's stressful job, for example, elicits parental distress, adversely affecting the child. The "macrosystem" pertains to the norms, expectations, and attitudes of culture/society. Finally, the "chrono-system" relates to changes and transformations experienced by individuals over their life-span—including historical events. The impact of the chronosystem on self-criticism will be discussed later in the chapter.[5]

Thus far, my discussion of criticism-based vicious cycles has only involved the microsystem—that is, transactions between a child's self-criticism and criti-cal expressed emotion from families, peers, and schools—and the mesosystem (interactions between families, peers, and school personnel that mediate criti-cism against the child). Let me now turn to the role exosystems and macrosys-tems play in the development of self-criticism.

I have already indicated that exosystems might burden parents in numerous ways, in turn derailing their ability to attune themselves to their child's authen-ticity. Conflicts at work, downsizing, and unemployment make for perturbed parents who are likely to vent their frustrations on their children. Even in the absence of any overt expression of angst, highly sensitive children—particularly vulnerable to cues from others in order to attain self-knowledge—may inter-pret parental distress as disapproval. Relocation is another exosystem-based event that might burden parents, in turn adversely impacting their children—sometimes directly (J. B. Kelly & Lamb, 2003). Some of my Israeli colleagues who have spent extended sabbaticals abroad, for example, have told me of the great effect this experience has had on their children. Having to master a new language while getting used to a new school environment, children run the risk of reacting with a considerable measure of self-doubt and self-criticism. They may also complain about needing to adjust to a competitive, academically-demanding school—their own in Israel having been essentially supportive and informal (if highly crowded).

Macrosystems have profound impacts on children/adolescents' self-criticism via microsystems and directly. Cultures vary tremendously with respect to the importance they attribute to authenticity, achievement, and self-evaluation. As the *Dead Poets Society* illustrates, North American prep schools—and their English public/boarding school equivalents—are highly competitive. Cultural norms shape media messages that are extensively consumed by both children and teens. The frightening escalation of cases of unipolar depression in contempo-rary Western society (Klerman & Weissman, 1989; Lewinsohn, Rohde, Seeley, & Fischer, 1993; Seligman, 1990; G. Shahar, 2001) has prompted several think-ers to characterize late modernity as the "age of melancholy" (Klerman, 1979). According to sociologist Anthony Giddens, "The modern world is a 'runaway world': not only is the *pace* of social change much faster than in any prior system, so also is its *scope*, and the *profoundness* with which it affects pre-existing social practices and modes of behavior" (1991, p. 16 [original italics]). Giddens identi-fies the mechanisms of this dynamism as (1) the separation of time and space, ren-dering the meaning of place ambiguous (e.g., I am residing in Israel while serving as editor of an American professional journal); (2) the disembedding of social institutions or the regulation of social exchanges via abstract and symbolic tokens (e.g., money); and (3) reflexivity—an emphasis on the construction of a coherent self-identity, gaps or holes arousing strong feelings of shame (a.k.a. self-criticism).[6]

Building on Giddens' theory—as well as a host of others—philosopher and existential psychoanalyst Carlo Strenger (2011) describes the devastating impact of globalization on the educated classes. Taking the form of an "information craze" that quantifies and rates human beings while raising expectations of achievement, it inculcates a chronic fear of insignificance: having failed to conquer the world, the best and brightest experience it as worthless.

Their historic sociological perspective leads both Giddens and Strenger to largely overlook individual differences. As I have previously argued, however, self-critical individuals appear to be particularly likely to embrace the norms of late modernity (including globalization):

> ... these [self-critical] individuals exemplify, or represent, modern society. Arguably, introjective individuals are sensitive not only to perfectionistic messages conveyed by their parents, but also to those conveyed by society as a whole. Lured into believing that an additional success would finally alleviate chronic feelings of shame and inadequacy, and that improved performance would ultimately yield acceptance by self and others, those individuals are trapped in a labyrinth of unsatisfying success that only serves to exacerbate their shame, inadequacy, and self-punitive stance (Blatt, 1995). Their collapse ... is evidence not only of their individual vulnerability, but also of the vulnerability of the society from which they scrupulously absorbed their values. (G. Shahar, 2001, pp. 236–237)[7]

Does this mean that **ACRIM** plays a lesser role in collectivist societies—in which individual achievement is subjugated to collective goals? As tempting as it may be to subscribe to this possibility, there are reasons to doubt it. In CHAPTER 3, I cited research attesting to the malignant effect of self-criticism even in collectivist cultures such as Japanese, Chinese, and Bedouin-Arab societies (Abu-Kaf & Priel, 2008; Kuwabara, Sakado, Sakado, Sato, & Someya, 2004; Yao, Fang, Zhu, & Zuroff, 2009). Sarah Abu-Kaf, Chris Henrich, and I have recently surmised that **ACRIM** might actually be as strong in collectivist societies as it appears to be in individualistic ones—albeit for different reasons (Abu-Kaf, Henrich, & G. Shahar, in preparation). Specifically, in collectivist cultures, the self is defined in terms of relationships (Markus & Kitayama, 1991). Thus, the "activation" of self-criticism might spill over into people's perception of others as critical toward the self, in turn increasing self-criticism. Cross-cultural research examining this possibility is currently under way.

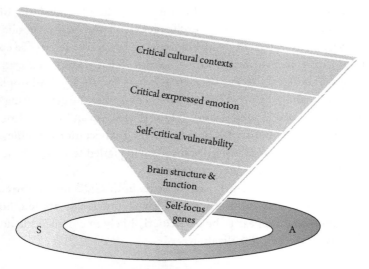

Figure 5.3 The full-fledged Axis of Criticism (*ACRIM*)

A Full-Fledged Axis of Criticism

Figure 5.3 integrates the *ASK* and *ACRIM* conceptualizations. In the previous chapter, I argued that, emanating from various constellations of the child's innate need for self-knowledge and parental criticism, self-criticism drives a wedge between authentic self-expression of one's talents, interests, and proclivities and accurate knowledge of this authentic self. Figure 5.3 suggests that the wedge is thicker than we might have initially imagined. Criticism from family members, peers, and school personnel augment one another, thereby consolidating and broadening criticism-based vicious cycles. The influence exerted by exosystems and macrosystems further contributes to the child/adolescent's evolving self-criticism, both via their impact on the microsystem (family, peers, and schools) and directly (e.g., through the media).

The Life-Span

Let us now consider the chronosystem—that is, the changes and transformations individuals experience over their life-span. Around the age of 18, adolescents transition into adulthood (Arnett, 2000). At this developmental stage, the level of parental supervision substantially decreases. Armed with a newfound level of freedom and independence, newly-ordained young adults enter social institutions they have never encountered before—in Western Europe and North America, colleges and/or workplaces; in Israel, compulsory army service (3 years for men, 2 for women). To a large extent, the way in which young people adjust to these unfamiliar contexts depends on their cognitive-affective schemas of self/others and the relationships they have developed over the first two decades of their lives.

It stands to reason that self-critical young adults will be influenced by the same criticism-based schemas and scripts that have governed their lives up to this point, continuing their generation of criticism and degeneration of nurturing and supportive environments. The extensive research on self-critical college students conducted across cultures confirms that this is indeed the case (e.g., Dunkley, Zuroff, Blankstein, 2003, 2006; Mongrain, 1998; Priel & G. Shahar, 2000).

Military conscription constitutes a culturally unique developmental phenomenon in Israel. Research conducted by Apter, Bleich, King, Fluch, Kottler, and Cohen (1993) demonstrates that here, too, self-criticism continues to create havoc. On the basis of psychological autopsies of the military records of 43 Israeli male soldiers who committed suicide while on duty, these investigators identified the feeling of having "fail[ed] to live up to [their] own or others' expectations" (1993, p. 140)—including those connected to military service (e.g., succeeding in a mission, being selected for a prestigious unit)—as a leading cause of suicide.[8] The latter scenario—selection for a prestigious unit—is particularly noteworthy in Israel. Service in an elite unit is a coveted goal among many young Israelis, not only because these units epitomize national ideals (see King, 2003) but also because they open doors to bright professional futures. It thus functions as a parallel to graduation from an American Ivy League university. I have personally known people who took their own lives after being honorably discharged from the Flight Academy despite being promised an extremely prestigious restationing. To its credit, the Israeli Defense Force takes the "suicide by the brightest" phenomenon very seriously, succeeding in markedly reducing suicide rates among recruits.

During their third decade of life, many young adults enter the work sphere. At this point, relationships with supervisors and coworkers become crucial—not only for occupational success but also for general well-being (Arnett, 2000, 2004). Here, too, I expect self-critical individuals to generate criticism-based vicious cycles involving critical expressed emotions from supervisors and coworkers. The consequent significant reduction in work satisfaction constitutes an outcome detrimental to both worker and workplace. The more adult patients I treat (older than 25 years), the more I am beginning to see this in the clinic. My curiosity regarding the role *ACRIM* plays in serious occupational outcomes, such as abusive supervisory relationships (Tepper, 2007), worker burnout and absenteeism (Maslach, Schaufeli, & Leiter, 2001), and job displacement, redundancy, and unemployment (e.g., Rege, Telle, & Votruba, 2011), is thus exponentially growing.

During the third and fourth decades of life, most people form crucial romantic relationships, leading to cohabitation and/or marriage. Studies suggest that childhood maltreatment predicts young-adult self-criticism (Dunkley, Masheb, & Grilo, 2010; Pagura et al., 2006; Sachs-Ericsson, Verona, Joiner, & Preacher, 2006; Soffer et al., 2008; for an excellent review, see in particular Zuroff, Santor, &

Mongrain, 2005). This, in turn, generates romantic dissatisfaction (Lassri & G. Shahar, 2012). Upon becoming adults, maltreated children tend to propel themselves into victimizing romantic relationships (Marx, Heidt, & Gold, 2005; Noll, 2005). I would therefore expect self-critics' romantic relationships to be marred by criticism-based vicious cycles. John Gottman's pioneering work identifies spousal criticism as one of the principal predictors of the success or failure of a marriage (e.g., Gottman, 1993). Self-criticism being likely to evoke spousal criticism (e.g., Mongrain, Vettese, Shuster, & Kendal, 1998; Zuroff & Duncan, 1999), it constitutes a contributing factor in dire romantic outcomes.

Most married couples (still) have children. As Priel and Besser and Luyten and his colleagues have independently demonstrated, self-criticism not only predicts postpartum depressive symptoms but also postpartum spousal conflicts and low social support (Priel & Besser, 1999, 2000; Vliegen, Casalin, & Luyten, 2014; Vliegen & Luyten, 2009). Anxious to become "good enough" caretakers, first-time parents usually consult with pediatricians and nurses at well-baby clinics regarding their parenting practices. Highly self-critical parents are likely to experience even mild forms of instruction and direction as criticism—or evoke it from practitioners (societal pressures on mothers to breastfeed also possibly contribute to this vicious cycle: see Ostry & Nathoo, 2009). A (highly self-critical) female patient told me that she sends her husband to the well-baby clinic with their 1-year-old to avoid facing criticism from nurses and pediatricians regarding her mothering skills.

Finally, self-criticism has been shown to lead to marked distress among the elderly (e.g., Besser & Priel, 2005). A relatively recent study conducted by Paul Gilbert's group suggests that people who take care of the elderly (this sample, it must be acknowledged, suffered from dementia) are likely to experience self-criticism (as well as shame, entrapment, and depression) related to the fear of not giving "good enough" care (Martin, P. Gilbert, McEwan, & Irons, 2006). Here, too, self-criticism in the elderly might interact with caretakers' criticism, leading to critical expressed emotions and—in some extreme cases—elder abuse (for information on the latter, see Sengstock, McFarland, & Hwalek, 1990).

Summary of CHAPTERS 4 and 5

How do **ASK** and **ACRIM** add to our knowledge and understanding of self-criticism beyond the theories reviewed in CHAPTER 3? In my opinion, they provide a straightforward explanation of the self-critical cascade identified in CHAPTER 1, according to which self-criticism constitutes a distorted form of self-knowledge that ultimately drives a wedge between an individual's evolving authenticity and accurate self-knowledge. Adversely impacting attempts to realize one's authentic self, self-criticism ensures that these are inept, awkward, and desynchronized. These abortive efforts widen the gap between authenticity and self-knowledge because they to elicit responses from others that are conducive to gaining accurate self-knowledge on the one hand and actively evoke criticism from others on the other. The larger the gap, the more likely self-critics are to interpret even benign responses from others as critical and self-select into a highly evaluative social environment. The latter move is driven by a conflicted attempt to align their principal personality tendency (self-criticism) with environmental values and norms while simultaneously inquiring about their true identity in the hope that it will be allowed to unfold and be affirmed by others. Tragically, this usually only serves to expose the person to increased competition, failure, and harsh evaluation. Finally, criticism-based vicious cycles are ongoing, repetitive, and iterative, unfolding over the life-span.

ASK/ACRIM makes no claims regarding Blatt's anaclitic-introjective distinction. By way of offering an integration of the two theoretical stances, I adopt the two-polarities model of personality development and psychopathology. According to this, personality develops along two trajectories—achievement and interpersonal relatedness. Placing the two trajectories squarely within the authentic self (*A*), I posit that some of our innate talents, interests, and proclivities are geared toward mastering the world (the achievement/introjective trajectory) while others are directed toward forming and securing relationships (the interpersonal/ anaclitic trajectory). I then extract self-criticism from the achievement trajectory, aligning it between the two trajectories because self-criticism may equally ensue from thwarted achievement and failed relating. In both cases, self-criticism drives a wedge between authenticity and self-knowledge. Although supported by research that suggests that self-criticism indeed constitutes an equally strong indicator of both achievement and relatedness concerns (Desmet, Coemans, Vanheule, & Meganck, 2008; Hong & Lee, 2001; G. Shahar, 2006b; G. Shahar, Soffer, & Gilboa-Shechtman, 2008), this theoretical maneuver circumvents the question of why self-criticism engenders more vulnerability than dependency.

Nor does *ASK/ACRIM* hold (like P. Gilbert et al.) that self-criticism must be submissive—a trait ostensibly incompatible with the tumultuous social environment self-critics inhabit. **ASK/ACRIM** also departs from Bandura's view that self-criticism (self-censure, self-reproach) serves as a way of meeting standards more closely. In fact, the present theory explains why self-critics *never reach self-standards*—due to their inadvertent generation of criticism from others. Finally, **ASK/ACRIM** disentangles what I regard as the authenticity/self-knowledge knot implied by Rogers's theory by providing a straightforward description of the link between the two processes—including the place of self-criticism in both. I also believe that **ASK/ACRIM** goes a good way toward delineating a multisystem, empirically testable, life-span, socially and culturally sensitive description of the evolution of self-criticism.

At the same time, ***ASK/ACRIM*** is profoundly influenced by all the theories reviewed in CHAPTER 3. The very notion of self-knowledge is strongly inspired by Blatt's cognitive-affective schemas or mental representations (imported from Piaget and Werner), Beck's modes, and Bandura's epistemic description of self-reproach. The notion of the internalization of criticism—most potently propounded by Blatt but also present in the theories of P. Gilbert, Bandura, and Rogers—plays a major role in the present theorization. While Blatt and Rogers imprint ***ASK/ACRIM*** via their emphasis on early parent-child relationships, P. Gilbert does so by means of his accentuation of the evolutionary basis of personality. In consequence, I coined the term "Particularized Mode of Adaptation."

Authenticity being, of course, the hallmark of Rogers' theory, I am a staunch Rogerian (and Winnicottian, Maslowian, etc.). Like Blatt, I find the notion of the psychodynamic unconscious useful—although I prefer operationalizing it in cognitive rather than psychoanalytic terms. I similarly believe that the stronger the self-criticism trait is, the more unconscious the striving for authenticity and the more inept the ways in which the latter is expressed will be. Like all theoreticians (perhaps barring Beck), I acknowledge the pivotal role of others in enabling the developing person not only to express his or her authenticity but also to know its nature. During childhood, these are primarily the parents. As the child grows older, more and more people—and social institutions—become directly involved in the quest for synchronizing authenticity and self-knowledge. Highly self-critical individuals require special interpersonal circumstances to allow their authenticity and self-knowledge to harmonize. These make up psychological treatment—the putative other being the therapist.

PART III

IN PRACTICE

Credo: A Philosophy of Treatment

Put the emphasis upon a single method of treatment no matter how diverse the problems which enter the office. Patients who won't behave properly according to the method should be defined as untreatable and abandoned. Once a single method has proven consistently ineffective, it should never be given up. Those people who attempt variations must be sharply condemned as improperly trained and ignorant of the true nature of the human personality and its disorders. If necessary, a person who attempts variations can be called a latent layman.

(Haley, 1969, p. 682)

. . . the "Renaissance Mind" is not broader than other intelligent minds but happens to cover a narrow swathe across the multi-dimensional space of knowledge that happens to cut across many disciplines which have divided up the space in other ways.

(H. A. Simon, personal e-mail, February 21, 2000;
cited in Dasgupta, 2007)

By now, I hope you have become somewhat curious to know how I *treat* self-criticism. Describing the treatment of a specific problem demands an elucidation of one's general approach to the art and science of psychological treatment. This forms the subject of the present chapter. Herein, I will share a set of convictions and therapeutic principles I have developed over two decades of clinical work. Some of these—in my opinion—are pertinent to all forms of psychological treatment and all patients. Others betray the particular nature of my clientele—primarily adolescents and young adults with (suicidal) depressive, personality, eating, and somatoform disorders. I will present these in bullet-point form, together with reference to their application to the treatment of self-criticism. Reference to specific interventions and techniques will be given in the following chapter.

Symptoms and the Symptomatic First

While I embrace the treatment of non-symptomatic, psychologically-well-off individuals who seek therapy primarily as a form of self-improvement and personal growth (e.g., I. Hirsch, 1994), I staunchly believe that this line of practice remains secondary to our true mission. Why? Because the threat of the pandemic we face leaves us no choice in the matter. As indicated in CHAPTER 1, the rate of mental illness/disorders is rising worldwide (e.g., Kazdin & Blase, 2011). Extant reports may in fact underestimate the problem, not taking into account subsyndromal manifestations of mental illness—that is, symptoms of psychological disorders that, while inflicting devastating interpersonal, occupational, economic, and health damage, do not meet the criteria for a binary diagnosis of mental illness (in the case of depression, see, inter alia, Judd, Akiskal, & Paulus, 1997). The charter bestowed upon us by governments, funding agencies, public health policymakers, and the public at large is to survive this tsunami. Our only chance of doing so is to direct our efforts toward treating symptoms and the symptomatic—and inspiring our best and brightest to join us in this urgent task.

We also must *because we can*. Clinical psychological and psychiatric science is flourishing, significant discoveries being made every year. Although key disagreements regarding diagnoses and the course of various mental illnesses remain (e.g., Frances, 2009; D. Watson, 2005), we are making important strides toward understanding affective, psychotic, eating, personality, conduct, and other disorders. I personally believe that the research on self-criticism reviewed previously constitutes a prime example of the advances that have been made. It is far from being the only or even the most important achievement, however. Progress is also being made with respect to the identification of specific interventions for specific symptoms and symptom clusters. Revisiting the comprehensive impact—and benefit—of these evidence-based interventions in the following, I contend that those who ignore them do so not only at their own but also at their patients' peril. An excellent illustration of this claim is the treatment of posttraumatic stress disorder (PTSD). As a citizen of a country chronically beset by military and terror-related traumas, I am aware first-hand of the tragic implications of past failures in treating PTSD (e.g., Solomon & Dekel, 2005). The development of several forms of treatment that have proven themselves capable of reducing symptoms (e.g., Prolonged Exposure—see Foa, Rothbaum, Riggs, & Murdock, 1991) is a priceless achievement, important caveats regarding their generalizability notwithstanding (e.g., Westen, Novotny, & Thompson-Brenner, 2004).

Symptoms and syndromes are not only costly, debilitating, and dangerous but also present a major obstacle to authentic self-expression. My work with seriously-depressed university students has taught me that while some students find themselves in the wrong (for them) academic program—depression thus serving as an important incentive to revisit their choices—others who feel they have made the right choice use their studies as a refuge from external stress and inner plight. Academic studies are very difficult to maintain when you are depressed, eating up resources and spreading adversely into virtually all life spheres (see, for instance, G. Shahar & Davidson, 2009). For students whose depression threatens their appropriately-selected academic vocation, expeditious and focused treatment might prevent them from becoming suicidal.[1] With respect to the treatment of self-criticism, the progress that has been achieved is important first and foremost because it allows us to minimize and neutralize debilitating disorders rather than merely relieve discomfort or mild distress (see G. Shahar & Davidson, 2009). It also means that controlling and managing affective, anxious, dissociative, psychotic, and other symptoms must be our first priority. This fact is backed up by research evincing that a failure to promptly alleviate symptoms predicts a poor treatment outcome (Gilboa-Shechtman & G. Shahar, 2006).[2]

Assessment and Case Formulation

Intimately related to the previous discussion is my conviction that assessment constitutes an integral element of responsible psychological treatment. How can we neutralize and/or minimize symptoms without having first evaluated their pattern or severity?

A proper discussion of my approach to clinical assessment lies beyond the scope of this book (hopefully to be addressed in another). Let me simply observe here that I advocate a complete and comprehensive assessment, focusing on symptoms and the symptomatic, for all types of treatments. First and foremost, assessment should be undertaken before treatment in order to establish the groundwork for case formulation and treatment planning. It should also be repeated at fixed intervals throughout the course of treatment—I usually assess every 4 months. Particularly pertinent to the present focus on self-criticism, assessment should move beyond identifying symptoms toward targeting risk factors and vulnerabilities.

The assessment of self-criticism presents us with the problem of methods that can be employed *in the clinic*. Assessment methods per se are not in short supply. As Table 6.1 demonstrates, we have at our disposal five leading self-report measures—the Depressive Experiences Questionnaire (DEQ), the Dysfunctional Attitudes Scale (DAS), the Personal Style Inventory, P. Gilbert's Forms of Self-Criticizing/Attacking and Self-Reassuring Scale, and the Attitudes Toward the Self Scale. Most studies conducted to date have used the DEQ and DAS. These also form a robust composite measure (e.g., G. Shahar & Priel, 2003). Blatt's Object Relations Inventory (ORI) likewise enables a semi-implicit (projective) measurement of self-criticism. Nachshon Meiran, Gal Sheppes, Eva Gilboa-Shechtman, Orr Spivak, and I have also developed a promising—albeit admittedly complex—computer task for the assessment of a lack of self-criticism (Sheppes, Meiran, Gilboa-Shechtman, & G. Shahar, 2008; Sheppes, Meiran, Spivak, & G. Shahar, 2010). None of these measures are really suitable for clinical practice, however. Norms are scarce, and even when they exist their use in a clinical setting is not straightforward. While a clinically-based scale exists for the

Table 6.1 **Self-Criticism Measures**

Measure	Description	Validated for Research	Guidelines for Practice
Self-Report Measures			
Depressive Experiences Questionnaire (DEQ; Blatt, D'Afflitti, & Quinlan, 1976)	66 items derived from patients' experience of depression (do not describe actual symptoms). Numerous versions exist, including STREALTH'S DEQ-SC6. Factor analysis yields three factors: dependency, self-criticism, and efficacy (see Table 1.1 for sample items from the DEQ).	Extensively validated (see footnote)	Although research norms are available (e.g., Nietzel & Harris, 1990), their use in clinical practice is not described.
Dysfunctional Attitudes Scale (DAS; Weissman & Beck, 1978)	40 items tap dysfunctional attitudes and beliefs implicated in (but not symptoms of) depression. Numerous versions exist (e.g., Cane, Olinger, Gotlib, & Kuiper, 1986). Factor analysis yields two factors: need for approval and performance evaluation (tantamount to self-criticism: e.g., "If I fail partly, it is as bad as being a complete failure").	Is extensively validated (e.g., was used in the TDCRP study)	None
Personal Style Inventory (PSI; Robins et al., 1994)	48 items assessing cognitive-personality vulnerability for depression. The measure captures sociotropy and autonomy, each possessing three subscales. Sociotropy: Concerns about what others think of self, excessive dependency, pleasing others. Autonomy: Need for control, defensive separation, and perfectionism/self-criticism. The latter is composed of four items only (e.g., "It bothers me when I feel that I am only average and ordinary").	Yes, for the entire PSI. The perfectionism/self-criticism subscale appears to belong to both sociotropy and autonomy, however, being associated with DEQ self-criticism rather than with measures of perfectionism (e.g., G. Shahar, 2006b).	None

Measure	Description		
Attitude Toward the Self (ATS; Carver, 1998).	A 9-item measure of self-regulatory vulnerabilities for depression composed of three subscales: High standards, generalization, and self-criticism. The latter includes three items (e.g., "I get angry with myself if my efforts don't lead to the results I wanted").	Yes, for the entire ATS. No data exist for the validity of the self-criticism subscale.	None
Forms of Self-Criticizing/Attacking and Self-Reassuring Scale (FSCRS; P. Gilbert, Clarke, Hempel, Miles, & Irons, 2004)	22 items assessing the thoughts typically entertained by depressed persons. The FSCRS is composed of three subscales: Inadequate Self (IS; "I can't accept failures and setbacks without feeling inadequate"), Hated Self (HS; 9 items—"I remember and dwell on my failings"), and Reassuring Self (8 items—e.g., "I still like being me").	Yes. No published data exists regarding the association between FSCRS and other self-criticism measures, however.	None

Projective Measures

Self-criticism subscale of the Objects Relations Inventory (ORI; Blatt, Chevron, Quinlan, Schaffer, & Wein, 1988)	The ORI was developed as an empirical instrument designed to assess individuals' internal representations via analysis of spontaneous descriptions of self (self-representations) and significant others (mother, father). Descriptions are rated for content and structural dimensions using a variety of subscales primarily based on Piaget's principles of concept development. As assessed by the ORI, self-criticism relates to the extent to which individuals judge and/or evaluate themselves harshly—frequently reflecting self-dissatisfaction.	Associations with other measures of self-criticism are unknown.	None

(*continued*)

Table 6.1 **Continued**

Measure	Description	Validated for Research	Guidelines for Practice
Computer Tasks			
A computer-task based on the task-switching paradigm has been developed by Nachshon Meiran, Sheppes, Gilboa-Shechtman, Spivak, and G. Shahar that assesses "anti-self-criticism"— that is, an aversion to engaging in self-critical tasks.	The task-switching paradigm pertains to the ease with which people are able to shift between cognitive tasks—indicating intact executive functions (Monsell, 2003). We developed a computerized procedure whereby participants are asked to shift between a self-critical task—linking the word "self" to negative words—and a neutral task. The findings indicate that young-adult participants with low levels of depressive symptoms found it more difficult to maintain a negative self-reference task than a neutral task, young adults with elevated levels of depressive symptoms not exhibiting such difficulties (Sheppes et al., 2008). This group also found that difficulties in maintaining a negative self-reference task—labeled by the authors as a "negativity aversion"— buffered against the prospective effect of exam failure on depressive symptoms (Sheppes et al., 2010).	Not yet. While a negativity aversion might be construed as an anti-self-criticism mentality, as with many implicit and cognitive measures of the self-concept, the correlation between the task-switching procedure and DEQ self-criticism was very small ($r = .13$, ns, unpublished). Only two studies have been conducted using the computerized procedure, although more studies are under way.	None

Note: STREALTH = Stress, Self, and Health Research Lab; TDCRP = Treatment for Depression Collaborative Research Program.
For additional information regarding the DEQ, see David Zuroff's website: http://www.psych.mcgill.ca/perpg/fac/zuroff/downdeq.htm

self-criticism subscale of the ORI, to the best of our knowledge the clinical use of this scale has not been subjected to any systematic examination to date.[3]

Another important assessment-related issue is case formulation—part of a general empirical hypothesis-testing approach to clinical work. The information gained during the assessment phase is translated into a formulation that draws together—in a brief narrative or diagram—the mechanisms causing and maintaining the patient's problems (e.g., symptoms, disorders, or difficulties in diverse domains), their origins, and current precipitants. As the treatment proceeds, the therapist repeatedly returns to the assessment phase, collecting data to monitor the process and progress of the therapy in order to revise the formulation and intervention as required (see Haynes, Leisen, & Blaine, 1997; Persons, 2012).

Researcher and psychoanalyst Dr. John Porcerelli and I have developed the action formulation (TAF; G. Shahar & Porcerelli, 2006). This constitutes an integrative approach to case formulation that focuses on the adaptive and maladaptive ways in which individuals create their social context. TAF is composed of four fundamental steps: (1) mapping the patient's social environment (e.g., sources of support, chronic interpersonal difficulties, and negative and positive life-events) and the role it plays in the clinical outcome; (2) identifying how patients actively shape or influence their environment in the context of their personalities, psychopathologies, and strengths in order to understand what role these play in generating vulnerability and resilience factors in the interpersonal realm; (3) differentiating maladaptive, risk-related interpersonal cycles from adaptive, protective-based ones; and (4) tailoring integrative techniques to counter the maladaptive cycles and strengthen the adaptive ones (see also G. Shahar, Horesh, & Cohen, 2008, for an application of TAF to the treatment of personality disorders).

The research reviewed in CHAPTER 1 demonstrates that self-criticism is likely to generate interpersonal strife, derail social support, and interfere with positive life-events, such as enjoyable activities, satisfying relational exchanges, and so forth. Applying TAF to the individual patient thus entails understanding the precise behaviors, coping strategies, and interpersonal deficits that propel him or her to generate life-stress and degenerate social support and stressful events. For instance, adolescent and young-adult patients with social anxiety might refrain from making new friends for fear of rejection. They thereby deny themselves the prospect of experiencing positive events and building support systems—or rely too heavily on friends (or family members). In this way, they induce the very rejection they dread, thereby maintaining their social anxiety (for an example of using TAF with a depressed, self-critical adolescent, see G. Shahar, Elad-Strenger, & Henrich, 2012).

TAF also calls for the identification of "virtuous," resilience-related cycles. In the clinic, I constantly remind myself that while patients may be highly self-critical they are *not only* self-critical. They always have other traits and qualities that counter the vicious self-criticism cycle with more adaptive interpersonal cycles. Thus, for example, the socially-anxious adolescent who generates stress and degenerates support and positive events may also be highly curious and technologically savvy, enabling him or her to develop online social networks that mitigate against feelings of loneliness. As described in CHAPTER 2, the presence of such traits as self-efficacy can similarly buffer against the adverse effect of self-criticism. Integrative therapeutic techniques may thus help patients who are both self-critical and self-efficacious utilize other traits or self-aspects in order to circumvent self-criticism. This notion is developed in the following chapter.

Individual Differences

Individuals suffering from the same psychopathology (e.g., depression) exhibit tremendous variability in terms of manifestation, course, etiological constellation, and response to treatment (e.g., evidence-based pharmacology and psychotherapy; see, for instance, Davidson & McGlashan, 1997). This variation calls for adjusting treatment to the individual patient's profile—an objective consistent with the current strong trend toward personalized medicine (e.g., Sikora, 2007).

While this focus on patient individuality appears to counter the emphasis I placed earlier on general psychopathological constructs such as depression, PTSD, and so forth, no contradiction exists in reality. What is evident is constant tension between the particular and the general, the nomothetic and the idiographic, the disorder and the person who suffers from it. Similar tensions exist in other branches of medicine (Manickaraj & Mital, 2012; Sikora, 2007) and the behavioral sciences—most predominantly in personality psychology (Allport, 1937; Hermans, 1988; Westen, 1996). Specifically, in the therapeutic context, tension means that rather than treating "just the disorder" or "just the person" we treat *this person* (say, "I") suffering from *this disorder* (e.g., "D"). In order to treat "ID," we have to consider all that is known about both. The person responsible for actively pursuing all extant and pertinent knowledge is the therapist.[4]

Individuality tends to complicate the presentation of clinical cases—and thus their treatment. This circumstance frequently leads to psychiatric comorbidity—that is, the co-occurrence of several psychiatric disorders. In psychopathology, comorbidity appears to be the rule rather than the exception—especially in the case of affective and anxiety disorders (e.g., Kendall & Clarkin, 1992; Maser & Cloninger, 1990).

What are the implications of psychiatric comorbidity for self-criticism? The fact that the trait may be embedded in various disorders necessitates a differential approach to its neutralization as a function of the putative disorder we are trying to treat. Treating a self-critical depressed patient, for example, will differ from treating a self-critical depressed patient who also suffers from OCD. In some clinical instances—patients with both unipolar depression and social anxiety being a case in point—self-criticism appears to contribute to both disorders, leading to a wide symptomatic alleviation when successfully treated. For others—bipolar spectrum disorders exhibiting with some personality disorder features, for example—the link between self-criticism and comorbid syndromes is neither apparent nor straightforward but requires increasing levels of sophistication and patience.

Chronicity is another noxious derivative of individuality. It is one thing to treat a self-critical young-adult suffering from his or her first major depressive episode and something completely different to treat another young-adult who—like Ilan in CHAPTER 4—suffers from double depression. If you recall, one of the central components in the self-critical cascade presented in CHAPTER 1 is the "scarring" effect, whereby symptoms—particularly of depression—increase self-criticism. Young adults with double depression who have long endured extensive depressive symptoms are likely to have a strongly harnessed self-criticism, making their depression refractory.

In addition to comorbidity and chronicity, case complexity also captures patients' individualized presentation of problems. As Larry Davidson and I have noted (G. Shahar & Davidson, 2009), case complexity refers to the presence of a host of risk factors—including personality vulnerability (e.g., self-criticism), stress, and demographic challenges. The more complex (multifaceted) the case is, the poorer the therapeutic response is likely to be (Blatt & Zuroff, 2005; Westen et al., 2004; but see Kazdin & Whitley, 2006). With respect to the treatment of self-criticism, this implies that its meaning, function, and vulnerability status may be affected by other factors. For example, how should a clinician address self-criticism in a depressed inner-city adolescent whose life is marked by poverty and exposure to violence as compared with a depressed self-critical adolescent from an affluent suburb? My own experience suggests that with the former—but not the latter—it is a major struggle simply to establish a therapeutic contract and secure stable attendance (see Altman, 2009, for a nuanced and moving account of treating economically-disadvantaged adolescents).

Patient individuality also bears on differential treatment response. The extensively described Treatment for Depression Collaborative Research Program (TDCRP) study epitomizes this by demonstrating the robust effect of pretreatment patient characteristics on treatment outcomes in the framework of state-of-the-art, evidence-based treatment for depression (see also Marshall, Zuroff, McBride, & Bagby, 2008; Rector, Bagby, Segal, Joffe, & Levitt, 2000). In addition to pretreatment self-criticism, analysis of the TDCRP data implicated other individual difference factors—such as pretreatment satisfaction with social relationships or a therapeutic alliance established after merely three psychotherapy sessions—as important predictors of outcome.

Several years ago, in a special issue of the *Israel Journal of Psychiatry* in honor of Sidney Blatt (G. Shahar, Zohar, & Apter, 2007), my former student Nirit Soffer (now Soffer-Dudek) and I estimated the percentage of TDCRP outcome variance accounted for by (1) evidence-based treatment, (2) pretreatment symptoms, (3) pretreatment self-criticism (erroneously labeled "perfectionism"), (4) pretreatment social relationships, and (5) a therapeutic alliance established after three sessions (Soffer & G. Shahar, 2007). In a multiple regression analysis that accounted for a respectable 22% of treatment outcome variance (measured via several symptom inventories), the treatment component only accounted for a statistically non-significant 1% of the overall 22% explained by the regression model! In this extremely expensive, carefully-designed clinical trial, patients' individual differences thus far outweighed the treatment component in determining outcome.[5]

The distinction between *intervention* and *treatment* is also closely related to the issue of patient individuality. Suppose we are treating a single, isolated problem—say an uncomplicated, first-onset panic attack—via a scientifically-validated intervention (e.g., interoceptive exposure [Kiyoe et al., 2006]). Then suppose the intervention "works," the symptoms abating or completely disappearing. In this case, the work may be over—without any need to distinguish between the intervention and the treatment. For this particular patient, interoceptive exposure constitutes both.

As is probably evident from the earlier discussion, however, this scenario is quite rare—particularly outside the psychotherapeutic research laboratory. In most cases, the patient presents various issues with which the therapeutic dyad repeatedly negotiates, the problems being tackled either sequentially or concurrently but virtually never in a linear fashion. Issues are also rarely completely resolved, tending to recur, change shape, prompt other problems, and so forth. Treatment in the real world—that is, in either public or private practice—is thus very different to that conducted in a scientifically-controlled setting, even if similar or identical interventions are adopted.

The cognitive-behavioral therapy (CBT) tradition epitomizes the use of prescriptive, clearly-articulated interventions. As I discuss the evolving and unfolding nature of psychological treatment with colleagues trained within this tradition, I am coming to understand that virtually all of them view treatment in the same way as I do. Does this mean that they are "cheating"—that they are not really practicing CBT? No. It simply means that they are practicing an integrative CBT—that is, a CBT tailored to the needs of the individual patient (e.g., Persons, 2012). When I point out to them that in this or that particular case they have actually employed non-CBT interventions (e.g., reflections, reframing, interpretations), they are completely unphased. "Call it whatever you wish," they usually say. "It works and I still perceive it as CBT."[6]

Implicit in this response is a distinction I believe most therapists make between "interventions" and "treatment." The former pertain to specific actions initiated by therapists in order to accomplish a certain therapeutic goal (e.g., symptom reduction). The latter refers to the ongoing, unfolding, complex process of care. Like my CBT-oriented colleagues, I subscribe to the notion that interventions should be clearly delineated, target-clear objectives, that are scientifically informed (i.e., evidence based). At the same time, I recognize that they are woven into the ebb and flow of an ongoing, flexible, potentially ever-changing treatment process that is governed by the patient's—and therapist's—individuality, including the shared intersubjective processes that unfold over time.

What does this mean for the treatment of self-criticism? First, the evolving and unfolding nature of any treatment necessitates a variety of interventions at different points in the treatment process. Here, timing is almost everything: some interventions might be useful in earlier phases, others at later stages.[7] Second, an extended treatment based on virtually all approaches and incorporating any type of intervention has to be beneficial for self-critical patients due to the "common factors" concept.[8] In the field of psychotherapy research, this relates to the beneficial processes that take place in most—if not all—forms of psychotherapy that lead to the alleviation of symptoms, better functioning, and personal growth (Arnow et al., 2013; Lambert & Ogles, 2004).

If you recall, the **ASK/ACRIM** theoretical perspective construes self-criticism as a distorted form of knowledge that drives a wedge between what the person fundamentally is (**A**uthenticity) and how he or she construes him- or herself (**S**elf-**K**nowledge). Rather than being static, this wedge expands dynamically and actively over time via criticism-based vicious interpersonal cycles. As is evident from the research reviewed in this book, these vicious cycles permeate therapeutic relationships, posing a potential threat to treatment. The very fact that therapists are determined to withstand therapeutic ruptures and are committed to continue empathizing with their patients and helping them survive in-the-world, however, means that they are in a prime position to offer self-critical patients a precious "corrective emotional experience" (Alexander & French, 1946). In this role, they are dedicated to enabling existence and exploring and helping patients to understand themselves, remaining resilient in the face of inept, awkward, and even aggressive overtures (Inquisitive Actions).

At the beginning of treatment, self-critical patients are frequently surprised by this possibility, regarding it as surreal—and certainly not to be trusted. They are thus likely to overlook it, distort it (i.e., assimilate it into their extant knowledge structure), and—more often than not—confirm or refute it by creating additional criticism-based ruptures. With time and therapist fortitude, however, this potentially corrective experience solidifies and actualizes into a genuine encounter. It is further reinforced when, together with the patient, the therapist verbalizes it, seeking to make sense of it in the context of the patient's life story, past and current interpersonal relations, present symptoms and problems, and future. When this is done sensitively and empathically—albeit insistently and consistently—patients gather the strength to re-examine what they think they know about themselves.

They can then revisit this knowledge structure on the basis of novel and more authentic experiences of themselves, particularly in their relationships with others. This in and of itself helps diminish the self-critical wedge between **A** and **SK**—in turn minimizing the criticism-based vicious cycles that underlie **ACRIM**.

Psychotherapy Integration

"What are you?" I was asked several years ago by a senior clinician during a professional gathering. Despite the ambiguous nature of the question, I knew precisely what he was after. He didn't want to know whether I was a human being or a UFO, Black or White, Ashkenazi or Sephardi, a prosperous entrepreneur or a starving poet. He wanted to know what kind of therapist I am. I truthfully replied that I am an integrative psychotherapist.

"Yes, but what are you *really*?" he insisted. "Are you 'integrative-dynamic'? 'Integrative CBT'?" "I'm an integrative-integrative psychotherapist," I replied. At this point, I was half bewildered, half amused. "Yes, integrative," was the response. "But you know, we therapists are like dogs, we need to sniff each other to know who belongs to whom." No longer bewildered or amused, I responded, "Perhaps I am a different kind of 'dog.'"

But really, I *am* an integrative psychotherapist—and certainly not the first or only one. Psychotherapy integration seeks to bridge different forms of treatment, including and transcending mainstream schools. The latter, it believes, can be fruitfully and strategically interwoven and applied as custom-fit, case-specific treatment plans (Ziv-Beiman and G. Shahar, 2015). The initial seeds of integration can be traced back to Freud himself, who as early as 1909 proposed the therapeutic benefits of confronting the phobic patient with the phobic object (exposure/desensitization) and experimenting with ways of inducing frustration and conflict (e.g., by setting time limits) in order to access deeper levels of the unconscious (Stricker & Gold, 1993).

It was not until the 1930s, however, that scholarly works began calling for the translation, assimilation, and integration of theoretical concepts from diverse schools (Dollard & Miller, 1950; Kubie, 1934). Attempts were then made to understand and decipher the sources of therapeutic change in general and identify the "common factors" present across therapeutic realms (for a review, see Norcross & Goldfried, 2005). The field greatly expanded following the inauguration of the Society for the Exploration of Psychotherapy Integration (SEPI) and the establishment of the *Journal of Psychotherapy Integration* (JPI)—of which I am honored to serve as chief editor as of writing.

Not only am I an integrative psychotherapist but I also staunchly subscribe to *theoretical* integration. The importance of a broad, in-depth, and comprehensive integrative theoretical basis derives from a number of factors, in my opinion.

First, psychopathology is by nature holistic. It consists of multiple dynamic and constantly interactive factors, both at the individual level (genetics, personality traits, physical attributes, etc.) and the contextual-environmental level (see the discussion of Bronfenbrenner's ecological theory of human development in CHAPTER 5). Psychopathology thus requires an integrative epistemology to capture, map, decipher, and treat it properly.

Second, our professional integrity demands it. While the complex nature of integrative theory and practice might be difficult to master and navigate, not to undertake the endeavor would be professionally inadequate—even irresponsible. Ultimately, it would translate into shortchanging the patients who seek our assistance and trust us to provide the most comprehensive (mental) care possible.

As is evident from observations in the field of applied psychology and reflective of the increasing emphasis on personalized health care, integrative modes of therapy are in fact being practiced—albeit sometimes subversively. The vast majority of clinicians identify themselves as either integrative or eclectic; many more incorporate several techniques within their practice (Norcross & Goldfried, 2005). The establishment of a guiding theoretical framework to tie these practical threads together has thus become a de facto necessity.

Last but not least, the understanding of clinical psychology as a field that strives to embrace both science and practice elicits the need for a comprehensive theory that can facilitate both the generation and systemic evaluation of the most suitable treatment/intervention for each patient.

Theoretical integration is highly compatible with Stricker and Trierweiler's (1995) notion of the therapist as a "local clinical scientist." Comparing the clinical setting with a metaphorical science lab, these scholars claim that the therapist must be familiar with and apply his or her scientific knowledge. At the same time, he or she must also recognize the treatment's specificity as a natural factor limiting the applicability of this knowledge and demanding real-time adjustments in order to provide local solutions to problems. On this view, the clinician is an *active* rather than merely an *applied* scientist—monitoring, weaving, and fine-tuning theoretical, scientific, and experiential knowledge together with context-specific factors (or a complex and dynamic context). This model also accentuates the clinician's need to think critically, examine scientific knowledge, and acknowledge his or her professional obligation to contribute to, encourage, and facilitate clinically-informed scientific research.

The shift toward the "local scientist" approach is further exemplified by the development of modular psychotherapy—a treatment model composed of "self-contained functional units (modules) that connect with other units, but do not rely on those units for their own stable operations" (Chorpita, Daleiden, & Weisz, 2005, p. 142). Different modules are selected and applied based on effectiveness (e.g., empirical support, evidence-based protocols, clinical experience, etc.), appropriateness (e.g., contextual and environmental setting, therapist characteristics, etc.), and patient profile/modalities/characteristics (e.g., pre-senting problem, symptomatology, developmental stage, treatment history, and preference; see Wetherell et al., 2009). This approach—which corresponds to the current emphasis on personalized medicine—challenges the one-size-fits-all idea by increasing the flexibility and adaptability of techniques. The rise of empirical studies assessing the use of modular psychotherapy in different settings attests to the increased attention this novel approach has been garnering in recent years (Weisz et al., 2012; Wetherell et al., 2009).

Of the various modalities of theoretical integration, I most strongly iden-tify with Paul Wachtel's cyclical psychodynamics (Gold & Wachtel, 1993; E. F. Wachtel & Wachtel, 1986; P. L. Wachtel, 1977, 1994, 1997, 2014). This rests on three notions: (1) the contextual unconscious—that is, unconscious processes are constantly manifested in interpersonal behavior; (2) the vicious cycle—that is, psychopathology emerges and is maintained by the individual's unintended construction of negative social relations; and (3) the ironic vision of behavior—that is, individuals create the very conditions they dread. The cyclical psychodynamic model depicts psychopathology as the consequence of interrela-tions between the unconscious, intrapsychic processes, and overt interpersonal behaviors (P. L. Wachtel, 1994), and it proposes a therapeutic approach that integrates insight-oriented work with active behavioral techniques. The former seeks to understand unconscious processes, the latter to reduce the likelihood of maladaptive interpersonal behaviors (P. L. Wachtel, 1977). As argued by Wachtel and his colleagues (e.g., Gold & Wachtel, 1993; E. F. Wachtel & Wachtel, 1986), insight and "action" techniques work synergistically (for additional versions of Wachtel's approach, see K. Frank, 1990; Gold & Stricker, 2001).

Self-criticism's modus operandi epitomizes Wachtel's notion of personal vul-nerability: Self-critics create an interpersonal cyclicity, leading to a psychopa-thology that reinforces personal vulnerability. Juxtaposing self-criticism research with Bandura's (1978) principle of reciprocal determinism (Sameroff, 2009; G. Shahar, 2006a), self-critical erosion can be understood as fundamentally inter-personal, transactional, and cyclical. This, in turn, highlights the need to focus on this cyclical behavior in assessment and treatment.

Wachtel's cyclical psychodynamic approach to therapy successfully addresses what I believe to be the major challenge facing psychotherapy integration—namely, the weaving together of an exploratory, insight-oriented therapeutic stance with a perspective/directive one. The major goal of the first approach is to help patients spontaneously experience themselves (A) and make sense of these experiences (SK). This position is thus conversational and flexible. Barring any clinical cri-sis (e.g., suicidality), patients come to therapy and are invited *to be*. They choose when to begin talking and about what.

The perspective/directive approach, in contrast, seeks to equip patients with specific information and skills. It is thus primarily educational and instructional.

The therapeutic states of mind involved in each stance are markedly different. While the former usually involves intuitive, associative, metaphorical, and emotionally expressive modes of being, thinking, and relating (e.g., T. H. Ogden, 1997, 1999), the latter focuses on the provision of information, instruction, and active teaching, calling for a clear, targeted, linear, and logical mental state (e.g., Rudd, Joiner, & Rajab, 2001).

Over the course of practicing and associating with practitioners, I have found that although most clinicians respond favorably to the prospect of an integration that incorporates various techniques from the same therapeutic stance (e.g., exploratory and prescriptive), they are reluctant to combine techniques from both. I am nonetheless convinced that such a twofold integration of insight and action (P. L. Wachtel, 1977) is precisely what most patients seek from us.[9]

The cyclical psychodynamic model nonetheless requires some significant modifications. Wachtel has always been suspicious of cognitive approaches and techniques, preferring to integrate the psychodynamic and behavioral (P. L. Wachtel, 1994). At a conference in Tel Aviv in 2011, he explained that his misgivings stem primarily from older, informational processing approaches to psychological care. The goal of these techniques is to correct dysfunctional cognitions (e.g., Beck, Epstein, Harrison, & Emery, 1983). They are thus incompatible with Wachtel's perception of the person as an actor rather than spectator (see also Coyne, 1994; G. Shahar, 2004, for a similar position). As Wachtel has told us (see also P. L. Wachtel, 2011), however, the recent "third wave" in CBT—which includes psychotherapeutic modalities based on acceptance and mindfulness (dialectical and behavior therapy and acceptance and commitment therapy, for example: see Dimeff & Linehan, 2001, and Hayes, Strosahl, & Wilson, 1999, respectively)—is much more consistent with his view of the person. He has thus recently integrated the "third wave" CBT into his cyclical psychodynamic approach (Wachtel, 2011, 2014).

Although I largely agree with Wachtel, I also acknowledge other developments within cognitive psychology and cognitive-affective neuroscience and seek to integrate these into a cyclical psychodynamic approach to therapy. I (G. Shahar, 2013b; see also Shahar & Schiller, in press) thus recently proposed a modified version of the cyclical psychodynamic model that draws on existential philosophy, psychology (Davidson & G. Shahar, 2007), and neurocognitive research (Amati & Shallice, 2007; Iacoboni et al., 1999). All these approaches understand people to be fundamentally goal directed and future oriented (see CHAPTERS 4 and 5). Calling this modified cyclical psychodynamic model "radical intentionalism" (G. Shahar, 2013b), I posited that "human suffering results primarily from the tendency to rigidly project a desired self into the future and work toward realizing what we think we should become" (G. Shahar, 2013b, p. 322; see also G. Shahar et al., 2012). Such an inflexible dedication might directly produce life-stress and interfere with generating positive events and social support.

Here, I would like to further update this position. I now suggest that the tendency to project a desired self into the future is inevitable. The intransigent projection of such desires—with the accompanying generation of a negative social context—nonetheless still derives from the wedge between **A** and **SK**. People being confused about their authentic self, they seek to become something that is consistent with their self-knowledge (i.e., what we think we should become). The rigidity and ineptitude with which they project and pursue the future derives from their oppressed authenticity. Struggling to find a voice within interpersonal relationships, their **A** ultimately and tragically shapes these relationships in a way that further dampens it (see CHAPTERS 4 and 5). I also believe that an inability to "stay in the present" and flexibly coordinate between present and future-oriented thinking contributes to the pathological intransigence of the projection of self-based plans into the future (Dunning & Fetchenhauer, 2013). It is the ability to stay in the present and discover who I am—drawing from various sources of information, including my past—that minimizes the wedge between **A** and **SK**, thus allowing me to launch my real, authentic self into the future.

Leaving specific interventions and techniques to the next chapter, my focus here lies on describing the optimally-beneficial therapeutic climate for self-critical patients. This is an environment as nurturing as it is curious that pays particular attention to criticism-based, vicious interpersonal cycles both within and outside treatment. This framework is dedicated to empathically examining the person's life narrative while also investigating—jointly with the patient—the present and future. It is a place that acknowledges the fact that the patient has a core being without overlooking his or her complexities and multiplicities. Perhaps most importantly of all, it is an environment that facilitates flexible shifts between perspective interventions designed to short-circuit self-critical cycles and enable exploratory work in a reflection of John Lennon's famous dictum: "Life is what happens to you while you're busy making other plans."

Therapist Subjectivity within the Intersubjective Matrix

Readers of this book who come from humanistic-existential or psychoanalytic-relational therapeutic perspectives (Aron, 1996; Mitchell, 1988; Schneider, 2007; Yalom, 1980) will probably regard the sentiment that the therapist's subjectivity—his or her history, life narrative, personality proclivities, and authentic self—plays a major role in the outcome of treatment as self-evident. For many decades, CBT and other prescriptive approaches have been criticized—even ridiculed—for trying to suppress therapist subjectivity in order to allow therapeutic tactics and techniques to dominate. While such criticism might once have been justified, it is no longer. Contemporary approaches to

CBT now acknowledge the importance of therapist subjectivity (e.g., Cartwright, 2011; Hayes et al., 1999; Leahy, 2008; Rudd & Joiner, 1997).[10]

Why does therapist subjectivity play an important role in the treatment of self-critical patients? I have enumerated various reasons (see G. Shahar, 2013b):

1. Allowing a glimpse into others' subjectivity might encourage people to share their own. Social psychological research attests to the contagious influence of self-disclosure in naturalistic interpersonal settings (the "stranger on the train" phenomenon—Rubin, 1975). Therapist self-disclosure may similarly facilitate patient disclosure and inner exploration, as well as strengthen the therapeutic alliance (Barrett & Berman, 2001; Ziv-Beiman, 2013). While self-disclosure by self-critics might also evoke dismay and distress in the therapist (Bareket-Bojmel & G. Shahar, 2011)—therapists not being immune to this potential impact—any disclosure on the part of any patient is arguably grist for the psychotherapeutic mill.

2. Experiencing the therapist as a real human being with his or her own struggles may reduce feelings of shame and concealment of subjectivity. Patients with elevated self-criticism are either convinced that they are inferior to others or afraid to be proven so in the course of relating. This is particularly true of young people (adolescents, young adults), who frequently believe competent grownups to be problem free. In the therapeutic context, young people naturally assume that therapists are competent grownups. Self-critics might experience a therapist who is a real person with weaknesses, vulnerabilities, struggles and capable of making mistakes as a deeply liberating encounter. This might further encourage them to expose shameful aspects of their own experience.

3. Awareness of the adaptive ways in which therapists regulate emotions might constitute a powerful modeling process. Having been a psychotherapy patient for decades, I have learned a great deal from my numerous therapists about how to regulate emotions. One of the most valuable lessons I have gained is that virtually any painful experience—however scary, surreal, shameful, or traumatic it may be—can be verbalized and made sense of. Like Harry Potter's "dementors," the worst monsters are those that are formless. Every day, patients observe therapists tolerating enormous amounts of affective pain—the pain they themselves bring to the therapy room. Watching closely how therapists modulate this pain, articulate its meaning, and shape it into something understandable, they begin to put it into practice in their own lives. Bandura would probably call this "vicarious learning," Roy Schafer "internalization," and Alexander and French (1946) a "corrective emotional experience." Call it by whatever name you prefer; the underlying point is that this process is enabled by therapists allowing patients to observe their (the therapists') subjectivity.

Therapists who are unable to experience are also unable to modulate experience. Therapy cannot work if we are not present "in-the-room."[11]

Self-critical patients learn all of this from their therapists. They may also gain another important skill—namely, how to regulate their self-criticism. I have already alluded to the possibility that self-critical patients may induce or evoke distress and dismay in their therapist. In fact, I would say that this is an inevitable hazard. Therapists immerse themselves in their patients' inner world—that of self-critical patients being marked by toxic criticism and punitive derogation. Criticism is also contagious (Bareket-Bojmel & G. Shahar, 2001). When I treat self-criticism, I myself become self-critical: Am I up to par? Am I doing my job? What am I missing? (G. Shahar, 2004). Sometimes, my judgmentalism spills over into other realms: "If I can't be there for this patient, how can I be there for my children? I'm a terrible father." When I am at my best, I am aware of this stream of consciousness. Obviously, I can't always be that. On occasion, my patients get annoyed with me and I get upset with them in turn. Sensing this, we find ourselves in a tense rupture. Maybe I've said the wrong thing or failed to say the right thing—creating a Kohutian "empathic failure." Therapists do fail—nothing ventured, nothing lost.

When this happens, the one place patients don't need me to be in is that of obsessive remorse. This only incurs guilt feelings in self-critical patients, in turn increasing their self-criticism and then escalating into anger. At this point, the rupture is here to stay. What patients need is for me to assume a benevolently curious stance, stimulating both of us to examine rather than wallow in the crisis. When I am at my best, I can do this. I go to the clinic every (other) day determined to be/do my best. With Ilan—to whom I referred in CHAPTER 4—I managed to do so in a "good enough" manner (i.e., more often than not). Ilan learned not only to believe in the possibility of withstanding rupture (with others and with me) but also that mistakes do not constitute cues for self-derogation—firstly mine and then his.

I once criticized the management style of one of my mentors. He replied, "You're right, you know. But I am not going to fire myself." I immediately added this to my list of wise pieces of advice that I pass on to psychotherapy supervisees: "Don't fire yourself. You run the risk of taking your patients with you if you do."

4. When therapists observe their subjectivity after having expressed it, they may understand the way they "use" the patient and how this might contribute to ruptures, thus enhancing exploration of their patients' self-criticism. More than a decade ago, I described a serious therapeutic rupture I experienced with a female patient during my early internship phase (G. Shahar, 2004). Only in the course of writing that article did I realize how much I needed her—and that this "need" might be fundamental to an ongoing, meaningful treatment

process. I will present a more detailed description of this case in the following chapter.[12]

In the context of *ASK*, one of the reasons we need other people is that they bear the potential of enabling us to become what we might be. When we act in coordination with another person's subjectivity, we might come closer to realizing this goal. Conversely, if I act despite of or against the other person's subjectivity, the potential for rupture increases precipitously.[13]

Like a host of other psychotherapy thinkers, I believe that the latter possibility is inevitable (Rudd, Joiner, & Rajab, 2001; Stolorow, Brandshaft, & Atwood, 1987; Safran & Muran, 2000). As I remarked earlier, therapeutic ruptures constitute not only a risk (i.e., patient dropout or premature termination) but also an opportunity for growth. Here, I am emphasizing one aspect of this opportunity. When I realize that a rupture with a particular patient stems from my "needing him or her" in a way that does not tally with his or her needs, my attention is automatically directed to the latter. Seeing him or her better, I can attend to his or her plight and help him or her make sense of it. In this way, I may help to diminish the self-critical wedge between his or her *A* and *SK*. The fact that I myself go through the same process—realizing my own needs and being empathic to them—is a useful (though not necessarily pleasant) byproduct of this intersubjective process.

5. Patient awareness of therapist subjectivity might facilitate a properly worked-through termination phase. Termination is a complex issue to which I cannot do justice in the present context. In the context of treating people with personality disorders, Guina Cohen, Neta Horesh, and I (G. Shahar, Cohen, & Horesh, 2008) examined the right timing for the termination of treatment with these difficult-to-treat individuals under the economic pressure of providing brief treatments. Drawing from action theory (Brandstädter, 1998; Lerner, 1982; G. Shahar, 2006a), we argued that, the major thrust of personality pathology being active generation of adverse social conditions, termination might be considered when vicious interpersonal cycles diminish and "virtuous"—positive—ones emerge.

Self-criticism being a highly noxious form of personality pathology (albeit distinct from personality disorders—see Chapter 2), the same recommendation applies. More specifically, I am proposing that termination with self-critical patients is most feasible when their tendency to engage in criticism-based vicious cycles—that is, being attracted to a critical environment and evoking criticism from others—diminishes. I believe that this is frequently first indicated by a decreased tendency to pressure therapists' into becoming critical toward them or interpreting their utterances as critical statements.

In my experience, one of the best ways to achieve this is via the "discovery" that I am human. Patients begin to make comments about my habits, peculiarities, dispositions, and style. Most of these are accurate and conveyed with a benevolent sense of humor. An atmosphere of friendship increasingly permeates the room—although we both know I am not acting as a friend.[14] The more this occurs, the more I am convinced that these patients—most of whom are adolescents and young adults—no longer *need me* for the potentially vicious Inquisitive Action described in CHAPTERS 4 and 5 (i.e., to evoke information about who they are). It is not that I no longer matter, but that I matter less—and perhaps in a different way. When this is accompanied by an apparent reduction in criticism-based vicious interpersonal cycles and when dangerous behavior (suicidality, nonsuicidal self-injury, restrictive eating) is no longer apparent, I begin to inquire—first within myself and then with the patient—whether the time is right to terminate.

Development and Systems: Become Familiar With Both

Diverse developmental stages bring about various biological changes (e.g., puberty in early adolescence, menopause in mid-adulthood), entail an onset of disparate psychological disorders (e.g., attention-deficit disorder in childhood but also throughout the life-span, bipolar disorder during adolescence and young adulthood), and present divergent psychological tasks (e.g., identify formation in adolescence vs. adjustment to parenting in adulthood). As I attempted to chart in CHAPTER 5, different developmental stages also place individuals in relationship to very different ecological systems (e.g., kindergartens vs. schools vs. [in Israel] the military vs. colleges vs. workplaces, etc.). The developmental period during which patients start treatment thus constitutes a crucial factor in shaping case formulation and treatment planning.

In light of this, developmental science—developmental psychology, biology, psychopathology, and so on—must constitute a quintessential base for psychotherapy, calling upon the therapist to constantly broaden his or her knowledge base in the field. Psychotherapeutic expertise in a specific developmental stage—childhood, adolescence, young adulthood, mid- or late adulthood—mandates an intimate acquaintance with the ecological systems pertinent to this stage. Child and adolescent psychotherapists must thus be well versed in the structure, function, and operation of school systems. Those who treat adults, on the other hand, must have a good grasp of the workplace. The treatment of individuals with medical issues necessitates an understanding of the health system—the operation of which changes in accordance with age (pediatric vs. geriatric settings). A developmental focus, of course, entails acquaintance with family and cultural psychology, the life-span being nested within families—broadly defined—and various cultural settings.

The stress I am placing on human development is linked to all the previously noted emphases related to psychological treatment—focus on symptoms and the symptomatic, individual differences, the distinction between interventions and global care ("treatment"), integrative psychotherapy, and the acknowledgment of therapist subjectivity and intersubjective processes. With respect to the latter, I would add that a developmental orientation is central to how therapists (should) create their own professional identities. The fact that patients at diverse developmental stages introduce different experiential themes (e.g., the discovery of sexuality in adolescence, heightened death awareness in old age) means that these themes are bound to interact with the particularities of therapist subjectivity. A therapist who finds him- or herself helpless in dealing with a particular developmental issue might want to steer clear of treating that age group.

I try to drive home this message to clinical psychology students and interns whenever I can, strongly encouraging novices to avoid the pitfall of attempting to "treat everyone" and concentrate on acquiring the knowledge and skills that will help them treat those patients (in particular, those age groups) that will imbue their work with a profound sense of meaning—a strong calling, an experience of "feeling real." I am discovering that when a patient's authenticity resonates with the therapist's, the therapeutic dyad can withstand formidable obstacles—including severe clinical crises and ominous therapeutic ruptures.

I knew from a very early professional age that I wanted to treat adolescents and young adults, particularly those struggling with affective, eating, personality, and psychosomatic disorders and suicidality. The vitality of adolescents and young adults (see, e.g., Arnett, 2006), the centrality of issues of identity and identity formation, the discovery of romantic and sexual life, the frequent walk on the margin of health (as manifested, for instance, by risky behavior), and the taking of crucial life decisions (selection of a profession and spouse) all resonate with my temperament, proclivities, interests, and life history.[15] These types of patients form the focus of the following chapter.

Specific Interventions and Guidelines

World is the structure of meaningful relationships in which a person exists and in the design of which he participates.

(May, 1958, p. 59)

Now I want to add that in certain stages of certain analyses the analyst's hate is actually sought by the patient, and what is then needed is hate that is objective. If the patient seeks objective or justified hate he must be able to reach it, else he cannot feel he can reach objective love.

(Winnicott, 1949, p. 71)

In this chapter, I will focus on specific interventions and guidelines for working with highly self-critical patients. My attention here is directed toward the treatment of symptomatic and psychiatrically-comorbid adolescents and young adults—that is, patients in the second and third decades of their lives. This clinical continuum is further delimited by the specific psychopathological constellations I treat—affective (depressive and [hypo]manic), eating, somatoform, stress related, personality disorders, and suicidal behavior. These are also the psychological constellations and age groups I study at the Stress, Self, and Health Research Lab. Because I ascribe great importance to clinical experience and acquaintance with specific scientific knowledge, I believe that the interventions and guidelines set out here are not automatically relevant to other developmental periods (e.g., the elderly) or psychopathological constellations (e.g., panic disorder, obsessive-compulsive disorder, or psychosis). My hope is that students—and readers—will build on my methods and theories and find effective ways for treating self-criticism in other developmental periods and psychopathological constellations.

The chapter is divided into two parts. First, I consider what is known—clinically and scientifically—regarding the behavior and response of self-critics to treatment. This includes the relatively little evidence for specific techniques aimed at alleviating self-criticism. This part concludes with my own evaluation of our extant knowledge of the treatment of self-criticism. I then present my own preferred interventions and guidelines. Timing being (almost) everything in the treatment of self-criticism, I will review the various interventions and guidelines recommended in the order I introduce them to patients, highlighting the links between them. This temporal order is, of course, merely prototypical. As with all clinical issues, individual characteristics take precedence over general principles.

Part I: How do Self-Critics Respond to Treatment? What are the Extant Evidence-Based Interventions?

The therapeutic alliance is important in all forms of psychotherapy and interventions. An abundance of evidence suggests that self-criticism impairs the therapeutic alliance (see CHAPTERS 1 and 2; G. Shahar, Blatt, Zuroff, Krupnick, & Sotsky, 2004; Whelton, Paulson, & Marusiak, 2007; Zuroff et al., 2000), thereby impeding the process of psychotherapy and its outcome (Horvath & Symonds, 1991).

Kannan and Levitt's (2013) comprehensive review of the way in which different psychotherapeutic orientations (psychodynamic, cognitive, and emotion-focused) treat self-criticism led them to conclude that the latter approaches all construe self-criticism as an automatic response whose presence the patient must first recognize. This includes becoming aware not only of the self-critical tendency itself but also of its process and early causes. The goal of the various treatment orientations is not to eradicate self-criticism in all its forms but to create a healthier and (more) constructive response to it.

Psychoanalytic frameworks perceive self-criticism as an internalized punishing "object" (Aronfreed, 1964) or punitive superego (Freud, 1917). An individual experiences self-critical thoughts as an internal process in which negative thoughts are directed inward. In voice therapy (Firestone, 1988)—a therapeutic approach geared toward treating destructive behavior—patients are encouraged to verbalize their self-critical thoughts in the second person as though someone else were talking to them, in order to shift them outward and separate them from their own rationales. In this way, they identify the sources of self-criticism in past life experiences and become aware of the way in which self-criticism affects their present behavior.

Cognitive therapy emphasizes the role of dysfunctional cognitions in behavior and emotion, self-critical thoughts being conceptualized as the result of maladaptive cognitive schemas. One of the building blocks of cognitive (and cognitive-behavioral) therapy—primarily for depression (Beck, Rush, Shaw, & Emery, 1979) but also for many other psychopathologies (for a review, see Huppert, 2009)—is "cognitive restructuring." This technique teaches patients to identify distorted, maladaptive, or irrational thoughts and fight them via various strategies, such as Socratic questioning (inquiring repeatedly about the premises on which maladaptive thoughts are based in order to expose their untenable nature), pinpoint cognitive errors (e.g., assuming an all-or-nothing perspective for gray areas), actively seek evidence to dispute irrational thoughts, and marshal counterarguments. The thoughts and cognitions usually targeted by cognitive restructuring relate to self-evaluation (including self-derogation), pessimistic thoughts about the future, assumptions regarding the avoidance of negative stimuli, and so forth. The technique requires considerable skill on the part of the therapist, as well as a high degree of cooperation on the part of patients, who must be willing to examine their core beliefs. In this spirit, cognitive-behavioral therapy (CBT) stresses *collaborative empiricism*—the expectation that patient and therapist will join forces in order to discover and correct distorted cognitions (Beck et al., 1979).

Only two forms of cognitive reconstructing have been tested specifically with respect to self-critical thoughts—compassionate mind training (CMT) developed by P. Gilbert and his colleagues noted earlier and trial-based thought record (TBTR; de Oliveira et al., 2012). In CMT (P. Gilbert & Procter, 2006), the patient is taught to adopt a more compassionate perspective by developing a relationship between the different parts of the self based on warmth, care, and compassion. Time is spent nurturing empathy for one's own distress in the past and present. Cultivation of the ability to self-soothe and be compassionate reduces the internal and external sense of threat.

TBTR (de Oliveira et al., 2012) is a form of cognitive restructuring that challenges dysfunctional negative core beliefs via the metaphor of a legal trial. A "prosecutor," "defense attorney," and "jury" present and weigh the evidence for and against core beliefs. A one-session intervention of a mixed sample of adult patients evinced a reduction in the strength of their self-critical core beliefs and corresponding emotions (de Oliveira et al., 2012).

Emotion-focused therapy (EFT)—developed by Leslie Greenberg and colleagues (L. S. Greenberg & Watson, 2006)—emerged out of Carl Rogers's person-centered therapy. This is a nondirective form of therapy in which the therapist's active listening and genuine, empathetic, and positive interaction help the patient focus on the present and become more aware and accepting of him- or herself (Rogers, 1951, 1967). Change occurs because the positive therapeutic interaction allows the patient to seek to fulfill what Rogers believes to be a natural human tendency—self-actualization, growth, and openness toward experiencing different possibilities in life as one's true self (Cepeda & Davenport, 2006). It contrasts with cognitive therapy, which focuses on informational processing as a vehicle for promoting change. In EFT, maladaptive and negative emotions are activated and new emotional experiences generated in order to create an enduring change in the emotional organization of the self (L. S. Greenberg & Watson, 2006). Explicitly targeting the "inner critic," EFT appears to be a credible approach for treating self-criticism in the context of depression (J. C. Watson, Goldman, & Greenberg, 2007).

My friend and colleague Ben Shahar (no family relation) and his colleagues (B. Shahar et al., 2012) have found that an emotion-focused two-chair dialogue intervention significantly reduced self-criticism and emotional distress among highly-self-critical individuals. In this brief intervention, patients are taught to identify their self-criticism, conceptualized as a conflictual split between two parts of the self—one harsh, critical, and punitive, the other weak and submissive. Patients are asked to act out both parts of the self in order to emotionally experience both aspects. The ensuing dialogue eventually leads to a resolution of the conflict and a more incorporated, less critical, and more compassionate self. This intervention was found to significantly reduce self-criticism, anxiety, and depressive symptoms and increase self-compassion and self-reassurance (B. Shahar et al., 2012).

Ben Shahar and his colleagues have recently demonstrated via a randomized controlled trial that loving-kindness meditation (LKM) was superior to a waitlist control group in reducing self-criticism and depressive symptoms and increasing self-compassion (B. Shahar et al., 2014). Impressively, therapeutic gains were maintained 3 months after the intervention. This appears to be the only study pursuing LKM as a potential avenue for the treatment of self-criticism. Hopefully, it will pave the way for future attempts.

Finally, an important clinical discussion of the treatment of self-criticism has been initiated by Elizabeth Schanche (2013). Correctly identifying self-criticism as a transdiagnostic phenomenon and linking it in particular with Cluster C personality disorders (e.g., avoidant, obsessive-compulsive personality disorders), Schanche adduces three sets of techniques that may be helpful in treating this vulnerability. The first—drawn primarily from Leigh McCullough's short-term psychodynamic model (L. McCullough, 1997)—is gradual exposure to previously avoided affects. The idea behind this set of interventions is as straightforward as it sounds—that is, it encourages self-critical patients to experience once-warded-off emotions (e.g., anxiety, sadness, anger, shame) in order to enable them to increasingly refrain from defensively assuming a self-critical stance (i.e., bashing oneself instead of experiencing emotions). The second set is drawn from P. Gilbert's CMT (see earlier). The third set is taken from P. Ogden, Minton, and Pain's (2006) sensorimotor approach, in which the therapist helps the patient employ soothing sensations (e.g., gentle stroking movements) in order to activate self-compassion (again resorting to P. Gilbert's influential theory; for a clinical illustration, see Schanche, 2013).

Evaluating Extant Scientific and Clinical Knowledge

This scientific and clinical literature on the treatment of self-criticism constitutes a great start. Considerable wisdom has been accumulated, some of which is even being scientifically validated. Nevertheless, it remains only a start. The gap between the decade-long, voluminous personality and psychopathology research on the detriment of self-criticism on the one hand and the relative dearth of scientifically-solid ways to mitigate it on the other is conspicuous. I hope that the next part of this chapter will advance us even further along the road.

By way of evaluating the literature reviewed in Part I and linking it specifically with the strategies recommended later, let me note the following:

1. As observed earlier, patient self-criticism presents a major obstacle to the construction of a beneficial therapeutic alliance, the latter being a strong predictor of psychotherapy outcome. The treatment of self-critical patients must thus view protecting the therapeutic alliance as a top priority.

2. Self-critical patients are likely to be intensely suspicious of active interventions presented at the beginning of treatment. More often than not, they perceive these as an indication of their current deficiency—as well as potential traps for future failure. Even benign overtures made by therapists (I shall discuss hostile overtures later) are bound to be interpreted by self-critical patients as judgmental. The findings from the Treatment for Depression Collaborative Research Program epitomize this reaction. Therapists should thus be actively prepared for it.

3. In light of these two points and the self-critical cascade described in CHAPTER 1—namely, that self-critics maintain their self-criticism by generating a negative social environment, which leads to distress—I anticipate that treatment of highly-self-critical patients is likely to be long term (Blatt, 1995; G. Shahar, 2001). There are simply too many interpersonal complications—both within and outside treatment—to address within the confines of brief treatment.

4. A patient, cautious, principally exploratory, warm, and empathic approach should thus be adopted during the first weeks—and sometimes months—of treatment. This therapeutic stance is necessary for the future employment of active techniques.

5. This cautious, warm, and empathic approach is likely to lead to many of the benefits exhibited by emotion-based therapies such as EFT, LKM, and McCullough's graded-exposure technique. Specifically, over the course of the first weeks (perhaps 2 to 3 months) of treatment, patients learn to be less afraid of both the therapist and the treatment (including the emotions it stirs). Personally, I prefer this naturally-occurring—if somewhat protracted—processing of painful emotions over the more structured EFT and other forms of brief treatment. My fear is that the latter interventions carry the potential for being experienced by patients as demands made by therapists.

6. Next to be employed are active techniques. These are geared primarily toward (a) training patients to identify non-self-critical self-aspects, (b) teaching them to shift away from self-critical cognitions, and (c) guiding them toward

managing daily activities and tense interpersonal exchanges. The majority of these active techniques are drawn from CBT, mindfulness-based therapy, and interpersonal therapy for depression (IPT). Others I have developed myself (see later).

7. All of the active interventions are presented via the use of existential terms, focusing on choice, freedom, destiny, and, of course, *A*uthenticity and *S*elf-*K*nowledge.

8. Although I have not yet encountered the need to employ compassion-based interventions, this might simply betray an oversight on my part. I am assuming, however, that the benefit of these techniques will be particularly pronounced during the latter stages of treatment, once the patient has come to trust the therapist and has learned to shift attention to non-self-critical self-aspects.

9. As highlighted later, a constant need exists to attend to the transference/countertransference exchanges that unfold in the course of treatment—in particular to therapeutic ruptures.

Part II: Recommended Interventions and Guidelines, Ordered Temporally

Some of the interventions described previously occur consecutively—such as active instillment of warmth, psychoeducation, empathic immersion in parents' wounds (for adolescents), multiple selves analysis, mindfulness and recentering, participation-engagement (behavioral activation, dereflection, and routine analysis), interpersonal inquiry and reframing of Inquisitive Actions, and trial-based cognitive restructuring. These interventions are iterative, being employed over and over again even after they have been successfully introduced in previous phases of the treatment. Guidelines pertaining to transference/countertransference exchanges, therapeutic ruptures, and enhancing the therapist's presence ("em-presentation") are relevant to all treatment phases.

Active Instillment of Warmth

I make every attempt to infuse the beginning of therapy with a warm, supportive, and nurturing atmosphere. This means that I almost never confront, preferring inquire rather offer interpretations. I use humor extensively—and hopefully also benevolently. With adolescents in particular, who come to therapy ambivalently at best and often under duress, I try to avoid a prolonged silence at the beginning of treatment, finding that they frequently use it as an excuse to drop out because "nothing is happening." The more treatment progresses, the more tolerant I become of silence, sometimes even encouraging it when it is clear that it is being used for constructive reflection rather than avoidance of the therapeutic encounter. During this latter phase, I follow the lead of psychoanalytic thinkers such as Bion (1984) and T. H. Ogden (1997, 1999) by reflecting on my own stream of consciousness as it unfolds during the silence and the relevance of my free association to my patients' inner lives.

What I am trying to create at the outset of treatment is an atmosphere of camaraderie. Self-critics find this difficult, of course, a voice within them viewing this attempt on my part with great suspicion. To the extent that it nevertheless feels good to them, however, it makes them *curious* about what will follow. Curiosity being essential for bridging the gap between *A* and *SK*, this is all it takes at this stage to get the treatment up and going—until the first rupture, of course.

Psychoeducation Regarding Self-Criticism and Critical Expressed Emotion

Psychoeducation is an evidence-based intervention that combines disorder-specific information with tools for coping and self-management. It is based on the notion that the patient and his or her family constitute important partners in the treatment process. Providing them with knowledge and strategies regarding its use in a proactive manner will thus help them become better allies, in turn positively affecting the outcome (Lukens & McFarlane, 2004). An important element of many psychological interventions, psychoeducation can also be used as an intervention in its own right. Studies have shown it to be effective in reducing distress and anxiety levels and improving treatment outcome and quality of life in numerous mental and physical conditions—including schizophrenia (McFarlane, Dixon, Lukens, & Lucksted, 2003), depression (Dowrick et al., 2000; Tursi, Baes, Camacho, Tofoli, & Juruena, 2013), cancer-related distress (Matsuda, Yamaoka, Tango, Matsuda, & Nishimoto, 2014), and chronic pain (Luciano et al., 2013).

At the beginning of treatment, I summarize the self-critical cascade described in CHAPTER 1. At this point, I submit to my patients—in lay terms—that science has found self-criticism to form a very serious dimension of vulnerability because it creates interpersonal havoc, leading to emotional distress. I then tell them what is known about critical expressed emotion (CHAPTER 5) and how I view its links with self-criticism. I then invite them to describe possible criticism-based cycles in their lives.

I hope to achieve three things hereby. First, by impressing upon them the negative consequences of self-bashing, I try to make them cease regarding it as a virtue. In essence, I'd like them to know that I strongly believe that self-bashing is bad for their health. Second, psychoeducation regarding self-criticism can work as a stress inoculator (Meichenbaum, 1977). By becoming aware of the hazards of self-criticism, patients begin to become prepared to defend themselves against future derogatory inner voices—particularly in the face of imminent failures (e.g., an important examination). While this does not happen immediately or exclusively on the basis of psychoeducation, it does set the stage for the development of anticipatory coping strategies (Aspinwall & Taylor, 1997) that can be called on to fight activations of the inner self-critic in the future.

Third, I hope to reinforce the therapeutic alliance. I am essentially telling patients that I have a good grasp of at least one of the forces contributing to their plight and am committed to helping them protect themselves against it. Potentially, this remoralizes patients—"I am not alone; this guy might be there for me." It might also elicit hostility and suspicion—"Yeah right! This guy thinks I am going to buy into his promises to be there for me?!" More often than not, however, both reactions occur. This is a good thing: I want patients to test my determination and wherewithal. While invariably challenging, this is never as frightening as the things patients themselves fear.

A caveat is in order at this point. If psychoeducation is employed rigidly and in an authoritarian manner rather than playfully (in the Winnicottian sense—i.e., with curiosity and humor), it runs the risk of *heightening* self-criticism because it conveys a persecutory demand ("Stop being self-critical—or else"). While I try my best not to be intransigent or authoritarian, I am aware that patients might experience me in this way. I thus attempt to preempt this possibility by calling patients' attention to it—"The trick here is to refrain from criticizing yourself for criticizing yourself. And of course, it is tough."

Psychoeducation does not stop with patients. Family members—parents and siblings—also need to be educated about the detrimental effects of derogatory criticism. Parental and family guidance are almost invariably perceived by family members as threatening: "Here comes the shrink to tell us how we screwed up our son's life." I am finding that the best way to circumvent resistance is via normalization and minimization. I first acknowledge that family can be a chaotic melting pot that inevitably involves stress, strife, and criticism. I then note that the research attesting to criticism's pernicious effect demands that we all strive to minimize its occurrence. I present it as a challenge worth taking on, frequently adducing examples from my own parenting, including my own failure to avoid being critical toward people in my family. (I will return to therapeutic self-disclosure later.) In this way, I seek to *externalize* the message by entrusting it to the science of self-criticism rather than to my own fallible hands.[1]

Schools also need psychoeducation regarding the adverse effects of self-criticism and critical expressed emotion. Constantly pressured by their ongoing responsibilities, teachers and other school personnel are often unaware of the difficult circumstances behind their self-critical pupils' criticism-evoking habits. As a therapist working with adolescents, I am a strong advocate for my patients, helping the pertinent school personnel understand why they behave the way they do and why derogatory criticism will only exacerbate the problem. In most of my encounters with school staff, this has yielded beneficial results. Teachers and school counselors are usually eager to gain a better understanding of their pupils and readily embrace therapist assistance in this direction. At times, such advocacy might change a developmental/educational trajectory and thus prevent serious consequences.

Many years ago, I treated a 12-year-old boy with a horrendously traumatic childhood—the most salient feature of which was blatant exposure to violence. Unsurprisingly, this adolescent became increasingly violent at school, to the point where he hit two classmates so hard they needed serious medical attention. He was immediately expelled. This was a calamitous event for the child's mother, who was struggling to extract herself and her child from poverty. Things then rapidly spiraled out of control. The mother lashed out at her son, who threatened to kill himself. Extremely alarmed by these events, I immediately set up an appointment with the school personnel and drove there within days to meet with the staff. I was met by a stern-looking group of teachers and counselors determined to keep my patient out of school. At the end of a very long meeting, having heard the boy's chilling story and understood just how important their perception of him was to him, the team changed its mind and decided on temporary suspension. Eventually, he was allowed to return to school. Criticism-based interactions between the mother and boy then abated, enabling us to examine some of the boy's—and mother's—deep-seated anxieties about his dropping out.

Empathic Immersion in Parental Wounds

I recently gave a clinical seminar to school psychologists about depression in schools. One of the dilemmas raised by the attendees related to the boundary between parental guidance and psychotherapy for parents of depressed children. The participants noted—appropriately in my opinion—that the treatment of depressed children requires parental counseling and guidance. They also noted that these guidance/counseling sessions quickly turn into therapeutic ones. Parents actively raising their own conflicts, traumas, and struggles (including, possibly, their own depression), they expect "treatment." The school psychologists expressed considerable concern that "getting into therapy with the parent" might compromise their role as the child's therapist. While they acknowledged the possibility of referring parents to treatment, this option was quickly deemed unsatisfactory, many parents not being able to pay for more than a single treatment in the family. They thus solicited my opinion.

Most were surprised to learn that I actually advocate "getting into therapy with the parent"—on condition that this is limited to as few sessions as possible. My rationale is that sessions with parents being inherently charged, they are bound to evoke parental self-criticism. Parents may experience the therapist's wish to "stay away from therapeutic encounters" as standoffish, experiencing the therapist as being there merely to provide psychoeducation or concrete guidance. The best way to circumvent this obstacle is to convince them that they are seeing someone who cares about them—even if this someone's principal responsibility is their child rather than themselves. This means actively and empathically immersing oneself in their pain, giving support, verbalizing their wounds as challenges, validating and normalizing the hurt, linking it to the parent-child relationship and child's depression, and expressing confidence that they are capable of coping with their own struggles without involving their children.

Up until a decade ago, Beersheba—the city in which I practice—was economically disadvantaged. It is currently flourishing, which is heartening to see, and has begun to attract upwardly mobile individuals from various areas in the Negev—and even from the center of Israel. Being upwardly mobile myself, I found treating self-critical adolescent children of my peers an illuminating experience. I am learning that these parents' determination and strong will inadvertently translate into impatience and intolerance regarding their children's difficulties. These parents find it genuinely hard to understand why their children "can't get it right." Some allege that "it's all about the child's seeking attention" and that he or she "simply isn't trying hard enough."

In trying to gain a deeper understanding of this attitude, I am finding out that, despite their apparent success, some upwardly mobile individuals feel they have fallen short of realizing their career goals. They thus deem themselves to be failures—despite evident professional, economic, and social success. As sessions with parents quickly accumulate, it becomes increasingly apparent that such self-criticism underlies the critical expressed emotion they direct toward their children. Simply conveying this to parents and expecting them to stop criticizing their children does not work. In fact, it further activates their self-criticism, in turn consolidating criticism-based vicious cycles. When I allow these issues to unfold naturally in sessions with parents, however—sometimes taking additional time and extending the length of the session or scheduling additional sessions—parents begin to develop a measure of self-empathy. This enables them to reflect candidly on their relationship with their children. Loosening the hold of critical expressed emotion on the parent-child relationships helps to set both parties free. Obviously, this must be an iterative process, repeated time and again throughout the child's treatment. Nor is it a substitute for treatment for parents—always the best solution for parental afflictions.

Although I presented this position to the seminar attendees I was grappling with the right way to label the counseling/guidance sessions. Help arrived from one participant, who said: "What you are actually doing is giving them a *therapeutic injection*." "Exactly!" I replied. In the absence of separate psychotherapy for the parent, I am giving them an empathy-based, Kohutian/Rogerian-like therapeutic injection. I try to do this every month or so.[2]

Multiple Selves Analysis and Personal Projects Analysis

Earlier, I acknowledged my alliance with the prevalent notion that the self-concept is multidimensional. Shared across numerous psychotherapy schools of thought (Bromberg, 1996; Lysaker & Hermans, 2007; Satir, 1978), this notion leads to the assumption that awareness of one's self-concept multiplicity is pivotal to well-being because it leads to greater self-knowledge and self-acceptance. This theoretical stance is largely supported by social-psychological empirical research attesting to the stress-buffering effect of self-complexity (Linville, 1987; McConnell, 2011; for mixed results, see the review by Rafaeli-Mor & Steinberg, 2002).

Particularly noteworthy is the use made of multiplicity by two forms of evidence-based psychotherapy—schema therapy (Young, Klosko, & Weishaar, 2003) and emotion-focused therapy (L. S. Greenberg & Watson, 2006; B. Shahar et al., 2012; see earlier for the description of Ben Shahar's work, which is particularly pertinent to self-criticism). Having recently described the method I employ for increasing patient self-concept multiplicity, focusing on the treatment of self-critical adolescents and young adults (G. Shahar, 2013b), I will expand on this here.

Multiple Selves Analysis (MSA) has three goals. The first is to convey to patients that their self-criticism is not "them" but merely a "side" or "voice" within them. The second is to get them to identify non-self-critical self-aspects or inner voices. The third is to train them to activate these benign self-aspects—particularly when distress and self-criticism are high. These three aims are introduced slowly, gradually, and iteratively throughout the treatment process.

My first task is to alter the language used by patients when they present their self-critical voice. Whenever they utter a self-derogatory statement, I gently localize and specify it. For instance, if a patient says, "I suck," I will immediately respond, "This side of you, this inner voice, says that you suck." At this point, I refrain from doing more. All I want at this stage is to pique the patient's curiosity. The best-case scenario is when patients are so intrigued by this change of vocabulary that they inquire—perhaps indignantly—about it. This is my cue to move on to the next task.[3] If they do not, I wait for several sessions—during which I persist in altering the self-critical language.

We thus return to the psychoeducation phase—but this time to situate all that we know about the detrimental effects of self-criticism within the context of self-concept multiplicity. I present the multiplicity notion to the patient, selecting phrases appropriate to his or her age and level of abstract thinking. The most important message to patients is that they have other, more benign, and even supportive sides. I expect strong objections from most self-critical adolescents and young adults: "You're wrong," they say, "You don't really know me," "You don't know what I'm talking about," "You're just saying I don't suck because that's what you're paid to do," and so on.

Arguing back is a trap. How can I convince young people who have been practicing self-criticism for over a decade—and often longer—that they don't actually "suck"? My patients' objections are best construed (to use Sullivan's phrase) as a "security operation" (Sullivan, 1953)—i.e., as a way to protect themselves from further anxiety. Self-criticism is what my patients *have*. It is their prominent form of **SK** (per CHAPTER 4). What do I offer them in return?

Whatever I do, is unclear to them at this stage. In fact, arguing with patients runs the risk of quickly colluding with a criticism-based vicious cycle. This makes them feel that I am criticizing them for being self-critical. There will be enough time and opportunities in the treatment process to experience and manage ruptures (see later)—we don't need to create artificial ones.

Instead of disputing with them, I attempt to engage **A**—that is, the forceful, authentic vector within my patients (and us all). I tell them I'm not going to debate with them because I don't feel I can convince them at this early stage of our acquaintance. I am nonetheless certain that if they only had a self-critical voice within them they wouldn't still be alive. They must have other sides to have gotten so far. If this is met with resistance, as it frequently is, I present the following paradoxical stance:

> Listen, one thing I think we would agree on is that, regardless of how accurately you describe or experience yourself, you're suffering. If you suck, telling me that you do pains you further. Given that you are here, expecting some relief, what I am proposing to you is to simply work with me to inquire about other potential sides within you. If you do, one of three things might transpire. You might be proven right, in which case I am colossally wrong and you are wasting your time with me. Better to realize this sooner than later, right? Or I'm right and you are going to find out you have favorable sides in you, of which you were not fully aware. This is a good thing, no? Or—the most likely scenario—neither of us is right and we will simply discover things that neither of us anticipated. Surely, this is still better than the current state of affairs?

Of course, the real answer to the latter question is "No, it isn't. There is indeed a worse scenario than the current one—to completely not 'know myself.'" The good news is that this is impossible. As Kierkegaard allegedly stated (Cooper, 1990), humans are the only beings who are infinitely interested in their own existence. If we look, we will find. The point here is to draw patients' attention to the fact that therapy is the place to be curious about things, to ensure them that I trust their ability to inquire, and to make it clear that I myself am 100% determined to embark on this journey alongside them.

If this does not work, I employ self-disclosure. I tell the patient that although he or she might believe I am simply a know-it-all psychologist who has forgotten what it is like to be an adolescent (or a young person), I do know or I would not have entered this profession in the first place (and have to face young people telling me I know nothing . . .). I tell them that in my youth I went through this journey myself, more than once—and then decided that I wanted to go through it over and over by way of a calling. I say that I am inviting them to take the journey with me—the journey being their lives. More often than not, this piques their curiosity about *me*. It makes them want to learn the "juice" about my life. Alas, however, business comes before pleasure. Gossip must be earned. I tell them that I will give them the goods later—if they set out on the journey with me.

The reader may or may not agree with my own personal style in practicing MSA. This matters not. Whatever advice I dispense to therapists must be channeled through their own particular **A**. There are many routes to achieve the same therapeutically-desired outcome—in this case, patients' awareness of their multiplicity. The important issue is that patients embrace the multiplicity notion. This is *huge* therapeutic progress, constituting the most important step toward putting the inner critic in its place. As I frequently say to patients, self-criticism *must* have a place within their soul. It should never be eradicated, because the possibility of being self-critical always carries with it the prospect of attempting to understand oneself. There is a world of difference, however, between having a place and taking over and being tyrannical.

"Tyranny" is an important term in this context. Adolescence and young adulthood are developmental stages during which politics and political thought become salient (Bhavnani, 1991). This is definitely the case in Israel—a profoundly political (and politically-polarized) nation. Invoking political metaphors and analogies is thus a useful technique with adolescents and young-adult patients. In discussing the impact of self-criticism on their lives, I often liken it to dictatorship: their inner critic oppresses all their other self-aspects. The goal in identifying these other sides is not to replace one tyrant with another but to allow all the self-aspects to have a voice, be in a state of dialogue, and coexist—just as in a democracy. As Churchill is credited with saying, while democracy might be problematic, it is better than the alternatives.

To some extent, democracy is predicated upon territory. For all the voices to exist, they must have a place to reign freely. In treatment, I find that the process of personification enables such a realm. Specifically, I ask patients to give a name to their self-critical self-aspect—and to all the other self-aspects we identify. As I have previously argued (G. Shahar, 2013b), giving a name to all self-aspects delimits and demarcates them. Later on, using additional techniques—particularly mindfulness and behavioral activation—the personification of self-aspects allows patients to shift flexibly between them and decipher their various functions.

Jennifer—a young-adult engineering student with sky-rocketing self-criticism *and* double depression—named her inner critic Gabriel. The name immediately evoking the biblical angel, we began discussing how self-criticism serves the role of a guardian angel—a sentinel that keeps spontaneity at bay in the interest of living the life one "should live."[4]

Personifying patient self-aspects is also conducive to the exploration of these self-aspects' development and life story. If you recall, in CHAPTER 1 I described how Rina named her inner self-critic Danny after a guy she had dated who had treated her badly. As with Rina, Jennifer and I spent several sessions tracing the first time Angel Gabriel appeared—at her fourteenth-birthday party, at which few of her classmates showed up. It is also interesting to learn when and under what circumstances other, non-self-critical voices emerge in patients' lives. This frequently reveals important people and relationships, as well as key events—both negative (e.g., ostracism at school) and positive (e.g., a vacation with grandparents during which the patient felt visible, attuned to, and cared for). This aspect of MSA renders it a truly integrative intervention, composed of both exploratory and perspective components.

Human beings seem to possess a profound need to anthropomorphize or personify the world (Bering, 2006; Epley, Waytz, Akalis, & Cacioppo, 2008; Epley, Waytz, & Cacioppo, 2007; Kwan & Fiske, 2008; G. Shahar & Lerman, 2013; Waytz, Cacioppo, & Epley, 2010). Individual differences in this tendency seem to impact vast areas of psychological functioning—including human/computer interaction, business, and law (Waytz et al., 2010). Personification is potentially adaptive because of its transformative nature—it changes an event or situation from an external obstacle into an internal sense of purpose and meaning. For these same reasons, however, it may also constitute a risk factor, inducing significant distress (G. Shahar & Lerman, 2013).

From a cognitive-linguistic point of view, personification/anthropomorphism may be construed as a particular case of metaphorical speech (e.g., Fadaee, 2011). Since Susan Sontag's landmark publication of *Illness as Metaphor and AIDS and Its Metaphors* (1978), both social science and medical literature have begun attending to the metaphorical framing of various medical conditions—reflecting the stigmatization attached to them (e.g., Barroso & Powell-Cope, 2000; Rollins, 2002; Rosenman, 2008; Sherwin, 2001). The metaphorization of illness is not necessarily a negative move; it can provide definite advantages. Breast cancer patients who view their disease as a "challenge" or "value" thus exhibit lower levels of depression and anxiety and a higher quality of life than those who regard it as an "enemy," "loss," or "punishment" (Degner, Hack, O'Neil, & Kristjanson, 2003).

Metaphors taken from art and literature have become an integral part of the diagnostic concept of depression, influencing both treatment and research (Rosenman, 2008). They are also employed in therapeutic interventions, such as self-management courses. These have shown that their use facilitated emotional expression among individuals suffering from chronic illnesses (McFarland, Barlow, & Turner, 2009). In general, metaphors play a significant role in influencing and creating moral, ethical, and political values—particularly in the context of illness (Rollins, 2002; Sherwin, 2001).

After patients' key self-aspects have been identified, personified, and situated within the patient's life narrative, we start taking on the future. Irvin D. Yalom is a major source of inspiration here: "Memory ('the organ of the past') is concerned with *objects*; the will is concerned with *projects*. ... Effective psychotherapy must focus on patients' *project relationships* as well as on their *object relationships*" (Yalom, 1980, p. 291 [original italics]). Focusing on personified non-self-critical self-aspects, I invite patients to imagine where these benign/benevolent sides are heading. Such personal project analysis (PPA) is a key component of MSA because it provides clues to patients' authentic personal projects. This stage also reveals some of the ways in which the self-critic interferes with this authenticity.

The prolonged and iterative nature of this process cannot be overemphasized. I am in no rush. Things happen in treatment while we are engaging in MSA/PPA. There are crises to address and symptoms to neutralize; some important phenomenological issues might surface and be in need of working through. Nor does completion of the MSA/PPA process guarantee a change in the self-concept. On the contrary, the process must be repeated over and again, each time being linked to other life circumstances, different segments of the patient's life story, and various stages in the development of the therapeutic relationship.

Within 6 to 9 months of treatment, however, patients usually no longer speak (or think) about themselves as a unified whole. They begin to talk in terms of "sides," "voices," and "aspects." Although they might complain about the formidability of the "self-critical voice," they acknowledge that it is not the only "voice" and that it is possible to experience the self "outside" this voice.

Possible—but very difficult. MSA/PPA is an intervention that seeks to change the *structure* of the self-concept. This might very well be resistant to change due to the patients' information-processing style—their ruminative, perseverative, inflexible, self-focused attention (see CHAPTER 2). Even if patients are aware of their other, benign/benevolent sides, they may find it difficult to mentally attune to these. Their mind simply doesn't always follow. In order to help them shift from one self-state to the other, I introduce mindfulness and recentering techniques.

Mindfulness and Recentering Techniques

Mindfulness is a (cognitive)-behavioral technique that originated in Eastern meditative practices. It requires the individual to actively pay attention to external and internal present experiences—including emotions, thoughts, and sensations—in a nonjudgmental way (Kabat-Zinn, 1994). Elsewhere, it has been described as attentional self-regulation (Evans, Baer, & Segerstorm, 2009). Mindfulness is a crucial component in several treatments, such as dialectical behavioral therapy (DBT; Dimeff & Linehan, 2001), mindfulness-based stress reduction (MBSR; Kabat-Zinn, 1982), compassionate mind training (P. Gilbert & Proctor, 2006), and acceptance and commitment therapy (ACT; Hayes, Strosahl, & Wilson, 1999).

Having practiced mindfulness meditation for over 15 years now—beginning while I was at Yale as a way of being able to live outside my own self-criticism—I am a staunch advocate of the technique. In fact, I see it as a fundamental mental and lifestyle stance, a cornerstone of mental hygiene—akin to the role of nutrition and exercise in physical self-care. It also resonates well with my philosophical convictions. As an existentialist, I am a fierce defender of freedom, deeming it a necessity for authentic expression. I also believe, however, that freedom/authentic expression are predominantly based on the way we manage our attention. In this regard, mindfulness is really an attention-control endeavor. I thus find it relevant to discuss the notion of freedom with my adolescent and young-adult patients before I introduce the idea of mindfulness. The practice faithfully follows Kabat-Zinn's instructions—and in this sense I add nothing new or innovative to the technique. Once I see that patients are beginning to routinize mindfulness, however, I immediately link it to MSA/PPA (Figure 7.1).

I explain that, in addition to the known benefits of mindfulness (M), practicing it should help shift attention from the self-critical inner voice or self-aspect (SA) to other voices/aspects.

At this stage, mindfulness enters the prolonged/iterative therapeutic mix, being repeatedly present in the sessions and consistently linked with MSA/PPA.

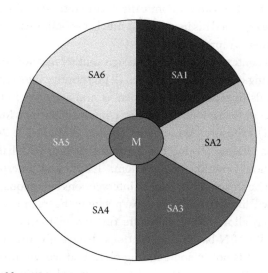

Figure 7.1 The self-aspects pie

The connections between mindful and nonmindful states of mind on the one hand and the unfolding of life experiences on the other are also continuously explored.

Participation-Engagement

Several years ago, Larry Davidson and I called for the implementation of philosophically-based guidelines for prioritizing interventions in the treatment of comorbid, chronic, and complex clinical cases. We labeled this guideline "participation-engagement" (PAREN; G. Shahar & Davidson, 2009). Inspired by Heidegger's notion of being "in-the-world," PAREN seeks to help patients actively pursue authentic personal projects. According to PAREN, symptoms and vulnerabilities that block an authentic expression must be the first target, other symptoms and vulnerabilities being relegated to later stages in the therapeutic process—if they are dealt with at all.

We (G. Shahar & Davidson, 2009) described a hypothetical case study and stressed the need for the therapist to prioritize when treating comorbidities. Our hypothetical patient, Jonathan, was an aspiring professional philosopher who suffered from multiple psychological conditions—agoraphobia, panic disorder, dysthymic disorder, a personality disorder, and impaired social skills. Jonathan reported that he was unable to study properly throughout the day due to difficulties falling asleep and waking up multiple times during the night. While all his other problems appeared severe and life disrupting, this particular symptom was denying him the chance to achieve his life goal—a successful career in academia. We decided on the order in which we would treat his problems, employing a CBT protocol to treat the insomnia before we addressed any of the other symptoms. Had Jonathan been an economically-secure retired businessman, he—and we—would have regarded his insomnia as much less ominous, most likely leading us to treat his other symptoms first.

In the present context, I would like to assign another meaning to PAREN. I view it as an overarching category that includes all prescriptive interventions seeking to involve individuals in meaningful experiences and activities in-the-world. These interventions include behavioral activation (Dimidjian, Barrera, Martell, Munoz, & Lewinsohn, 2011), exposure (Abramowitz, Deacon, & Whiteside, 2011), social skills and assertiveness training (Fodor, 1992), routine analysis (G. Shahar & Davidson, 2009), dereflection (Frankl, 1975; Yalom, 1980), and interpersonal inquiry (Buechler, 2004; Levenson, 1991). Not all interventions being equally relevant to the present focus, I will limit myself to the most potent in the treatment of self-criticism.

First, however, allow me to elaborate further on the philosophical underpinnings of all PAREN-based interventions. I have already quoted Jean-Paul Sartre's dictum: "It is not in some hiding-place that we will discover ourselves; it is on the road, in the town, in the midst of the crowd, a thing amongst things, a human among humans" (1939) (see Chapter 4). These words bring home (pun intended) the realization that we must express, create, and understand our authentic self (the term "discover" pertains to expression, creation, and understanding) in-the-world—as opposed to in our thoughts, minds, or the clinic. Sartre's political philosophy posits *engagement* as a principal virtue for intellectuals. In other words, they are called to take an active stand in worldly political affairs and be politically active (Heter, 2006).

Paul Tillich, another great existential thinker, used the term "participation" to elucidate the existential nature of anxiety and the way humans can transcend it. In his seminal treatise *The Courage to Be* (1952), he promotes self-affirmation—being what one is—as well as participation in circles of activities broader than that of the self. Anticipating Bakan's (1966) and Blatt's (1974, 2004, 2008) later scholarship, he argued that both strategies are crucial for overcoming existential anxiety:

> The self affirms itself as participant in the power of a group, of a movement, of essences, of the power of being as such. Self-affirmation, if it is done in spite of the threat of nonbeing, is the courage to be. But it is not the courage to be as oneself, it is the "courage to be as a part." . . . We are threatened not only with losing our individual selves but also with losing participation in our world. (1952, p. 89)[5]

What is *our world*? Tillich being one of Rollo May's key mentors it is no wonder that May—a prominent leader in existential psychoanalysis and psychotherapy—defined "world" as the "structure of meaningful relationships in which a person exists and in the design of which he participates" (as quoted at the beginning of this chapter).

Let me now turn my attention to four extremely pertinent interventions relating to the alleviation of self-criticism—behavioral activation (BA), dereflection, routine analysis, and interpersonal inquiry.

Exemplifying the proverb "With food comes appetite," BA entails systematically encouraging patients to pursue meaningful and pleasurable activities in order to combat depressive anhedonia. The basic aim of this strategy is to reinstate the biopsychological reward system underlying operant conditioning, prompting patients to inject "positive mood" into their psyche. The theoretical underpinnings of this intervention are Skinnerian behavioral and Banduran social-learning principles (Jacobson, Martell, & Dimidjian, 2001). As a psychological treatment of unipolar depression, BA possesses a very impressive evidence base (Dimidjian et al., 2011; Soucy-Chartier & Provencher, 2013). "Dismantling" studies in which various components of CBT are compared suggests that BA may be superior to the cognitive component of CBT for depression (Dimidjian et al., 2011). Another of BA's noteworthy advantages is that it strongly tallies with basic psychological science attesting to the protective effect of positive life events on mental health. Specifically, positive events prospectively predict a reduction in distress and buffer against the adverse effects of life-stress (G. Shahar & Priel, 2002). Positive events also facilitate recovery from a depressive episode (Needles & Abramson, 1990).

I introduce BA to my patients after we have consolidated the MSA/PPA and mindfulness-based techniques. BA can neutralize self-critical ruminations in two ways. First, it reduces depressive symptoms directly, thus preventing depressive scarring—the final component of the self-critical cascade (CHAPTER 1). Second, it increases the accessibility of benign or adaptive self-aspects, which are put into action in-the-world. When patients *go out-in-the-world* and experiment with novel behaviors, they can thus experience themselves differently from the way in which they had when subject to their self-critical voice.

Returning to Rina's treatment, toward termination she raised the prospect of going away on a skiing vacation with two of her female friends. At the time, she was both recovering from a painful romantic breakup and between jobs. I therefore strongly agreed with the idea of her taking time for herself and enjoying herself. After I had endorsed the vacation, however, Rina began to backtrack. We then had the following email exchange (also presented in G. Shahar, 2013b, p. 324):

Rina: Hi Golan, I am having difficulties accepting the idea that I am going skiing for a week. . . . I feel bad about spending the money. However, I don't have the guts to tell my friends I'm not going. What should I do?
Golan: You should go skiing (smiling).
Rina: Shouldn't I do this with a clear mind?
Golan: When will this happen?
Rina: It's unclear, if ever.
Golan: QED.[6] That's why I support your exploring new options and activities.
Rina: OK, thanks.

During the trip, Rina enjoyed the sightseeing and the resort's unique ambiance. Discovering that she did not really like skiing, however, she dropped out of the course while her friends continued. Feeling depressed, she called her ex-boyfriend—only to be met by coldness and indifference. To top it off, she then had an unsatisfying fling with a man she met at the resort. On the positive side, she survived the week's vacation, her ability to share the painful phone call with her friends not only strengthening her relationship with them but also fortifying her desire for close female friendships. Our discussion of the fling also deepened our understanding of her yearning for love—which so easily disintegrates into premature physical contact. An event that commenced as part of a BA regimen thus turned into a complex experience consisting of enjoyment, frustration, loneliness, and friendship. This enhanced her **SK**, helping her discover her preferences and choices—and thus her **A**.

Dereflection is a cornerstone of Viktor Frankl's logotherapy (Frankl, 1958, 1966)—a well-known form of existential psychotherapy (Yalom, 1980). In an article entitled "Paradoxical Intention and Dereflection" published in *Psychotherapy*, Frankl propounded:

> Instead of striving for potency and orgasm, the patient should be himself, give himself. And instead of observing and watching himself, he should forget himself. In order to implement this process, in other words, in order to counteract the patient's hyper-reflection, another logotherapeutic technique . . . has been developed: "dereflection." (1975, p. 234)

While paradoxical intention seeks to help patients restore control over undesirable behaviors (e.g., obsessions), dereflection is designed to enable them to execute *desirable* behavior (e.g., sexual activity). Hyper-self-focused awareness constituting a major obstacle for executing desirable behavior, it must be circumvented. The patient is encouraged to "forget" or "put aside" the behavior he or she strives for and "go do something else." Because outward-directed attention prevents hyperreflection (self-focused attention) and no longer blocks the behavior, the latter will then spontaneously come to the fore.

This technique is still frequently used (for more recent use of dereflection in burnout, depression, food addiction, and psychosomatics, see Bulka, 1984; Herion, 2011; B. Z. Hirsch, 2008; Lukas, 1981). Although I am not aware of any systematic empirical research examining its efficacy, it may be argued to fall under BA—which also encourages patients to be involved in activities in-the-world (BA is, of course, admirably empirically supported). When juxtaposed with Paul Tillich's notion of participation, however, I believe that dereflection may also be used to encourage patients to do something for others in order to feel better about themselves.

Any clinician worth his or her salt will know what I am talking about. As demanding as it is to immerse oneself in other people's plights (Sussman, 1995), being a therapist also offers tremendous solace. We forget about our own problems in the process. I talk about this all the time with my wife, Rachel, who is a clinical psychologist and suffers from a chronic physical illness. According to Rachel, nothing remoralizes her more when her illness flares up than seeing patients. Is it because one gains perspective on one's own dire situation? Possibly. I believe that it is also because it directs our attention outward.

I thus encourage my patients to do things for others. Specifically, I encourage them to volunteer for a charity or other health and social care organizations, citing voluminous empirical research attesting to the health-related benefits of volunteering—both physical and mental (e.g., Oman, Thoresen, & McMahon, 1999; Post, 2007; Poulin, 2014; see also Mongrain, 2014, on compassion toward others and self-esteem). I try to entice them into finding an avenue for volunteering that is particularly suited to them—in other words, an activity consistent with their Authenticity that offers them opportunities to participate in things at which they excel, stand for a cause that resonates with their plight, exemplify their convictions, or, in the best-case scenario, all the above.

Here is an illustration. For someone like me—who is extremely passionate about issues of authenticity and self-expression—working with gay individuals struggling to own their sexual preference is deeply moving. Coming "out of the closet" can leave young gay men disoriented and isolated. Despite some notable progress in acknowledging gay rights, Israeli society—for all sorts of reasons I cannot detail here—still lags behind other Western societies in exercising tolerance for gays. Being both internally disoriented and externally marginalized is, of course, a major precipitant for self-criticism in all young people. Fortunately, the gay community in Israel is well aware of this, actively seeking to reach out to youngsters to provide help and support. Most activities organized by the gay community being run by volunteers, I am tireless in encouraging my gay patients to get involved: "You're needed. You're intelligent and articulate and you've been through the process. Let others lean on you throughout theirs."

When they do, it invariably leads to the expected benefits—one of which is becoming more aware of their compassionate side. This increases the **SK** that accurately pertains to their **A**. In consequence, the self-criticism wedge is diminished. In similar fashion, I encourage adult patients who have lost family members to suicide to volunteer in a nonprofit suicide-survivors organization and those with chronic physical illnesses to volunteer in illness-related support groups. Patients do not need to have a particular "brand of suffering" for me to suggest that they volunteer, however. There is enough suffering in the world to go around for everyone.

Importantly, these encouragements are not meant as "commands." Patients and I always examine whether these suggestions are indeed appropriate under their specific circumstances. Even if they don't get actively involved, however, the very notion of volunteering paves the way for an investigation of how they feel about helping others. This in and of itself is grist for the self-exploration mill.

Routine Analysis

Larry Davidson and I have suggested that daily activities might reflect the struggle with one's authenticity (G. Shahar & Davidson, 2009). Specifically, time being a finite resource, what people do with it is likely to reflect the things they care about the most—that is, their projectuality (G. Shahar, 2011). This speculation is consistent with the idea of "revealed preference" in economics (Samuelson, 1948). This propounds that consumer preference is best identified by purchasing habits. Things are more complicated in psychology, of course. How people spend their time might reveal their authentic self—*or, equally, their attempt to avoid it.*

Let me give an illustration from my own life here. This book is very important to me. Not only is it my first but it also represents the product of two decades of professional self-creation. When I began, I embarked on an enthralling, thrilling writing spree. Then I experienced something new. I had serious writer's block, which lasted for months. I was quite baffled. Writing comes naturally to me. It is a central component of my **A**. When I write, *I feel real*. When I stopped writing, I thus had a hard time realizing that I in fact had writer's block. I misled myself time and again, telling myself, "I don't have time for this. I'm incubating. This is a really tough challenge. I must ponder all the implications of my theory. How can I be expected to write a book when I need to write grants and furnish my lab? How can I be expected to write a book when I am treating suicidal adolescents? I will get back to it just after this task/the holidays/when I have swum a hundred laps."

What enabled me to discover what was going on was conducting my own routine analysis. Specifically, I realized that even though I could schedule specific times for writing, I was unwittingly making sure that these were hijacked by crises: this student's manuscript has to be edited because it will affect his or her career; this grant proposal must be submitted or I won't have research funds for the next 5 years; this is exactly the right time for me to call this patient's psychiatrist and confer. When I looked at my schedule and understood my self-distractions, I began to grasp that the problem was not my inability to fight for—in the words of Virginia Woolf—"a room of my own" but repeated sneaking out of it. I always had a good reason not to write.

The reason was my **SK**. More precisely, it was my SB or SJB—standing for Sidney J. Blatt. Not my late mentor—who had always encouraged me to be independent, even if this meant departing from his teaching ("You may even attack my theory," he once told me, only half joking, knowing full well that there is no world in which this is possible). No, it was the internal Sid Blatt, the one who regarded me dismissively as though to say, "Hey, punk! Who the hell do you think you are, thinking that you can write your own statement about self-criticism?" Or "Oy vay. After all I've done for you, you're going to go against me?" (my friend Carlo Strenger calls this Jewish jiu-jitsu). It was this internal SB, representing my own self-criticism, that had infiltrated my **SK** and hijacked my **A**—the price of which was not writing. It was this internal SB I had to circumvent in order to get back to writing the book. I achieved this primarily by conducting a routine analysis.

Interpersonal Inquiry and the Reframing of Inquisitive Actions

One of the things I like most about the interpersonal psychoanalytic school of thought led by Harry Stack Sullivan, Clara Thompson, Erich Fromm, Frieda Fromm-Reichmann, and others is its adherence to *pragmatism* (G. Shahar, 2011). Consider, for example, Sullivan's dry and witty remark at the close of one of his case descriptions: "You will note that I have not discussed the latent content of the dream; but in psychotherapy, as I've come to consider it, one is occupied chiefly in benefiting the patient" (1953, p. 339).

The interpersonal psychoanalytic school of thought is adequately represented by numerous therapeutic features. One of the most prominent of these is *interpersonal inquiry* (Buechler, 2004; Levenson, 1991). This is guided by the question: "What is the patient trying to do?" According to Sullivan (1924; cited by Blechner, 1999), this query was posed by the legendary psychiatrist William Alanson White, after whom the interpersonal psychoanalytic institute in New York is named. The technique consists of a down-to-earth, collaborative, highly-detailed inquiry of patients' unfolding in-the-world occurrences, focusing primarily on interpersonal exchanges. In order to understand why such inquiry—rather than dreams or free associations—is propounded as constituting the "royal road to the unconscious," we must address Sullivan's notion of the Not Me (Sullivan, 1953).

Sullivan distinguishes between three types of self-representations—the Good Me, the Bad Me, and the Not Me, all of which develop in the context of the parent-child relationship (primarily with the mother). An anxious mother severs the bond with her child and threatens his or her need for satisfaction. The child then experiences her as a Bad Mother. Because representations of mother and self are intertwined, the child develops a corresponding Bad Me representation. When the mother-child relationship is working well, on the other hand, the mother's calmness enables the child to experience her as a Good Mother, the child thus developing a corresponding Good Me representation. The Not Me representation develops when the mother is not just anxious but overwhelmingly so. Such an experience is so threatening that it prompts the child to dissociate a large segment of his or her self-representations. This becomes the Not Me.

According to Sullivan and other interpersonalists, when patients are invited to closely observe their interpersonal conduct in the context of a secure and safe therapeutic environment, they are able to see themselves with people differently from their normal pattern (i.e., from their current **SK**). The unraveling of the Not Me via interpersonal inquiry enables patients to see all sorts of self-aspects—masochistic, aggressive, sadistic, needy, ignorant, prejudiced, and so on (see Mitchell & Black, 1995).

For these reasons—and a myriad of others—I am a big fan of interpersonal inquiry (G. Shahar, 2010). When treating self-criticism, I use it extensively to investigate all sorts of interpersonal occurrences—predominantly quarrels and fights. Most of my patients being adolescents and young adults whose romantic lives are both formative and fluctuating, abundant opportunities for the use of this technique arise. What my patients and I discover—again and again—is that the self-critical voice within them contributes to romantic spats and altercations by evoking criticism from others, more often than not by way of an Inquisitive Action. Propelled by their self-criticism, patients actively contribute to criticism-based quarrels/fights in an awkward attempt to understand who they are. They ask a question—but do so indirectly and critically. They receive the wrong answer—namely, criticism—because they have framed the question ineptly. Feeling unseen or attacked, they ask again, more critically—thereby perpetuating the vicious cycle.

I began this book with an illustration of this process—Rina picking fights with her then-boyfriend immediately after they had professed their love for one another. We only understood the link between the two events when we embarked on a detailed inquiry into the quarrels and their temporal proximity to the moving/mutual profession of love. Recognizing the juxtapositioning enabled us to examine the thematic link, helping us to realize that the real question underlying the fights was: "Can I really be loved?"

Why does Rina doubt that she can be loved? Any reader can come up with the right answer: she's felt unloved her whole life. Her mother—a smart, passionate, but extremely stormy woman—used to verbally abuse Rina. Her father, a shy and timid person, was emotionally absent. Oscillating between being verbally abused and emotionally neglected, how could Rina develop a sense of being lovable? When love was offered to her, it felt bogus and counterfeit. She was determined to get the truth out—ferociously, if need be.

Leonard, a gay patient of mine, is an incredibly psychologically astute young-adult who frequently acts as a lay psychotherapist for his friends—male and female. One of these friends was a young man whom he had dated in the past. Although they split up, they remained friends. About a year and a half ago, this friend of Leonard's lost a close family member. Being the compassionate and sensitive person he is, Leonard supported his friend steadfastly through the extended mourning period. This inevitably bringing the two closer, it resuscitated Leonard's romantic feelings toward his ex-lover-turned-friend.

A fragile situation indeed! Leonard addressed it by turning laconic and ignoring his friend's frequent text messages. This, in turn, evoked the friend's irritation and frustration, leading to increasing relational tension. Leonard was inadvertently trying to down-regulate the level of intimacy in the relationship. Although he didn't want to terminate it, he was apprehensive about making a romantic move lest he be rejected. Instead, he tested his ex-lover, taking a step backward to see whether he would come closer—"to haunt me," Leonard said to me self-mockingly.

This only confused matters more. Now relying on Leonard's emotional support, the friend actually *did* haunt him, prompting both hope and dread in Leonard (Mitchell, 1990). This, too, we understood in treatment via careful interpersonal inquiry. Leonard then made the brave move of acknowledging his romantic feelings. The friend immediately responded that he did not feel the same way. The two thus decided to keep a distance for a while. Leonard kept me posted by a text message, which ended with the words "I am sad." In our last session, however, he noted that his sadness was rapidly diminishing, being replaced by an emerging relief.

As we continued to ponder these events, I realized that as well as relief Leonard was suddenly re-experiencing a sense of self-respect. I communicated this to him, and he agreed with me. I said to myself—as I am now saying to Leonard—that by openly sharing his romantic feelings with his ex-lover he was asking two questions. The first—to his friend—was "Do you love me?" The reply was negative. The second—to himself—was "Am I worthy of love?" The reply to this question was (cautiously) positive—hence the self-respect.

Trial-Based Cognitive Restructuring

For years, I have been reluctant to utilize cognitive restructuring in my clinical practice, for reasons as numerous as they are complex. Quite candidly, it took me a long time to overcome my original psychoanalytic indoctrination and consider the possibility that CBT might work. Cognitive restructuring epitomizes the prescriptive and directive nature of CBT. I thus "picked on" this technique, refusing to even contemplate using it. When I had finally served my "indoctrination period," I adopted a model of psychotherapy integration—Wachtel's cyclical psychodynamics—that was primarily psychodynamic-behavioral in nature. Wachtel originally being suspicious of cognitive interventions, I followed suit.

Another reason for my reluctance to employ cognitive restructuring relates to my early adherence to developmental-interpersonal theories that emphasize active person-context transactions—epitomized in Bandura's reciprocal-determinism principle. A central philosophical pillar of the current model (G. Shahar, 2006a) is that many people—albeit inadvertently—bring their suffering upon themselves. This means, however, that whatever causes the pain *actually exists*. For instance, people may become depressed due to interpersonal ruptures to which they themselves contributed and perceive correctly (Hammen, 1991; Joiner, 1994; G. Shahar, Cross, & Henrich, 2004). I have consequently always feared that impressing upon patients the need to correct their inaccurate/irrational perceptions might gravely miss the mark. Therapists' insistence that their patients have incorrectly perceived reality—with its implication that they, the therapists, are the only ones capable of correct perception—is likely to be taken as offensive. Finally, I used to assure myself that there is no point in using cognitive restructuring because its efficacy is not really supported by empirical research (e.g., Longmore & Worrell, 2007).

Accumulated clinical experience has led me to change my position. I now deem cognitive restructuring as a potentially useful technique, provided that it (1) seeks to demarcate and delimit negative cognitions rather than utterly refute them and (2) is introduced later in the treatment process. Consistent with third-wave CBT approaches (e.g., ACT and DBT), I am convinced that the principal aim of treatment is to help patients gain cognitive flexibility—for instance, by increasing attention control—rather than to perceive reality more accurately or think more positively. I have already opined about the futility of trying to help individuals correctly grasp the reality they themselves have created. Research also suggests that to the extent that negative cognitions are avoidable—a dubious assumption at best—these cognitions are not necessarily or invariably bad (Andrews & Thomson, 2009). The damage negative cognitions inflict stems primarily from their persistence and rigidity. Once cognitive flexibility is introduced, the power of negative cognitions—and thereby their adverse effect—is considerably diminished.

I thus regard the primary aim of cognitive restructuring as training patients to create an inner dialogue that runs counter to their self-critical voice. Rather than attempting to defeat it, they should devote their efforts toward signaling to the entire mental system that more than one voice is present. In line with the political metaphor adduced earlier, I seek to train patients to drag other voices into an internal "town hall" to prevent the bully from hogging the platform. The best way I know to do this is the Trial-Based Cognitive Restructuring developed by de Oliveira et al. (2012), which has shown itself useful in reducing self-criticism.

Following de Oliveira et al. (2012), I ask patients to conduct a mini-trial. The self-critical voice is the "prosecutor," another voice inside them serving as the "defense attorney." I ask them first to voice the plaintiff's claims by *aggravating* self-derogation. After a sufficient amount of self-bashing, I then ask them to summon the defense attorney to counter the prosecutor's arguments. If they object that the prosecutor is correct and nothing else can be said, I ask them to try anyway. What begins as a hesitant and bewildered attempt at verbal self-defense quite often turns into a playfully enthusiastic manifestation of the patient's debating skills. The point is not to talk the prosecutor into submission, but simply to make patients aware that they can have their day in court while the jury is (constantly) out.

This particular use of cognitive restructuring is highly consistent with recent developments in cognitive psychotherapy that encourage the introduction of metaphor, imagination, and dramatization alongside standard cognitive therapeutic work (e.g., Kellogg, 2004; Riskind, Rector, & Taylor, 2012). It also closely corresponds to Winnicott's notion of play as inherently healthy, as well as to some forms of paradoxical interventions in which heightening the symptom (self-derogation) increases the patient's sense of control, thereby leading to symptom reduction.

I never introduce the intervention early in the treatment process, however, because I first want patients to (1) get a sense that the therapist is fundamentally supportive—even if they initially cannot acknowledge this possibility; (2) realize that their inner dialogues are a manifestation of their self-concept multiplicity; (3) be exposed to the idea of attention control (mindfulness, recentering) and receive training in its use; and (4) learn that their actual behavior might lead to positive mood changes (via behavioral activation). Once these accomplishments have been achieved and consolidated, patients can be introduced to TBCR as a natural continuation of the previous stages.

In illustration of this process, take Michael, a 26-year-old undergraduate who has been working with me for about 8 months. Having sought treatment for a mixture of mood and anxiety disorder features, he has made substantial progress over the course of our relatively brief work together. During the past couple of months, however, he has experienced a string of stressful events—a romantic breakup, the death of a close friend's father from cancer, a severe and refractory ear infection—that have thrown him back symptomatically and morale-wise. The following is a verbatim account of a session in which we employed cognitive restructuring:

Prosecutor: I'm worried about not completing my degree, about not being able to acquire the skills grownups must acquire in order to get along in the world. I'm just waiting for the day that it will catch up with me. I won't be able to manage the academic bureaucracy so as to complete my degree. City taxes, water and electricity bills, everything will be disconnected. I won't be able to manage financially or handle upcoming troubles.

Defense attorney: I've been in treatment for 8 months and I've made considerable progress in such a short time. Given that I've been facing considerable stress recently, this is excellent progress. Someone looks after me. I will get through each day at a time armed with the understanding that I have a safety network. This will give me strength to cope.

Prosecutor: The psychologist cannot solve all my problems or do things instead of me. Practically, it's difficult to rely on another person at all times at the age of 26.

Defense attorney: Thus far, I've tackled each challenge independently, so there's no reason to think I won't manage this one as well. I only want to get to the end of the race and I have to accept the fact that there are things that take time.

Prosecutor: This crisis caused me significant damage, taking away all my powers of functioning. It feels impossible.

Defense attorney: Lots of things felt impossible before you began treatment and were eventually overcome. I can't determine in advance the timeframe needed for getting out of this crisis. This depression is irrational. It's my childhood speaking. One shouldn't listen to an irrational voice.

Prosecutor: These responses are somewhat comforting, but they don't alleviate the fear. It's hard to see the light when you are surrounded with fears that play in your head like a broken record. It's difficult to argue against past failures.

Defense attorney: It's irrational, no matter how frightening this is, and supposedly relies on past instances. One must not listen to a voice devoid of genuine logic. This only harms me. It derails my goals.

I pointed out to Michael two noteworthy features of this exchange. First, rather than becoming completely convinced, the prosecutor becomes bewildered and curious ("These responses are somewhat comforting"). This is crucially important, because the goal is not to persuade the patient that the prosecutor's point of view is utterly wrong—bad things might indeed happen—but to make the prosecutor aware that they do not *have* to happen (i.e., convince him or her of the existence of "reasonable doubt"). Second, TBCR gravitated spontaneously into the future, centering on life goals. This, too, is supremely important, the objective being to get the patient to evaluate the "efficacy"— rather than the factual accuracy—of the prosecutor's and defense attorney's statements. Do they help the patient toward his or her goals or distract him or her from achieving them?

Transference, Countertransference, and Therapeutic Ruptures

Relational psychoanalysis emerged onto the psychotherapy scene in the late 1980s, receiving immediate attention and a standing ovation (e.g., Aron, 1996; Ghent, 1989; Mitchell, 1988, 1990). The laudation continues. Paul Wachtel, for instance, believes that these psychoanalytic strands should serve as the basis for integrative psychotherapy (P. L. Wachtel, 1997). Although I do not regard myself as a relational-psychoanalytic psychotherapist (I am a truly integrative dog), I do embrace the approach's "two-person psychology" credo (Ghent, 1989) and its explanation of the construction of transference (the impact of a patient's past relationships on how he or she experiences the therapist) and countertransference (the same thing but from the therapist's perspective). Specifically, the relational-psychoanalytic school departs from the classical view of transference as a projected manifestation of early interpersonal relations. Influenced by the pioneering writings of Morton Gill (e.g., 1979), relationalists construe it as an expression of both early relations *and* actual aspects of the patient-therapist exchange. Similarly, therapist countertransference is no longer seen as a less-than-professional impediment to the treatment process to be "analyzed away" in the therapist's own treatment but rather the inevitable expression of the therapist's subjectivity and something to be used as an important source of information relating to the patient's and therapist's own inner worlds (cf. Aron, 1996; Ghent, 1989; I. Hirsch, 1994; Mitchell, 1988).

In the context of the present focus, I would expect the very same criticism-based vicious cycles characterizing patients in their ongoing interpersonal relationships to be *transferred* onto/into the therapeutic relationship.[7] This is likely to occur not only because of patient self-criticism but also arguably because therapists are also likely to be self-critical. Both parties will thus jointly introduce the theme of criticism into the therapeutic session.

Previously, I described a clinical case I oversaw while interning in Israel many years ago (G. Shahar, 2004). Mrs. J. was a highly-self-critical middle-aged woman who had just recovered from a serious depressive episode that led to inpatient treatment. I treated her with an evidence-based time-limited form of psychodynamic psychotherapy (Mann, 1973; Shefler, 2001). After an expected "honeymoon" phase of five sessions, a major rupture erupted. This is how I described it over a decade ago:

> Much less exhilarating was the next session. Despite the fact that I had been aware of Mann's prediction that patients express ambivalence toward treatment during the second part of time-limited psychotherapy, I was still unprepared for Mrs. J.'s stern demeanor. She demanded a major shift in the treatment's style and focus. She sought my advice for what I vaguely recall as a marital dilemma and was outraged when I did not offer such advice. Instead, I insisted that we explore her need for such advice in the context of the central psychodynamic issue. This made her even more furious. As the session progressed, Mrs. J. and I succumbed to silence. About 30 min. later, she abruptly left the room. I was devastated. "So much for your becoming a practitioner-researcher," I belittled myself. "Clearly, you are not in the right profession." (G. Shahar, 2004, p. 374)

It was only my supervisor's sensitive and wise intervention and encouragement that I cajole the patient back into therapy that saved the treatment process, ultimately leading to a planned and successful termination. Here is how I conceptualized the rupture in the 2004 article:

> A relational-psychoanalytic perspective illuminates the interpersonal patterns involving Mrs. J. and myself. These patterns consisted of a meeting between two self-doubting and self-critical individuals. Mrs. J., the woman who vowed to exercise total control over her life but doubted her ability to do so, sought help from me, an ambitious, control-oriented, albeit highly-inexperienced intern who was looking at this therapeutic encounter as an opportunity to build my relatively fragile (professional) identity. Coming from very different demographic and psychological backgrounds, Mrs. J. and I shared the quest of shaping our own self-image. Mrs. J.'s self-image, threatened by her marital difficulties, was further put at risk when she confronted my refusal, or rather my inability, to advise her in this setback. My inability to advise her further jeopardized my own self-image, already on shaky grounds given the dearth of my psychotherapeutic experience. To protect her self-image, Mrs. J. pressured me to provide her with advice. To protect mine, I pressured her back into "psychodynamic work." Ironically

(Wachtel, 1977), the very similarity of our quests led to their mutual frustration. (G. Shahar, 2004, p. 382)

Overall, this case description and related conceptualization (G. Shahar, 2004) strongly adheres to relational psychoanalysis's two-person psychology credo. I now realize, however, that I introduced two—relatively minor—modifications to the relational approach that were precursors of the present **ASK/ACRIM** (Axis of Criticism) theory. First, I emphasized the role of goal-directed action and future-oriented thinking in patient-therapist co-creation of transference/countertransference exchanges. Drawing on the voluminous empirical research on goal concepts in (neuro)psychology, this ultimately led to my notion of projectuality (G. Shahar, 2011). Specifically, I argue(d) that, in the context of the therapeutic relationship, the patient and therapist are likely to inadvertently experience one another as both vehicles for and obstacles to projectuality, using one another—in the Winnicottian sense—for the purpose of "becoming what they might." Mrs. J. (thought) she needed my advice so that she could improve her relationship with her husband and move away from marginalization (see the article) toward personal control. I, on the other hand, (thought I) needed Mrs. J. in order to become the therapist I wanted to become (and avoid becoming the one I feared I might become). Both of us exerting pressure on the other to reach our independent destinations, a nasty rupture erupted.

Generally speaking, when self-criticism is involved, patients and therapists are likely to use one another for the purpose of exoneration. In other words, they make attempts to extract signs of approval from one another in order to stop feeling deficient. Because these efforts are invariably mediated via self-critical voices on both sides, they are bound to be inept, leading to the inverse response (P. L. Wachtel, 1977, 1997). The ensuing rupture is likely to be of a tacit "blame game" sort, both parties exerting pressure on the other to identify with the wrong-doing/deficient side in order to exonerate themselves. I call this "two-person politics" (G. Shahar, 2004).[8]

Politics being inherently adversarial, they are a potentially nasty business. Politics are also where things get done, however. In line with a long line of clinical thinkers, I believe that ruptures constitute a powerful opportunity for self-exploration (Atwood, Stolorow, & Trop, 1989; Mitchell, 1988, 1995). The one proviso I demand is that therapists use them to resurrect the question Mitchell (1995) insisted we ask our patients: "How do we end up doing this over and over again?"

In the context of treating self-critical patients, I propose what I call "turning ruptures into questions" (TRIQ). This consists of asking the following question: "What does this rupture tell us about our presumed deficiency?" This should lead to another question: "What are we asking about ourselves when we presume this deficiency?" To go back to G. Shahar (2004), TRIQ enabled Mrs. J. and me to become aware of our presumed deficiencies—Mrs. J.'s that she couldn't get along with her husband "like normal people," mine that I can't keep patients in treatment like a competent therapist. We could then recognize our authentic projectualities—Mrs. J.'s to be included rather than marginalized, mine to be professionally competent and capable of combining research and clinical voices (a proxy for a general struggle for self-cohesion).

Obviously, this is easier said than done—which leads to the second modification. With many highly self-critical patients—Mrs. J. being a case in point—the level of emotional pain brought up by criticism-based therapeutic ruptures is so great that it is very difficult to contain, modulate, and regulate on one's own. There is always a serious risk of therapists acting out their hurt and projecting their perceived deficiency onto their patients. This will often happen covertly and unconsciously, most therapists being responsible and conscientious and committed to not hurting their patients. Here, too, however, I subscribe to Mitchell's dictum that "hate and aggression often tend to become deeply embedded in character . . . and play a central role in intimate relations" (1990, p. 529; see also Muller, 1999). The therapeutic relationship is—inherently and invariably—an intimate relationship, perhaps doubly so when the sword of suicidal depression and other forms of severe psychopathology hang over the therapeutic dyad.

In the case of Mrs. J., my supervisor was the one protecting her against her therapist's unconscious self-critical "acting out" by *seeing through* my anxiety, *naming* my sense of deficiency, *validating* the painful reaction it aroused, *linking* it to my authentic struggle, and then *instructing* me to do the same for Mrs. J. Hereby, my supervisor essentially diminished the self-critical wedge between my *A* and *SK*, making me both more authentic and self-aware. Immensely grateful, I then assumed—more accurately, hoped—that a day would come when I would no longer need supervised help. Years later, when I published this clinical case (G. Shahar, 2004), I already subscribed to a different—and perhaps surprising—perspective. I have come to the realization that one never gets over the need for supervision—certainly not when working with self-critical, severely-symptomatic patients.

I say "surprising" because this is the feedback I get from students, interns, and psychotherapy supervisees when I voice it. Now a senior practitioner known to be working with difficult cases, junior clinicians look up to me—not expecting to learn that, like them, I also need "holding and containing" when I practice. It shatters not only their projected view of me as a master therapist but also the very notion of master therapists. I believe that it is very important to burst this bubble. *There are no master therapists.* Yes, there is quite a lot to be learned in our creed, particularly if you—like me—adhere to the scientist-practitioner model of practicing. Because it is so powerful, however, the clinical encounter is invariably baffling, puzzling, and at times stifling. Although virtuosity is not impossible—we do sometimes manage to perform outstandingly creative and moving therapeutic feats—the only way we manage to do so is through our authenticity.

So yes, supervision is necessary at all times, for all therapists—junior and senior—engaged in treating the symptomatic and, a fortiori, the self-critical. Whether conducted with a more experienced practitioner or a wise and committed peer, it must be employed. I also recommend personal therapy—preferably a prolonged and ongoing one. Psychotherapy is a profession—a calling, really—to which many of us are drawn in order to feel real. When we practice it, we practice our *A*. As I wrote a decade ago (G. Shahar, 2004), it takes a village to cultivate an authentic therapist.

Em-Presentation: The Intentional Introduction of Therapist Subjectivity

In the previous chapter, I suggested that patients' measured access to therapists' subjectivity may be therapeutically beneficial in general and highly beneficial with self-critical patients in particular. Here, I will describe some of the ways in which therapists might intentionally present their subjectivity to their self-critical patients.

Taking a Stand

"So give me back my razor," he said mischievously.

I looked at Yoni sternly. "Forget about it," I said. "The razor stays here."

"But I told you," Yoni protested, "I'm out of the woods. I'm not going to cut again!"

"I believe you," I said, trying to hide my tension. "But in case you change your mind, or be pulled into acting differently, you will have to get another razor, because this one stays here."

"But you know, it *is* my razor."

"It is certainly your razor. But it stays here."

"Till when?"

"Till forever. It is yours forever, but it also stays here forever."

I didn't really know why I insisted upon keeping Yoni's razor in my office drawer. He was indeed in good shape. Two years after we had started working together in therapy, he was very far from the extremely-depressed, self-hate-ridden 16-year-old he had been when we first met. Herculean efforts to put a halt to his repeated self-mutilation had borne fruit. His family—previously highly tumultuous—had calmed down. Yoni was about to be conscripted into a prestigious combat unit in the army. He and I were very proud. It felt safe to give him back the razor he had used to cut himself with. Besides, razors are easy to obtain (and broken glasses are easy to come by), so keeping Yoni's at my office wouldn't have prevented him from cutting. And yet, the razor stayed with me.

In retrospect, I realize that what I did by insisting on keeping the razor was *symbolically take a stand*. I made it clear to Yoni that, when he left my office, the part of him that cut stayed there. I insisted on being a *container* (Bion, 1963) of that part of him that self-mutilates, enabling him to move on.[9]

Reminiscing about Yoni's treatment takes me to a formative experience I had while interning at Yale. One of my psychotherapy supervisors—a very astute clinical psychologist—told me about one of her treatments with a self-mutilating young-adult. Her female patient, who was drawn to abusive and sadomasochistic sexual relationships, stood up during the session, took off her shirt, and showed her the whiplash marks from her previous night's sexual encounter. "What happened," my supervisor went on, "was that I was so horrified that I immediately burst into tears. To my amazement, the patient was profoundly moved by this 'spontaneous gesture.'[10] It made her open up to depths she had never ventured into before. We were able to understand the humiliation that these sadomasochistic sexual relations cause her and how they serve her self-hate."

I recall being profoundly impressed by this story. This wasn't a therapist who easily cried in front of patients, and it was clear to me that her response was driven by a profound internal logic informing this particular therapeutic exchange. But what? I now believe that she was reacting to her patient's need for a caring adult to take a stand against the enormity of her suffering and show her that she was there—deeply involved, ready to fight on her behalf.

Taking a stand is tricky. Patients generally come to therapy to shape their own identities and form their own views about life. By design, therapists hold tremendous power in their hands, the overwhelming consensus being that this should not be used for purposes of indoctrination. Therapists who repeatedly and routinely take a stand about issues in a patient's life—or other worldly issues—run the risk of pressuring their patients into submission and assuming the therapist's views rather than developing their own.

What I have just described is a different form of taking a stand. First, it is—or should be—only undertaken in extreme situations. Second, it addresses more than the destructiveness of the patient's act. It targets the patient's humanity, his or her right to be cared for and protected. It says to the patient: "I am a human being who has emotions and I am using these to let you know that I am here for you and that you are not alone."[11]

Stepping Out

Another way to em-present is to step out of the therapy office and work therapeutically on behalf of patients in-the-world. Advocating for patients constitutes a powerful example of stepping out. Earlier, I described how I worked with school personnel to deal with the violence exhibited by my 12-year-old patient. With Yoni, I routinely met with the staff at his boarding school. With patients with a chronic physical illness, I make a point of maintaining close contact with their treating physicians, frequently meeting them face to face at specialty clinics or in general hospitals. With young-adult women suffering from chronic, restrictive anorexia nervosa, I do house calls during periods when the patient—captivated by her zeal to lose weight—refuses to come to my office (see Strober, 2004, for a sobering discussion of the treatment of patients with chronic, treatment-resistant anorexia).

Central to my "stepping out" of the clinic is the issue of agency. By stepping out, I manifest to my patients my determination to work on their behalf. This determination reflects my agency, which in turn summons theirs. The message they thus receive is that now that they are not alone and can take charge of their own lives.

This is, of course, a theoretically integrative message. The focus lies on humanistic-existential agency (see Shumaker, 2012). The expectation that patients will follow suit, exhibiting their own agency, emanates directly from Bandura's social-cognitive notions of vicarious learning and modeling. This process is tacitly informed by psychodynamic object relations theory—according to which changes in representations of other people (in this case, a benevolent caretaker) invariably lead to changes in self-representations (the patient's). Finally, my involvement in patients' homes/schools/medical care reflects an appreciation of a family-systems approach to psychopathology.

Stepping out of the office is also tantamount to "witnessing," another empowering therapeutic stance (e.g., Ullman, 2006). Witnessing strengthens the therapeutic alliance by convincing the patient that (now that I have stepped out of my office and gone to where he or she lives) I am taking pains to understand where the patient is (literally) and what he or she is going through. This, in turn, helps the patient to embrace self-sympathy rather than self-criticism.

Increasing the Frequency of the Therapeutic Encounter

There are no big mysteries here. If one wants to introduce his or her subjectivity into patients' lives, one should increase the frequency of the therapeutic encounters. A weekly multisession is no longer unique to psychoanalysis or psychoanalytic psychotherapy, being practiced by various forms of CBT and DBT. The more symptomatic the patient—and the more dangerous his or her symptoms (e.g., suicidality, self-mutilation, restrictive anorexia nervosa)—the greater the need for increased frequency. For most of my patients, twice-weekly sessions are important.

The DBT protocol even allows for brief and focused out-of-session telephone conversations between patients and their therapists on an ongoing basis (as opposed to limited to crises). I embrace this in my work. The advent of new technology now allows for easy, rapid, and therapeutically quite effective ways of communication (e.g., texting, WhatsApp, etc.). I use these extensively. They are effective because many self-critical patients are reluctant to "bother me" with a phone call when they are in crisis but will text me because it feels less intrusive.

Therapist Disclosure: Spontaneous and/or Self-Initiated

Self-disclosure—therapists' revealing of information about themselves to patients—has been the focus of much therapeutic scholarship over the past three decades (for an extensive review, see Ziv-Beiman, 2013). Although self-disclosure has been most copiously discussed within relational psychoanalysis (e.g., Aron, 1996), its potential benefit is now acknowledged across numerous schools of thought—including the humanistic-existential (Geller, 2003; M. H. Williams, 1997) and cognitive-behavioral (Freeman, Pretzer, Fleming, & Simon, 1990; Goldfried, Burckell, & Eubanks-Carter, 2003).

I admit to being somewhat ambivalent about self-initiated therapeutic disclosure. Some of this ambivalence stems from strong needs for privacy (which, some would say, rivals some of the exhibitionistic features in my character. The latter allegation is surely farfetched!). Observing and reading about profoundly self-serving instances of self-disclosure on the part of the therapist that are devoid of any real therapeutic benefit has done nothing to make me feel better about the practice. Over time, however, I have come to recognize that therapeutic disclosure is simply inevitable and can—at certain times—be tremendously beneficial.

Therapeutic disclosure is inevitable because we currently live online (Strenger, 2011). A lot of what we have done or are currently doing is documented on the internet and is therefore easily accessible via search engines. This is probably even truer in Israel—a small country with a highly informal social structure in which individual paths frequently cross (e.g., a patient's relative might serve with me on reserve duty in the army). Practicing in a small university town, many of my patients are students. I am thus quite likely to know someone sitting in one of my undergraduate or graduate classes. "Gathering intelligence" is virtually (pun intended) trivial.

Adam, the patient I described in CHAPTER 2, was struggling with dysthymia and a chronic experience of being stuck. About a year ago, I published a volume of poetry "treating" such psychological issues as self-development, depression, and the state of psychoanalysis. Some of the material is emotionally and biographically revealing. Adam incidentally stumbled upon the book (which was far from being a bestseller). Having kept this information from me for many weeks, he then referred to in a session in which we were speaking about guilt: "Yes, ashmavet"—a neologism I coined from the Hebrew words for "guilt" (ashma) and "death" (mavet).

Confessing that he had read the book, Adam asked what I meant by the term. I explained that it was an attempt to convey how painful guilt is, especially when one is feeling guilty about not meeting standards that one strongly values. I then volunteered that I feel like that as a parent—frequently having the sense that I am falling short of being a "good enough" parent. This self-disclosure enabled Adam to more fully explore his own guilt about not actualizing his intellectual potential and investigate with me the developmental and familial factors that derailed his self-actualization.

With respect to self-initiated disclosure, two frameworks in particular appear to be potentially beneficial—especially with self-critical patients—in my opinion. If I have worked with a patient for years and the occasion arises for queries regarding my physical and mental health, I will share with patients that I have experienced bouts of depressive distress. I find that this is most helpful for patients who also hope to become therapists or physicians and are ashamed of their own vulnerability.

With young suicidal patients, I might also disclose my experience of the devastating consequences of parental suicide. For instance, I routinely administer Linehan's Reason for Living Scale—which assesses a host of reasons for not committing suicide in patients who are not yet parents (Linehan, Goodstein, Nielsen, & Chiles, 1983). Some patients report that the prospect of having children might act as a restraint against them harming themselves. I then note that—based on my own personal experience—the impact of parental suicide on children is catastrophic. Although the initial reaction is usually one of great surprise, the disclosure quickly enhances the therapeutic alliance. It also increases patients' awareness of the suffering they might inflict upon their loved ones if they kill themselves, as well as impressing upon them the hazards of succumbing to the inner critic who drives their suicidal wishes.

Chapter Summary

This chapter introduced specific guidelines and interventions used in the treatment of self-critical patients. In my opinion, the multiplicity and complexity of the antecedents and consequences of self-critical vulnerability require a multitude of interventions at different therapeutic stages. The need to bring other key members into the patient's social environment is another basic component in the treatment of adolescents and young adults with high levels of self-criticism.

Faithful to my integrative psychotherapeutic proclivities, I have drawn on various schools of thoughts in utilizing the previously described interventions. The overarching "music" of my therapeutic approach is conversational and open ended, following numerous humanistic-psychodynamic perspectives. It also strikes prescriptive chords, however, drawing primarily from cognitive-behavioral and interpersonal therapies, with a strong family-systems appreciation.

In therapy, the patient learns to personify distinct self-aspects and acknowledge the multifaceted structure of the self-concept. By identifying positive and negative components of the self, combined with mindfulness and acceptance strategies, the patient also learns to achieve self-regulation and shift between self-aspects. The therapist must assist the patient in identifying authentic life projects and prioritize the order in which the symptoms that prevent him or her from achieving these goals are treated. Emphasis should also be placed on the patient's interpersonal patterns and the way in which they manifest in treatment, highly self-critical individuals frequently exhibiting maladaptive interpersonal patterns.

Final Thoughts and Future Directions

Character is destiny.
(attributed to Heraclitus)

The purpose of this postscript is to anchor this treatise in several concluding reflections and point to future directions for self-criticism scholarship (theory and research) and practice.

Concluding Reflections

I opened this book by describing my passion for bridging science and practice ("projectuality"). I believe that self-criticism scholarship attests to the viability of this passion. Specifically, thinkers from various schools of thought have shown that robust, empirical research of a single dimension of vulnerability might (1) ensue from profound theories, (2) inform these theories, and (3) lead to innovative clinical assessment and intervention.

Although it took me two decades of self-creation to get to the point of being able to combine science and practice, this does not have to be the case. My own journey—so I hope—might inspire eager young minds and hearts in the mental health field to make their own contribution to the conjoining of research and practice. When I look at my Stress, Self, and Health Research Lab (STREALTH) students, I realize they will find that route much more easily and expeditiously than I did. I know that such is also the case in other labs across the world. In the mental health field, the best is yet to come.

The second important lesson to be learned from self-criticism scholarship pertains, in my opinion, to the superiority of systems approaches—from the mathematical and biological to the psychological and political (Flood & Carson, 1993; Thelen & Smith, 2006). Systems approaches regard the systems in which organisms are embedded as vital components in their functioning. They also postulate that organisms—both human and nonhuman—actively cope with the changing environment by controlling and altering their perceptions and behaviors (Bronfenbrenner, 1979).

Self-criticism scholarship illustrates the importance of acknowledging these bidirectional interactions between the systems in which the individual is nested (see CHAPTER 5). These social-environmental systems—from the ones that constitute the child's and adult's immediate social environment to the wider cultural systems within which they operate—augment one another to create criticism-based vicious cycles. These vicious cycles spill over from one system to the other, widening the wedge between A(uthenticity) and S(elf-) K(nowledge), thereby contributing to the individual's heightened self-criticism. Considering these complex interactions within a social environment promotes a holistic rather than reductionist perspective on self-criticism.

Intimately linked to the importance of systems approaches is the centrality of life-span and human development. In fact, when it comes to understanding a particular human experience, development might be said to be the "prime mover"—dictating what systems will confront individuals (e.g., kindergartens, schools, workplaces, cultural/political systems, etc.), which cultural gatekeepers are going to orchestrate this confrontation, and to what extent the person-context exchange will be coordinated with an individual's biological maturation and innate proclivities.

Development plays a key role in a systems-based perspective on self-criticism. In addition to determining which systems will be encountered in every developmental stage, the changes and transformations experienced by individuals over the life-span themselves constitute a "chronosystem" (Bronfenbrenner, 1977, 1979, 1994) that affects—and is affected by—individuals' self-criticism. Specifically, adjustment to newly-encountered systems during the life-span depends on the cognitive-affective representations of self and others and the interactions individuals have developed in earlier developmental stages (see CHAPTER 3) Criticism-based schemas govern self-critical individuals' interactions with the environments they encounter later on. Through interaction with these systems, self-criticism is likely to remain a stable and destructive force in their lives, tending to cause further developmental difficulties. In particular, self-criticism obstructs the two cornerstones of healthy self-development—action in the world and sufficient knowledge about the authentic self (see CHAPTER 4).

Another key lesson to be learned relates to personality psychology. I admit that I am chronically perturbed by the *zeitgeist* of the personality field, represented primarily by atheoretical trait approaches. Within normal personality research, this zeitgeist is brought to bear via the dominance of the Five Factor/Big Five model of personality traits. In psychopathology, personality is most strongly represented by similar atheoretical approaches—such as the *Diagnostic and Statistical*

Manual of Mental Disorders' personality-disorder clusters. That a small group of—mostly distinguished—investigators critical of this zeitgeist (e.g., Luyten & Blatt, 2011) exists is far from sufficient.

Proponents of trait approaches respond to this criticism by invoking the issue of criterion validity. "It might be true that we have no theory," they say, "but our models *work*." By this, they mean that trait measures predict important clinical and health outcomes. While I acknowledge this truth, I also note that self-criticism does as well—if not better—my concern is that other personality traits in the criterion validity arena. Self-criticism, however, is easily linked to a *personality structure*, anchoring it within an overarching theory of the psyche. The theories reviewed—and the novel one presented—are but specific examples. Others are possible. Further self-related dimensions should thus be of interest—e.g., self-efficacy, self-concept clarity.

Building on theory, my final reflection pertains to the crucial role of integration in science and practice. Take, for example, the **ASK/ACRIM** theory proposed herein. Assuming that it is of some use, it clearly derives from diverse sources of theoretical influence, spanning social-cognitive, humanistic-existential, family-systems, biological-psychology approaches, and social interaction sociological theory. If such a wide range of theories are needed to account for the origins and operation of a single self-related dimension, an attempt to account for the entirety of the human psyche is even more suggestive of the need for integration.

Future Directions

Assuming that **ASK/ACRIM** does in fact possess some merit, the theory must become both broader and more accurate. Links between *ASK* and other key personality constructs and processes (e.g., defensive processes, affect regulation, and coping strategies) must be theorized and put to empirical test. Much more thinking about the evolutionary basis of *ASK* must be engaged upon—a factor barely touched upon here. For instance, from an evolutionary-psychology point of view, without strong benefits self-criticism would not survive. No research thus far has shown that elevated levels of self-criticism—measured using the instruments described here—predict adaptive outcomes. I think that such effect exists and that we simply have not looked sufficiently hard to date.

Vulnerability-resilience research implies that many of the psychosocial factors that are classified into clear-cut vulnerability versus resilience categories actually embed elements of both. This complex vulnerability-resilience dynamic is well exemplified in a number of psychosocial dimensions—dependency, self-concept, social support, positive life-events, and passive coping strategies, for example (for a review, see G. Shahar, Elad-Strenger, & Henrich, 2012). It has also been demonstrated in regard to ideology-related variables, such as religiosity (e.g., Maltby & Day, 2000), ideological commitment, and national attachment (Elad-Strenger, Fireman, Schiller, Besser, & G. Shahar, 2013). Self-criticism also embeds elements of both risk and resilience. While setting high self-standards increases vulnerability to depressive symptomatology and decreases functioning due to high self-punitiveness, it may also promote high achievements and entail social rewards such as recognition and appreciation—at least in the short run—as a result of intense dedication.

ACRIM—a subset of the theory developed here—awaits empirical validation. For example, the hypothesized links between individual self-criticism and critical expressed emotion in families and other systems must be empirically and critically examined—preferably by as many labs as possible (see Auerbach, Ho, & Kim, 2014). STREALTH is currently empirically testing it in two realms—chronic illness and adolescent risky behavior. We are only beginning, however. The road to a clear pattern of findings stretches toward the horizon.

ACRIM's sphere of influence also needs to be expanded. Most self-criticism research has focused on psychopathology, initially with unipolar depression and then expanding to other disorders. Recently, Avi Besser, Patrick Luyten, and I—all Sid Blatt's "sons"—have independently built on our mentor's attempt to link self-criticism with health psychology and behavioral medicine (Blatt, Cornell, & Eshkol, 1993). Publications reflecting this attempt focus primarily on obstetrics and gynecology, chronic fatigue syndrome, chronic pain and other functionally somatic diseases. Much more needs to be done in this area.

Other fascinating fields in behavioral science await the benefits of self-criticism research. These include forensic psychology and political science. As a risk factor for depression, self-criticism may specifically shed light on various depression-related behaviors associated with outward aggression—such as adolescent delinquency (e.g., Leadbeater, Kuperminc, Blatt, & Herzog, 1999). Introducing the concept of self-criticism into the field of political science may also help us gain insight into various political phenomena—from out-group hostility and prejudice to violent activism and terrorism. A wide range of political stressors have been identified as strong predictors of political violence and intergroup hostility—including exposure to political conflict (Canetti, Rapaport, Wayne, Hall, & Hobfoll, 2012; Echebarria-Echabe & Fernandez-Guede, 2006; Gordon & Arian, 2001; Skitka, Bauman, Aramovich, & Scott Morgan, 2006), collective trauma (e.g., Carmil & Breznitz, 1991), and symbolic worldview threats (e.g., Elad-Strenger & G. Shahar, under review; McGregor et al., 1998). In many cases, these relationships are mediated by psychological distress—particularly depression and posttraumatic stress (e.g., Canetti-Nisim, Halperin, Sharvit, & Hobfoll, 2009; Hobfoll, Canetti-Nisim, & Johnson, 2006). Because self-critics tend to generate high levels of life-stress (e.g., Zuroff, 1992), self-criticism may play an important role in predicting perceived threat and distress following stressful events. It may thus shed light on radical political attitudes and behaviors. Research examining the role of self-criticism in predicting perceived political threat is now under way.

The biological basis of self-criticism must also be explored in future research. As noted in CHAPTER 4, Longe et al. (2010) have reported an association between self-criticism and activation in specific brain areas involved in conflict-processing and inhibition. These findings are limited, however, because they overlook the connectivity patterns involved in the reported cortical regions *and* limbic structures—such as the amygdala. Such connectivity plays a crucial role in regulating emotional behavior in affective disorders, particularly through its involvement in facial-expression processing (Hariri et al., 2005). In our future studies, we thus hope to employ functional magnetic resonance imaging (fMRI) paradigms and other advanced neuroanalytic techniques to examine functional and anatomical connectivity patterns within different brain areas in response to negative stimuli (e.g., angry facial expressions, maternal criticism, social exclusion) and resting states. Establishing the type, direction, and strength of these connections may help elucidate the underlying mechanisms that affect and even distort perception and its relation to self-criticism. We predict that, like carriers of the S allele of the functional 5-promoter polymorphism of the serotonin transporter gene (Hariri et al., 2005), self-critical individuals will show reduced connectivity between anterior cingulate and elevated amygdala activation during the processing of negative stimuli and in resting states.

We also hypothesize a clear linear relationship between genes implicated in affective disorders (such as the serotonin 5-hydroxytryptamine-transporter-linked polymorphic region [5-HTTLPR] and brain-derived neurotrophic factor Val66Met polymorphisms) and self-criticism and from self-criticism to stress generation (see Starr, Hammen, Brennan, & Najman, 2012, for a recent demonstration of the effect of 5-HTTLPR on stress generation). Self-focused attention—a crucial component of **SK**—is likely to play a part in this causal chain by mediating the link between genes and self-criticism and between self-criticism and stress generation and depression (Hilt, Sander, Nolen-Hoeksema, & Simen, 2007; R. O'Connor & Noyce, 2008). When participants are asked to retrieve or rate personal information in fMRI scans, we can also expect self-criticism to modulate activation in brain areas associated with personal information—such as midline structures (see CHAPTER 4). The use of resting-state paradigms—that is, when participants are not engaged in a predefined cognitive activity (e.g., Biswal, Yetkin, Haughton, & Hyde, 1995)—will enable us to examine functional connectivity and observe self-focus attention and its relation to self-criticism during ongoing streams of consciousness.

A potential avenue for the development of practice-friendly assessment of self-criticism is the transformation of extant self-report questionnaires—based on continuous scores—into a set of binary items, each representing a "self-criticism sign." Psychometric research might then be conducted to determine how many signs must be endorsed to predict the clinical cutoff of, say, depression (as measured by the Beck Depression Inventory or Center for Epidemiological Studies-Depression Scale) or serious suicidality (e.g., the existence of a concrete suicidal plan). Such research should also examine whether several such "signs" are more predictive of clinical cutoff or risky behavior than others. This in turn might lead to construct-validity-based research into the meaning of self-criticism. Although I am of course biased, the Depressive Experiences Questionnaire's Self-Criticism 6's brevity and sound criterion validity make it an ideal instrument upon which to base such a program of psychometric research.

In the area of treatment, research examining the response of self-critics to various forms of intervention is far from exhaustive. I already mentioned Ben Shahar's attempt to treat self-criticism via experiential (empty chair) and loving-kindness meditation techniques and P. Gilbert, Zuroff, and their colleagues' efforts to treat self-criticism with compassion-based techniques. As I argued earlier, my position is that virtually any clinical problem—including self-criticism—requires treatment based on multiple interventions and their integration. STREALTH is now examining the impact on self-criticism of one of the interventions described in CHAPTER 7—namely, Multiple Selves Analysis.

Importantly, however, self-criticism should not only be treated but must—and in my opinion can—be prevented. A Jewish proverb states: "A fool may throw a stone into a well which a hundred wise men cannot pull out." Although in principle this is prevention-science's raison d'être, self-criticism's pervasively pernicious effect (see CHAPTER 1) and social-systemic nature render it an ideal candidate for preventive intervention. To the best of my knowledge, no studies have been conducted in this direction to date. Given the particularly strong effect of self-criticism on unipolar depressive symptoms, a reasonable starting point would be to look at extant preventive interventions for depression and extract components useful for the prevention of self-criticism.

My bet lies on those that are consistent with behavioral activation—namely, those which encourage individuals to immerse themselves in enjoyable and meaningful activities. This wager is based on my general preference for action-theory perspectives, which emphasize the potentially active nature of human behavior and the potential that enjoyable activities carry for bolstering individuals' A, thereby diminishing the self-critical wedge between A and SK. Other potentially pertinent preventive interventions are as follows:

1. Those drawn from the autonomy-support construct within self-determination theory. This has already yielded several interesting interventions for increasing autonomy—particularly autonomy-supportive interventions in health-related contexts (for a review, see Fortier, Duda, Guerin, & Teixeira,

2012) and educational contexts (e.g., McLachlan & Hagger, 2010; Reeve, 1998; Vansteenkiste, Simons, Lens, Sheldon, & Deci, 2004).

2. Interventions developed on the basis of the emotional-intelligence literature that seek to increase emotional self-awareness for various purposes—from promoting academic achievement to boosting mental health (for a review, see Schutte, Malouff, & Thorsteinsson, 2013). In the terms of the theory developed here, the latter interventions are likely to increase accurate **SK**, thus diminishing the wedge separating it from **A**.

Developmentally speaking, the age range in which I think prevention of self-criticism should commence is early adolescence (i.e., around age 11). The rationale behind this developmental premise is straightforward: early adolescence represents a key developmental period concerning self-awareness and identity formation, also constituting a time when unipolar depression peaks. Both vicissitudes are highly relevant in the pursuit of self-criticism prevention.

A Final Word (Not Really)

When I began writing this book, I thought it would constitute my last word on self-criticism. I felt ready to move on to other fields and other realms of inquiry (e.g., heroism in self and society—see G. Shahar, 2013a). Now that I have completed it, I realize how naïve that thought was. There is so much more to do! STREALTH and I are determined to undertake at least some of it.

So it looks like self-criticism and I are stuck with each other. It is rather ironic that this has become clear as I turn the final page on such a prolonged (two-decade) segment of my life's work. But according to my own theoretical allegations, one only finds out about one's direction when one acts "in-the-world." Actions are questions. I have **ASK**ed—and sure enough, I have been answered.

NOTES

Chapter 1

1. All the names of patients referred to herein are pseudonyms.
2. To the best of my knowledge, the first to describe the two types of vulnerability to depression in academic clinical psychology was Blatt (1974).
3. Laboratory experimental clinical research might actually be integrated with naturalistically-observational research, in turn bolstering our understanding of depressive vulnerability. For instance, studies in which self-criticism and related cognitions are "activated" in the lab using priming techniques have shown that individual differences in participants' reactivity to such "primes" predict depressive relapses (e.g., Jarrett et al., 2012).

Chapter 2

1. D. T. Campbell and Stanley (1966) described five types of construct validity: internal validity (pertaining to the extent to which we may conclude that X causes Y), external validity (the extent to which the effect of X on Y may be generalized to various conditions), construct validity of the cause (described previously), construct validity of the effect (same as construct validity of the cause, only for Y), and statistical-conclusion validity (relating to the extent to which the statistical conditions applied in a study are adequate for drawing valid conclusions).
2. Based on their two-factor model solution, Clara et al. (2003) surmised that neuroticism is hierarchically superior to self-criticism, such that self-criticism is a facet within neuroticism. In my opinion, this constitutes a non sequitur, the data neither justifying the conclusion nor ruling out the inverse possibility—namely, that neuroticism is a facet of self-criticism. Another possibility—that both constructs are causally related—also remains to be examined.
3. "Positive perfectionism" is not always positive. Thus, for example, Taranis and Meyer (2010) found that the personal standards subscale of the Frost Multidimensional Perfectionism Scale (Frost et al., 1990) is associated with compulsive exercise. This effect was mediated by self-criticism.

Chapter 3

1. My clinical experience, and that of others, suggests that a submissive self-criticism might be more characteristic of patients with social anxiety than of those with depression and other forms of psychopathology. To the best of my knowledge, this premise has yet to be subject to any empirical examination.

2. Kaufmann (1974, p. 159) argues that Nietzsche asserts in the *Gay Science*: "What does your conscience say?—You shall become who you are." This formulation may derive from Pindar, *Pyth*. II, 73 (*genoi hoios essi*). My thanks go to Professor Jacob Golomb for bringing this dictum to my attention.

Chapter 4

1. Reprinted from Sullivan (1953), with the kind permission of W. W. Norton.
2. Reprinted from Davidson and Shahar (2007), with the kind permission of Johns Hopkins University Press.
3. See other research on late blooming in adulthood, however: Masten and Wright (2009).
4. In their wonderful treatise invitingly entitled "Know Thyself and Become What You Are: A Eudaimonic Approach to Psychological Well-Being," Ryff and Singer (2008) also appear—in my estimation—to fall into the same trap, namely, assuming that knowing oneself is relatively straightforward, thereby readily enabling authenticity (which the authors equate with actualizing one's virtues).
5. Winnicott's greatness in my mind lies in his constituting a truly humanistic thinker, similarly to Rogers and Maslow.
6. An allele is one of a number of alternative forms of the same gene. In this example, the polymorphic region is in the promoter region—namely, that which initiates gene transcription. The polymorphism results from different lengths of the repetitive DNA sequence due to insertion/deletion. A polymorphic region is a variation in the DNA sequence that arises from point mutations or insertion/deletion in the DNA sequence. A synaptic cleft is a region between two neurons.
7. The amygdala is an almond-shaped group of nuclei forming part of the limbic system that plays a primary role in emotion processing and memory. The subgenual cingulate gyrus is part of the brain's limbic system, located below the genu of the corpus callosum—that is, Brodmann area 25.
8. Homozygous means carrying two identical pairs of alleles. The serotonin 1A receptor polymorphism 5-HTR1A is a receptor that performs a regulatory role in the serotonergic system.
9. Midline structures are midbrain regions.

Chapter 5

1. In chaos theories and dynamic systems, attractors are shapes or forms toward which systems tend to gravitate (Gleick, 1988).
2. My thanks go to Prof. Joel Elizur of the Hebrew University of Jerusalem for pointing out to me that my proposed "Inquisitive Action" term closely corresponds to the notion of "probes" in family therapy (Joel Elizur, personal e-mail communication, February 21, 2014). Probes are minimalistic interventions that challenge family patterns and narratives to assess and search for flexibility (see also Elizur & Minuchin, 1989). They differ from Inquisitive Actions, however, in being naturally occurring and mostly unconscious interpersonal exchanges that take place both outside and within therapy.
3. See, for instance, the hilarious children's book *Rabbit Food* (Gretz, 2001), which describes Uncle Bunny's heroic—albeit abortive—attempt to persuade little John to like rabbit food. Substituting for parents is all but easy.
4. Yu and Gample (2009) reported that lack of warm and elevated maternal-power assertion was associated with child self-criticism, in turn predicting low levels of social competence. Their study relied neither on the conceptualization nor the measurement of EE, however. Wedig and Nock (2007) conducted a cross-sectional evaluation of 36 adolescents residing in the community assessing parent critically expressed emotion, adolescent

self-critical cognition, and self-injury. Their findings indicate that critically expressed emotion predicted self-injury. When testing the hypothesis that adolescent self-criticism mediates the link between critically expressed emotion and self-injury, the investigators found that the latter two were not linked ($F_{[1,34]}$ = 1.65, p = .21). It must be noted, however, that they employed a single-item measure of self-criticism worded as follows: "If others criticize me, they must be right." Single-item measures are highly unreliable and invalid. This item's content also differs substantially from that of items in established measures of self-criticism (e.g., Blatt, 2004), appearing to tap into individuals' *evaluation* of others' precision of perception rather than self-criticism per se. A statistically-significant interaction between critically expressed emotion and self-criticism in predicting self-injury was nonetheless reported. Adolescent self-criticism was related to self-injury when parental criticism was medium and high—but not when low (Wedig & Nock, 2007, Figure 1, p. 1176).

5. Diagrammatical depictions of Bronfenbrenner's theory abound online: for example, https://www.google.co.il/search?q=bronfenbrenner+theory&biw=1366&bih=622&tbm=isch&tbo=u&source=univ&sa=X&ei=dIsfVaCWAZbvaJ6sgfgG&ved=0CCwQsAQ

6. Per my Authenticity and Self-Knowledge (**ASK**) theory, I would argue that, while such an emphasis on self-knowledge has been evident throughout human history (cf. the Delphic maxim "Know thyself" and Vico's account of self-knowledge in *The New Science* [Bergin & Fisch, 1968]), it is a particularly salient feature of (post)modernity.

7. First published as "Personality, Shame, and the Breakdown of Social Ties: The Voice of Quantitative Depression Research" in *Psychiatry: Interpersonal and Biological Processes, 64* (2001), 229–238. Used with permission from Guildford.

8. A psychological autopsy is a scientific procedure that seeks to identify the causes of completed suicide (see Isometsä, 2001).

Chapter 6

1. For the role authenticity plays in prioritizing interventions when confronted with a comorbid presentation of symptoms, see later.

2. For those who view my emphasis on symptoms and the symptomatic as trivial, an examination of Israeli clinical psychology is in order. The mental health reform currently under way in the country (Aviram, 2010) threatens overwhelming cuts in the allocation of resources to the treatment of mental disorders and the training of future psychotherapists alike. While I have yet to be convinced that this reform is based on scientific rather than economic factors, I nonetheless sympathize with consumers who argue that the current situation is completely unacceptable from the point of view of treatment, (lack of) accountability, and focus. What I find most disheartening, however, is that opponents of the reform—principally psychologists—invoke the International Classification of Diseases' Code Z as an argument against its implementation. This stipulating that patients who experience numerous life-stressors deserve treatment whether or not they exhibit psychological symptoms, the current reform would preclude such care. I find this argument embarrassing for two reasons. First, it reveals a total lack of understanding of how scarce extant resources are, how pernicious psychological symptoms can be, and the importance of allocating the greatest resources to the ones suffering the most. Second, it betrays a deep-seated ignorance of human resilience. Although many people who have experienced serious life-stress find a way to function in an at least provisionally psychiatrically intact form, opponents of the mental health reform regard them all as being in need of treatment.

3. The Stress, Self, and Health Research Lab is thus now developing a semi-structured interview for the assessment of self-criticism we call SCRINTERVIEW (Self-Criticism-Interview). Building on the development of previous, focused, relatively brief, successful semi-structured interviews for the assessment of symptoms, stress, and personality, we are currently gathering psychometric data pertaining to it.

4. This tension between abstract categories representing disorders and specific patient characteristics may be located within the traditional discussion regarding universals in philosophy (see Armstrong, 1989). For a relevant debate with respect to psychiatric comorbidity, see Cramer, Waldrop, van der Maas, and Borsboom (2010) and Fried (2015).

5. The treatment-aptitude perspective—according to which psychotherapy outcome is determined by an interaction between the type of treatment and patients' characteristics—was formulated by Lee Cronbach (1953; see also Blatt & Felsen, 1993; Blatt & G. Shahar, 2004a). In this case, as in others (Rector et al., 2000; G. Shahar & Blatt, 2005), aptitude outweighed treatment type in predicting outcome.

6. They are fine, however, with the "integrative CBT" label.

7. For a discussion of the nature and timing of interventions pertinent to self-criticism, see CHAPTER 7.

8. Common factors are also sometimes known as "nonspecific factors."

9. Mary Connors' self-psychological integrative approach to therapy (Connors, 1994, 2001), the schema therapy noted earlier, Diana Fosha's accelerated experiential dynamic psychotherapy (Fosha, 2000), Leigh McCullough's anxiety regulating therapy (e.g., L. McCullough, 1997), and other forms of therapy also share the same objectives.

10. Despite the very different jargon, psychoanalysis and CBT both understand therapist subjectivity in very similar ways. Symington (1983), for example, refers to an expression of the analyst's subjectivity as "the analyst's act of freedom." If this is viewed as an agent of therapeutic change, causing a therapeutic shift in the patient as well as being freeing, it implies a primary-process-level form of communication between the patient and analyst. Rudd and Joiner (1997) suggest the therapeutic belief system (TBS) as an alternative conceptual framework. This addresses therapeutic relationship variables—specifically, the transference-countertransference conceptualization in cognitive therapy. Through TBS, the therapist can understand, organize, discuss, and ultimately address aspects of the therapeutic relationship for the patient and him- or herself. The detailing of his or her response to each treatment component makes the subjective objective, the implicit explicit, transferring what was emotional and reactive into the realm of the structured and responsive.

11. In psychoanalysis, terms such "projective identification" (in the Kleinian tradition) and "containing" (in the Bionian tradition) describe processes in which patients regulate painful affect through their use of the therapist's affect modulation.

12. Winnicott addresses the question of why we need patients and in what way in "The Use of an Object" (1969). Herein, he differentiates between object relating and object usage. The former is an experience of the subject that can be described in terms of the subject as an isolate, thereby preventing him or her from perceiving the reality of an object as separate from him or her. In the latter, in order to be used an object must be real in terms of being part of a shared reality. In other words, the object is not only meaningful as a bundle of projection (subjective object) but its nature and behavior are also taken into consideration (object as part of external reality). According to Winnicott, being able to use an object is a more sophisticated capacity than merely relating to one.

13. Corresponding to Martin Buber's *I and Thou* (1937), Maslow's *Towards a Psychology of Being* (1968), and Stolorow et al.'s (1987) construction of intersubjective psychoanalysis.

14. Corresponding to Heinz Kohut's (1971) notion of "twinship transference."

15. Later on, owing to familial vicissitudes, I added adults suffering from chronic illness to my clientele. Yale doctoral students call their dissertation project a "Me-Search."

Chapter 7

1. This therapeutic position might be related to T. H. Ogden's (1994) notion of the analytic third—a point of view situated between subject and object (e.g., patient and therapist) that observes both.

2. Provisionally, and as a complement to the general empathic stance I employ with parents, I also use the relational reframe (RR) technique. This is designed to treat depression in adolescents in the context of attachment-based family therapy (Diamond, Diamond, & Levy, 2014). It focuses on improving the adolescent patient's attachment relationship rather than on the identified patient's presenting symptoms. The technique is composed of three phases: (1) joining and understanding the depression, (2) shifting to attachment themes, and (3) contracting relational goals. The aim of the initial phase is to attain an extended and accurate assessment of the present symptoms, their outcomes, and the familial context in which they developed. In the second stage, the therapist shifts from intake to exploring attachment themes—specifically, relational ruptures—and vulnerable emotions, identifying the negative outcomes of these maladaptive relational patterns in the family's everyday life. Finally, the therapist works with the adolescent and family on how to resolve the conflict in their relationships, emphasizing the desire to achieve positive change and create positive parents.

3. This is in line with Winnicott's "squiggle" technique, developed particularly for treating children. The therapist and patient take turns in completing one another's drawings. Located beyond the context of child psychotherapy, I see it as exemplifying the intersubjective processes that underlie all treatments.

4. Karen Horney (1950) speaks of the "tyranny of the shoulds."

5. Reprinted from Tillich (1952), with the kind permission of Yale University Press.

6. *Quod erat demonstratum*. In Hebrew, *mashal* (*ma she-haya-le-hochiach* ["what should have been demonstrated"])—a common expression in Israeli parlance.

7. This might also be described as "enactment" in relational psychoanalytic treatment (Jacobs, 1986), a term I dislike because it denudes the behavior of its goal-directed, future-oriented action.

8. It was actually Prof. Niza Yanai, a former mentor and longtime friend, who offered me the term.

9. Bion's notion of the container (1962) has received extensive attention not only in psychoanalysis but also in other forms of psychotherapy. Its precise meaning cannot be elucidated without a detailed exposition of Bion's theory of the mind—a task that lies beyond my present scope. I use the term here in reference to the human ability to tolerate, think about, verbalize, and modulate the painful affect expressed by other people.

10. According to Winnicott, the child gradually individuates out of the "mother–infant matrix," in which full dependency is encouraged and afforded, into the True Self (see CHAPTER 4). The more the child individuates, the more he or she is able to signal to his or her mother what he or she needs—a process Winnicott terms a "spontaneous gesture" (1987).

11. In Hebrew, the word "empathy" is pronounced *empatia*, which sounds very similar to the word for "caring for" (*ichpatiut*). I frequently say that the focus in treatment should be more on *ichpatiut* than on *empatia*. The point I am trying to make is that patients value their therapists' determination to care for them more than they value their ability to decipher their inner experiences—the latter task often being downright impossible (Levenson, 1972).

GLOSSARY

AGENTS IN RELATIONS (AIR): This term seeks to replace the extensively used "object relations" term. AIR highlights the role of will and goal-directed action in interpersonal relationships.

AUTHENTICITY: Defined here as an individual's talents, interests, and physiological-cognitive-emotional proclivities (including temperament).

AUTHENTICITY AND SELF-KNOWLEDGE (ASK): A theoretical postulate indicating that mental health is contingent upon the congruency between authenticity and knowledge about the self-concept (i.e., who we believe we are). Self-criticism is construed here as a distorted form of self-knowledge, which creates a wedge between true self-knowledge and authenticity.

AXIS OF CRITICISM (ACRIM): Multisystemic impact of criticism-based variables on the self. *ACRIM* consists of a genetic makeup presumed to be involved in self-knowledge, as well as trait self-criticism, critical expressed emotion, and critical cultural contexts (see Figure 5.2).

CRITICAL EXPRESSED EMOTION (CEE): The tendency of family members to be critical and hostile toward one of the family members. CEE has been shown to be implicated in the onset and/or exacerbation of mental and physical illness.

EM-PRESENTATION: An active attempt by the therapist to introduce his or her subjectivity into the treatment process. This can be achieved via numerous channels and is assumed to be highly conducive to the treatment of self-critical adolescents and young adults.

EVENTUALITY: All stressful events—chronic or acute—that block authentic goal-directed action.

INQUISITIVE ACTION: Action taken by individuals geared—at least partially—toward deciphering their identity. It usually involves an inadvertent question posed to others about one's identity, manifested in the form of action. When maladaptive, it actually backfires, prompting rejection, rejection, confrontation, and loss. For example, an adolescent might exhibit rebellious behavior in the attempt to understand—from others' responses—what is allowed or disallowed. This, in turn, brings about hostile responses from others, informing rebellious adolescents that they are "bad."

MULTIPLE SELVES ANALYSIS/PERSONAL PROJECTS ANALYSIS (MSA/PPA): An active and structured psychotherapeutic technique that seeks to increase self-concept awareness—in particular, an accurate awareness of one's authentic self. It consists of asking patients to name and personify various self-aspects, focusing on those that are neither punitive nor self-critical. Patients are then invited to inquire into their future plans or the goals ("projects") characterizing these self-aspects, being encouraged to act based on the aspects and projects. The overarching goal is to help patients "live outside of their self-critic."

MSA/PPA is introduced after (1) a therapeutically warm atmosphere has been established, (2) patients have been educated regarding the detriments of self-criticism, and (3) significant others directing criticism toward patients have been empathically attuned to and consulted.

PARTICULARIZED MODEL OF ADAPTATION (PMA): My own (cursory) attempt to explain why authenticity, as defined here, is evolutionarily important. Specifically, I argue that, due to enormous individual differences within the human species, individuals may only survive if they decipher and adhere to their own particular nature—their strengths, proclivity, and temperament.

PROJECTUALITY: The tendency to project oneself into the future in order to become what one thinks one might—achieved via goal-directed action.

SELF-CRITICISM: An intense and persistent relationship with the self characterized by (1) an uncompromising demand for perfection in performance and (2) an expression of hostility and derogation toward the self when that perfection inevitably fails to materialize.

SELF-CRITICAL CASCADE: A pattern of results emanating from extant empirical research, whereby self-criticism brings about negative social conditions, in turn leading to emotional distress, culminating in an increase in self-criticism. This pattern appears to be particularly salient during adolescence.

TURNING RUPTURES INTO QUESTIONS (TRIQ): A therapeutic stance aimed at utilizing therapeutic ruptures for the purpose of inquiring with patients into their inquisitive action (see earlier)—that is, the way they launch behaviors, often ineptly, in order to inquire about their self-identity.

TWO-PERSON POLITICS: The inevitable—albeit potentially useful—power struggle between the self-critical patient and his or her (self-critical) therapist.

REFERENCES

Abela, J. R. Z., Fishman, M. B., Cohen, J. R., & Young, J. F. (2012). Personality predispositions to depression in children of affectively-ill parents: The buffering role of self-esteem. *Journal of Clinical Child and Adolescent Psychology, 41,* 391–401.

Abela, J. R. Z., & Skitch, S. (2007). Dysfunctional attitudes, self-esteem, and hassles: Cognitive vulnerability to depression in children of affectively ill parents. *Behavior Research and Therapy, 45,* 1127–1140.

Abela, J. R. Z., & Taylor, G. (2003). Specific vulnerability to depressive mood reactions in schoolchildren: The moderating role of self-esteem. *Journal of Clinical Child and Adolescent Psychology, 32,* 408–418.

Abela, J. R. Z., Webb, C. A., Wagner, C., Ho, M. H. R., & Adams, P. (2006). The role of self-criticism, dependency, and hassles in the course of depressive illness: A multiwave longitudinal study. *Personality and Social Psychology Bulletin, 32,* 328–338.

Abraham, K. (1924). The influence of oral eroticism on character formation. *International Journal of Psychoanalysis, 6,* 247–258.

Abramowitz, J. S., Deacon, B. J., & Whiteside, S. P. H. (2011). *Exposure therapy for anxiety: Principles and practice.* New York, NY: Guilford.

Abu-Kaf, S., Henrich, C. C., & Shahar, G. *Self-critical vulnerability and the Axis of Criticism: A cultural perspective.* Manuscript in preparation.

Abu-Kaf, S., & Priel, B. (2008). Dependent and self-critical vulnerabilities to depression in two different cultural contexts. *Personality and Individual Differences, 44,* 689–700.

Adan, A., Archer, S. N., Hidaglo, M. P., Di-Milia, L., Natale V., & Randler, C. (2012). Circadian typology: A comprehensive review. *Chronobiology International, 29,* 1153–1175.

Albee, G. W. (2000). The Boulder Model's fatal flaw. *American Psychologist, 55,* 247–248.

Alexander, F., & French, T. M. (1946). *Psychoanalytic therapy: Principles and applications.* Oxford, England: Ronald.

Alford, B., & Beck, A. T. (1997). *The integrative power of cognitive therapy.* New York, NY: Guilford.

Allport, G. W. (1937). *Personality: A psychological interpretation.* New York, NY: Holt Rinehart and Winston.

Allport, G. W. (1955). *Becoming.* New Haven, CT: Yale University Press.

Altman, N. (2009). *The analyst in the inner city: Race, class, and culture through an analytic lens.* New York, NY: Routledge.

Amati, D., & Shallice, T. (2007). On the emergence of modern humans. *Cognition, 103,* 358–385.

American Psychiatric Association. (2005). *Diagnostic and statistical manual of mental disorders* (4th ed.; DSM-4). Washington, DC: American Psychiatric Association Press.

American Psychiatric Association. (2013). *Diagnostic and statistical manual of mental disorders* (5th ed.; DSM-5). Washington, DC: American Psychiatric Association Press.

Aminoff, E. F., Clewett, D., Freeman, S., Frithsen, A., Tipper, C., Johnson, A., Grafton, S. T., & Miller, M. B. (2012). Individual differences in shifting decision criterion: A recognition memory study. *Memory and Cognition, 40,* 1016–1030.

Amitay, O., Mongrain, M., & Fazaa, N. (2008). Love and control: Self-criticism in parents and daughters and perceptions of romantic partners. *Personality and Individual Differences, 44,* 75–85.

Anderson, G., & Horvath, J. (2004). The growing burden of chronic disease in America. *Public Health Reports, 119,* 263–270.

Andrews, P. W., & Thomson, J. A., Jr. (2009). The bright side of being blue: Depression as an adaptation for analyzing complex problems. *Psychological Review, 116,* 620–654.

Angyal, A. (1951). A theoretical model for personality studies. *Journal of Personality, 20,* 131–142.

Antonovsky, A. (1979). *Health, stress, and coping.* San Francisco, CA: Jossey-Bass.

Antony, M., & Swinson, R. (2009). *When perfect isn't good enough: Strategies for coping with perfectionism* (2nd ed.). Oakland, CA: New Harbinger.

Apter, A., Bleich, A., King, R. A., Fluch, A., Kottler, M., & Cohen, D. J. (1993). Death without warning? A clinical postmortem study of suicide in 43 Israeli adolescent males. *Archives of General Psychiatry, 50*(2), 138–142.

Armstrong, D. M. (1989). *Universals: An opinionated introduction.* Boulder, CO: Westview.

Arnett, J. J. (2000). Emerging adulthood: A theory of development from the late teens through the twenties. *American Psychologist, 55,* 469–480.

Arnett, J. J. (2004). *Emerging adulthood: The winding road from the late teens through the twenties.* New York, NY: Oxford University Press.

Arnett, J. J. (2006). In search of vitality: Reflections on editing JAR, one year in. *Journal of Adolescent Research, 21,* 3–6.

Arnow, B. A., Steidman, D., Blasey, C., Constantino, M. J., Klein, D. N., Markowitz, J. C., . . . & Kocsis, J. H. (2013). The relationship between the therapeutic alliance and treatment outcome in two distinct psychotherapy for chronic depression. *Journal of Consulting and Clinical Psychology, 81,* 627–638.

Aron, L. (1996). *A meeting of minds: Mutuality in psychoanalysis.* Hillsdale, NJ: Analytic Press.

Aronfreed, J. (1964). The origin of self-criticism. *Psychological Review, 71,* 193–218.

Asarnow, J. R., Tompson, M., Hamilton, E. B., Goldstein, M. J., & Guthrie, D. (1994). Family expressed emotion, childhood-onset depression, and childhood-onset schizophrenia spectrum disorders: Is expressed emotion a nonspecific correlate of child psychopathology or a specific risk factor for depression? *Journal of Abnormal Child Psychology, 22*(2), 129–146.

Aspinwall, L. G., & Taylor, S. E. (1997). A stitch in time: Self-regulation and proactive coping. *Psychological Bulletin, 121,* 417–436.

Atwood, G., Stolorow, R., & Trop, J. (1989). Impasses in psychoanalytic therapy: A royal road. *Contemporary Psychoanalysis, 25,* 554–573.

Auerbach, R. P., Ho, M. H. R., & Kim, J. C. (2014). Identifying cognitive and interpersonal predictors of adolescent depression. *Journal of Abnormal Child Psychology, 42,* 913–924.

Austin, J. T., & Vancouver, J. B. (1996). Goal constructs in psychology: Structure, process, and content. *Psychological Bulletin, 120,* 338–375.

Aviram, U. (2010). Promises and pitfalls on the road to a mental health reform in Israel. *Israeli Journal of Psychiatry and Related Sciences, 47,* 171–194.

Bacchiochi, J., Bagby, R. M., Cristi, C., & Watson, J. (2003). Validation of the connectedness and neediness dimensions of the dependency construct. *Cognitive Therapy and Research, 27,* 233–242.

Bagby, R. M., Parker, J. D., Joffe, R. T., Schuller, D., & Gilchrist, E. (1998). Confirmatory factor analysis of the revised Personal Style Inventory (PSI). *Assessment, 5,* 31–43.

Bagby, R. M., & Rector, N. A. (1998). Self-criticism, dependency and the Five-Factor Model: A factor-analytic approach. *Personality and Individual Differences, 24,* 895–897.

Bakan, D. (1966). *The duality of human existence.* Chicago, IL: Rand McNally.

Baker, D. B., & Ludy, T. B., Jr. (2000). The affirmation of the scientist-practitioner: A look at Boulder. *American Psychologist, 55,* 241–247.

Bandura, A. (1977). Self-efficacy: Toward a unifying theory of behavioral change. *Psychological Review, 84,* 191–215.

Bandura, A. (1978). The self-system in reciprocal determinism. *American Psychologist, 33,* 344–358.

Bandura, A. (1986). *Social foundations of thought and action: A social cognitive theory.* Englewood Cliffs, NJ: Prentice Hall.

Bandura, A. (1991a). Social cognitive theory of self-regulation. *Organizational Behavior and Human Decision Processes, 50,* 248–287.

Bandura, A. (1991b). Social cognitive theory of moral thought and action. In W. M. Kurtines & J. L. Gewirtz (Eds.), *Handbook of moral behavior and development* (Vol. 1, pp. 45–103). Hillsdale, NJ: Erlbaum.

Bandura, A. (1997). *Self-efficacy: The exercise of control.* New York, NY: Freeman.

Bandura, A. (2001). Social-cognitive theory: An agentic perspective. *Annual Review of Psychology, 52,* 1–26.

Bareket-Bojmel, L., & Shahar, G. (2011). Emotional and interpersonal consequences of self-disclosure online. *Journal of Social and Clinical Psychology, 30,* 732–760.

Bargh, J., McKenna, K. Y., & Fitzsimons, G. M. (2002). Can you see the real me? Activation and expression of the "true self" on the internet. *Journal of Social Issues, 58,* 33–48.

Bar-Haim, Y., Lamy, D., Pergamin, L., Bakermans-Kranenburg, M. J., & Van IJzendoorn, M. H. (2007). Threat-related attentional bias in anxious and nonanxious individuals: A meta-analytic study. *Psychological Bulletin, 133,* 1–24.

Barnett, P. A., & Gotlib, I. H. (1988). Psychosocial functioning and depression: Distinguishing among antecedents, concomitants, and consequences. *Psychological Bulletin, 104,* 97–126.

Barrett, M. S., & Berman, J. S. (2001). Is psychotherapy more effective when therapists disclose information about themselves? *Journal of Consulting and Clinical Psychology, 69,* 597–603.

Barrom, C. P., Shadish, W. R., & Montgomery, L. M. (1988). PhDs, PsyDs, and real-world constraints on scholarly activity: Another look at the Boulder Model. *Professional Psychology: Research and Practice, 19,* 93–101.

Barroso, J., & Powell-Cope, G. M. (2000). Metasynthesis of qualitative research on living with HIV infection. *Qualitative Health Research, 10,* 340–353.

Bartelstone, J. H., & Trull, T. J. (1995). Personality, life events, and depression. *Journal of Personality Assessment, 64,* 279–294.

Bateson, G., Jackson, D., Haley, J., & Weakland, J. (1956). Toward a theory of schizophrenia. *Behavioral Science, 1,* 251–264.

Baumeister, B. F., Smart, L., & Boden, J. M. (1996). Relation of threatened egotism to violence and aggression: The dark side of high self-esteem. *Psychological Review, 103,* 5–33.

Baumgardner, A. H. (1990). To know oneself is to like oneself: Self-certainty and self-affect. *Journal of Personality and Social Psychology, 58,* 1062–1072.

Beck, A. T. (1983). Cognitive therapy of depression: New perspectives. In P. J. Clayton & J. E. Barrett (Eds.), *Treatment of depression: Old controversies and new approaches* (pp. 265–290). New York, NY: Raven.

Beck, A. T. (1996). Beyond belief: A theory of modes, personality, and psychopathology. In P. Salkovskis (Ed.), *Frontiers of cognitive therapy* (pp. 1–25). New York, NY: Guilford.

Beck, A. T., Epstein, N., Harrison, R. P., & Emery, G. (1983). *Development of the Sociotropy-Autonomy Scale: A measure of personality factors in psychopathology.* Unpublished manuscript. Philadelphia, PA: University of Pennsylvania.

Beck, A. T., & Haigh, E. A. P. (2014). Advances in cognitive theory and therapy: The generic cognitive model. *Annual Review of Clinical Psychology, 10,* 1–24.

Beck, A. T., Rush, A. J., Shaw, B. F., & Emery, G. (1979). *Cognitive therapy of depression.* New York, NY: Guilford.

Beck, A. T., Steer, R. A., & Brown, G. (1996). *BDI-II: Beck Depression Inventory-II manual.* New York, NY: Psychological Corporation.

Beevers, C. G., Gibb, B. E., McGeary, J. E., & Miller, I. W. (2007). Serotonin transporter genetic variation and biased attention for emotional word stimuli among psychiatric inpatients. *Journal of Abnormal Psychology, 116,* 208–212.

Belar, C. D. (2000). Scientist-practitioner # Science + Practice: Boulder is bolder. *American Psychologist, 55,* 249–250.

Benight, C. C., & Bandura, A. (2004). Social-cognitive theory of posttraumatic recovery: The role of perceived self-efficacy. *Behaviour Research and Therapy, 42,* 1129–1148.

Bergin, T. G., & Fisch, M. H. (1968). *The new science of Giambattista Vico.* Ithaca, NY: Cornell University Press [1774].

Bering, J. M. (2006). The folk psychology of souls. *Behavior and Brain Science, 29,* 453–462.

Besser, A., & Priel, B. (2005). Interpersonal relatedness and self-definition in late adulthood depression: Personality predispositions, and protective factors. *Social Behavior and Personality, 33,* 351–382.

Bevan, W. (1991). Contemporary psychology: A tour inside the onion. *American Psychologist, 46,* 475–483.

Bhavnani, K. (1991). *Talking politics: A psychological framing for views from youth in Britain.* Cambridge, England: Cambridge University Press.

Bhugra, D., & McKenzie, K. (2003). Expressed emotion across cultures. *Advancement in Psychiatric Treatment, 9,* 342–348.

Bion, W. R. (1962). *Seven servants.* New York: Aronson.

Bion, W. R. (1963). *Elements of psychoanalysis.* London, England: Heinemann.

Bion, W. R. (1984). *Second thoughts: Selected papers on psychoanalysis.* London, England: Marsfield Library.

Bion, W. R. (1990). *Brazilian lectures, 1973 Sao Paulo; 1974 Rio de Janeiro/Sao Paulo.* London, England: Karnac.

Biswal, B., Yetkin, F., Haughton, V., & Hyde, J. (1995). Functional connectivity in the motor cortex of human brain using echo-planar MRI. *Magnetic Resonance in Medicine, 34,* 537–541.

Blaney, P. H., & Kutcher, G. S. (1991). Measures of depressive dimensions: Are they interchangeable? *Journal of Personality Assessment, 56,* 502–512.

Blass, R. B., & Carmeli, Z. (2007). The case against neuropsychoanalysis: On fallacies underlying psychoanalysis' latest scientific trend and its negative impact on psychoanalytic discourse. *International Journal of Psychoanalysis, 88,* 19–40.

Blatt, S. J. (1974). Levels of object representation in anaclitic and introjective depression. *Psychoanalytic Study of the Child, 24,* 107–157.

Blatt, S. J. (1991). Depression and destructive risk-taking behavior in adolescence. In L. Lipsitt & L. Mitnick (Eds.), *Self-regulatory behavior and risk-taking: Causes and consequences* (pp. 285–309). Norwood, NJ: Ablex.

Blatt, S. J. (1992). The differential effect of psychotherapy and psychoanalysis on anaclitic and introjective patients: The Menninger Psychotherapy Research Project revisited. *Journal of the American Psychoanalytic Association, 40,* 691–724.

Blatt, S. J. (1995). The destructiveness of perfectionism: Implications for the treatment of depression. *American Psychologist, 12,* 1003–1020.

Blatt, S. J. (1998). Contributions of psychoanalysis to the understanding and treatment of depression. *Journal of the American Psychoanalytic Association, 46,* 723–752.

Blatt, S. J. (2004). *Experiences of depression.* Washington, DC: American Psychological Association Press.

Blatt, S. J. (2008). *Polarities of experiences.* Washington, DC: American Psychological Association Press.

Blatt, S. J., Auerbach, J. S., Zuroff, D. C., & Shahar, G. (2006). Evaluating efficacy, effectiveness, and mutative factors in psychodynamic psychotherapies. In *Psychodynamic diagnostic manual* (pp. 537–572). Silver Spring, MD: Alliance of Psychoanalytic Organizations.

Blatt, S. J., Chevron, E. S., Quinlan, D. M., Schaffer, C. E., & Wein, S. (1988). *The assessment of qualitative and structural dimensions of object representations* (rev. ed.). Unpublished research manual. New Haven: Yale University.

Blatt, S. J., Cornell, C. E., & Eshkol, E. (1993). Personality style, differential vulnerability and clinical course in immunological and cardiovascular disease. *Clinical Psychology Review, 13,* 421–450.

Blatt, S. J., D'Afflitti, J. P., & Quinlan, D. M. (1976). Experiences of depression in normal young adults. *Journal of Abnormal Psychology, 95,* 383–389.

Blatt, S. J., & Ford, R. Q. (1994). *Therapeutic change: An object relations perspective.* New York, NY: Plenum.

Blatt, S. J., & Homann, E. (1992). Parent-child interaction in the etiology of dependent and self-critical depression. *Clinical Psychology Review, 12,* 47–91.

Blatt, S. J., & Lerner, H. D. (1983). The psychological assessment of object representation. *Journal of Personality Assessment, 47,* 7–28.

Blatt, S. J., & Luyten, P. (2009). A structural-developmental psychodynamic approach to psychopathology: Two polarities of experience across the life span. *Development and Psychopathology, 21,* 793–814.

Blatt, S. J., Quinlan, D. M., Pilkonis, P. A., & Shea, M. T. (1995). Impact of perfectionism and need for approval on the brief treatment of depression: The National Institute of Mental Health Treatment of Depression Collaborative Research Program revisited. *Journal of Consulting and Clinical Psychology, 63,* 125–132.

Blatt, S. J., & Shahar, G. (2004a). Psychoanalysis: With whom? For what? And how? Comparison with psychotherapy. *Journal of the American Psychoanalytic Association, 52,* 393–447.

Blatt, S. J., & Shahar, G. (2004b). The dialectic self: Adaptive and maladaptive dimensions. In A. Werner (Ed.), *Psychoanalysis as an empirical, interdisciplinary science: An Anglo-American perspective* (Vol. 2, pp. 285–309). Stuttgart, Germany: Kohlhammer.

Blatt, S. J., Shahar, G., & Zuroff, D. C. (2001). Anaclitic (sociotropic) and introjective (autonomous) dimensions. *Psychotherapy, 30*(4), 449–454.

Blatt, S. J., & Shichman, S. (1983). Two primary configurations of psychopathology. *Psychoanalysis and Contemporary Thought, 6,* 187–254.

Blatt, S. J., Zohar, A., Quinlan, D. M., Luthar, S., & Hart, B. (1996). Levels of relatedness within the dependency factor of the Depressive Experiences Questionnaire for adolescents. *Journal of Personality Assessment, 67,* 52–71.

Blatt, S. J., Zohar, A., Quinlan, D. M., & Zuroff, D. C. (1995). Subscales within the dependency factor of the Depressive Experiences Questionnaire. *Journal of Personality Assessment, 64,* 319–339.

Blatt, S. J., & Zuroff, D. C. (1992). Interpersonal relatedness and self-definition: Two prototypes for depression. *Clinical Psychology Review, 12,* 527–562.

Blatt, S. J., & Zuroff, D. C. (2005). Empirical evaluation of the assumptions in identifying evidence based treatments in mental health. *Clinical Psychology Review, 25,* 459–486.

Blatt, S. J., Zuroff, D. C., Quinlan, D. M., & Pilkonis, P. A. (1996). Interpersonal factors in brief treatment of depression: Further analyses of the National Institute of Mental Health Treatment of Depression Collaborative Research Program. *Journal of Consulting and Clinical Psychology, 64,* 162–171.

Blechner, M. J. (1999). Psychoanalytic approaches to the AIDS epidemic. In H. Kaley, M. Eagle, & D. Wolitsly (Eds.), *Psychoanalytic therapy as health care* (pp. 199–220). Hillsdale, NJ: Analytic Press.

Bollas, C. (1987). *The shadow of the object: Psychoanalysis of the unthought known.* London, England: Press Association Press.

Bonime, W. (1965). A psychotherapeutic approach to depression. *Contemporary Psychoanalysis, 2,* 48–53.

Bornstein, R. F. (1995). Interpersonal dependency and physical illness: The mediating roles of stress and social support. *Journal of Social and Clinical Psychology, 14,* 225–243.

Bornstein, R. F. (1998a). Depathologizing dependency. *Journal of Nervous and Mental Diseases, 186*, 67–73.

Bornstein, R. F. (1998b). Interpersonal dependency and physical illness: A meta-analytic review of retrospective and prospective studies. *Journal of Research in Personality, 32*, 480–497.

Brandstädter, J. (1998). Action perspectives on human development. In W. Damon & R. M. Lerner (Eds.), *Handbook of child psychology* (pp. 807–863). New York, NY: Wiley.

Bromberg, P. M. (1996). Standing in the spaces: The multiplicity of self and the psychoanalytic relationship. *Contemporary Psychoanalysis, 32*, 509–535.

Bronfenbrenner, U. (1977). Toward an experimental ecology of human development. *American Psychologist, 32*, 513–531.

Bronfenbrenner, U. (1979). *The ecology of human development: Experiments by nature and design.* Cambridge, MA: Harvard University Press.

Bronfenbrenner, U. (1994). Ecological models of human development. In *International encyclopedia of education.* Oxford, England: Elsevier. (Reprinted in M. Gauvin & M. Cole, Eds., *Readings on the development of children*, pp. 37–43. New York: Freeman)

Brown, G. W. (1985). The discovery of expressed emotion: Induction or deduction? In J. Leff & C. Vaughn (Eds.), *Expressed emotion in families* (pp. 7–25). New York, NY: Guilford Press.

Brown, G. W., & Harris, T. O. (1978). *The social origins of depression.* New York, NY: Free Press.

Brown, G. W., & Harris, T. O. (1989). Depression. In G. W. Brown & T. O. Harris (Eds.), *Life events and illness* (pp. 49–93). New York, NY: Guilford.

Browning, M., Holmes, E. A., & Harmer, C. J. (2010). The modification of attentional bias to emotional information: A review of the techniques, mechanisms, and relevance to emotional disorders. *Cognitive, Affective and Behavioral Neuroscience, 10*, 8–20.

Brunstein, J. C. (1993). Personal goals and subjective well-being: A longitudinal study. *Journal of Personality and Social Psychology, 65*, 1061–1070.

Buber, M. (1968). *I and thou* (trans. W. Kaufmann). New York, NY: Charles Scribner's Sons [1937].

Buechler, S. (2004). *Clinical values: Emotions that guide psychoanalytic treatment.* Hillsdale, NJ: Analytic Press.

Buhrmester, D. (1990). Intimacy of friendships, interpersonal competence, and adjustment during preadolescence and adolescence. *Child Development, 11*, 425–450.

Buhrmester, D., & Furman, W. (1987). The development of companionship and intimacy. *Child Development, 58*, 1101–1103.

Bulka, R. P. (1984). Logotherapy as an answer to burnout. *International Forum for Logotherapy, 7*, 8–17.

Burgdorf, J., Panksepp, J., & Moskal, J. R. (2011). Frequency-modulated 50 kHz ultrasonic vocalizations: A tool for uncovering the molecular substrates of positive affect. *Neuroscience and Biobehavioral Reviews, 35*, 1831–1836.

Buss, D. M. (1987). Selection, evocation, and manipulation. *Journal of Personality and Social Psychology, 53*, 1214–1221.

Buss, D. M. (Ed.). (2005). *The handbook of evolutionary psychology.* New York, NY: Wiley and Sons.

Buss, D. M., & Hawley (2010). *The evolution of personality and individual differences.* Oxford, England: Oxford University Press.

Bussey, K., & Bandura, A. (1992). Self-regulatory mechanisms governing gender development. *Child Development, 63*, 1236–1250.

Butzer, B., & Kuiper, N. A. (2006). Relationships between the frequency of social comparisons and self-concept clarity, intolerance of uncertainty, anxiety, and depression. *Personality and Individual Differences, 41*, 167–176.

Campbell, D. T., & Stanley, J. C. (1966). *Experimental and quasi-experimental designs for research.* Chicago, IL: Rand McNally.

Campbell, J. D. (1990). Self-esteem and certainty of the self-concept. *Journal of Personality and Social Psychology, 56*, 538–549.

Campbell, J. D., Trapnell, P. D., Heine, S. J., Katz, I. M., Lavallee, L. F., & Lehman, D. R. (1996). Self-concept clarity: Measurement, personality correlates and cultural comparison behavior. *Journal of Social and Clinical Psychology, 11*, 167–180.

Cane, D. B., Olinger, J., Gotlib, I. H., & Kuiper, A. (1986). Factor structure of the dysfunctional attitude scale in a student population. *Journal of Clinical Psychology, 42*, 307–309.

Canetti, D., Rapaport, C., Wayne, C., Hall, B., & Hobfoll, S. E. (2012). An exposure effect? Evidence from a rigorous study on the psycho-political outcomes of terrorism. In J. Sinclair & D. Antonius (Eds.), *The political psychology of terrorism fears* (pp. 193–212). New York, NY: Oxford University Press.

Canetti-Nisim, D., Halperin, E., Sharvit, K., & Hobfoll, S. E. (2009). A new stress-based model of political extremism: Personal exposure to terrorism, psychological distress and exclusionist political attitudes. *Journal of Conflict Resolution, 63*, 363–389.

Cantor, N. (1990). From thought to behavior: "Having" and "doing" in the study of personality and cognition. *American Psychologist, 45*, 735–750.

Caprara, G. V., Alessandri, G., & Eisenberg, N. (2012). Prosociality: The contribution of traits, values, and self-efficacy beliefs. *Journal of Personality and Social Psychology, 102*, 1289–1303.

Carmil, D., & Breznitz, S. (1991). Personal trauma and world view: Are extremely stressful experiences related to political attitudes, religion beliefs, and future orientation? *Journal of Traumatic Stress, 4*, 393–405.

Cartwright, C. (2011). Transference, countertransference, and the reflective practice in cognitive therapy. *Clinical Psychologist, 15*, 112–120.

Carver, C. S. (1998). Generalization, adverse events, and development of depressive symptoms. *Journal of Personality, 66*, 609–620.

Carver, C. S., & Scheier, M. F. (1990). Principles of self-regulation: Action and emotion. In E. T. Higgins & R. M. Sorrentino (Eds.), *Handbook of motivation and cognition: Vol. 2. Foundations of social behavior* (pp. 3–52). New York, NY: Guilford.

Caspi, A., Hariri, A. R., Holmes, A., Uher, R., & Moffitt, T. E. (2010). Genetic sensitivity to the environment: The case of the serotonin transporter gene and its implications for studying complex diseases and traits. *American Journal of Psychiatry, 167*, 509–527.

Caspi, A., & Moffitt, T. E. (2006). Gene-environment interactions in psychiatry: Joining forces with neuroscience. *Nature Reviews Neurosciences, 7*, 583–590.

Caspi, A., Sugden, K., Moffit, T. E., Taylor, A., Craig, I. W., Harrington, H., . . . & Poulton, R. (2003). Influence of life stress on depression: Moderation by a polymorphism in the 5-HTT gene. *Science, 301*, 386–389.

Centers for Disease Control and Prevention, National Center for Injury Prevention and Control. (2010). Web-based Injury Statistics Query and Reporting System (WISQARS) Retrieved from http://www.cdc.gov/injury/wisqars/index.html

Cepeda, L., & Davenport, D. (2006). Person-centered therapy and solution-focused brief therapy: An integration of present and future awareness. *Psychotherapy, 43*, 1–12.

Chang, E. C. (2008). Introduction to self-criticism and self-enhancement: Views from ancient Greece to the modern world. In E. C. Chang (Ed.), *Self-criticism and self-enhancement: Theory, research, and clinical implications* (pp. 3–15). Washington, DC: American Psychological Association Press.

Chang, E. C., Chang, R., Sanna, L. J., & Kade, A. M. (2008). Self-criticism and self-enhancement: From complexities of the present to a complex future. In E. C. Chang (Ed.), *Self-criticism and self-enhancement: Theory, research, and clinical implications* (pp. 247–265). Washington, DC: American Psychological Association Press.

Chiao, J. Y., & Blizinsky, K. D. (2010). Culture-gene coevolution of individualism-collectivism and the serotonin transporter gene. *Proceedings of the Royal Society, 277*, 529–537.

Chorpita, B. F., Daleiden, E. L., & Weisz, J. R. (2005). Identifying and selecting the common elements of evidence based interventions: A distillation and matching model. *Mental Health Service Research, 7*, 5–20.

Cicchetti, D., & Sroufe, L. A. (2000). Editorial: The past as prologue to the future: The times, they've been a-changin'. *Development and Psychopathology, 12*, 255–264.

Cisler, J. M., & Koster, E. H. W. (2010). Mechanisms underlying attentional biases towards threat: An integrative review. *Clinical Psychology Review, 30*, 203–216.

Clara, I. P., Cox, B. J., & Enns, M. W. (2003). Hierarchical models of personality and psychopathology: The case of self-criticism, neuroticism, and depression. *Personality and Individual Differences, 35*, 91–99.

Clara, I. P., Cox, B. J., Enns, M. W., Murray, L. T., & Torgrudc, L. J. (2003). Confirmatory factor analysis of the multidimensional scale of PSS in clinically distressed and student samples. *Journal of Personality Assessment, 81*(3), 265–270.

Clark, L., Chamberlain, S. R., & Sahakian, B. J. (2009). Neurocognitive mechanisms in depression: Implications for treatment. *Annual Review in Neuroscience, 32*, 57–74.

Cohen, J., Jami, F. Y., Hankin, B. L., Shuqiao, Y., Xiong, Z. Z., & Abela, J. R. Z. (2013). Personality predispositions in Chinese adolescents: The relation between self-criticism, dependency, and prospective internalizing symptoms. *Journal of Social and Clinical Psychology, 32*, 596–618.

Conan-Doyle, A. (1890). *The sign of the four*. London, England: Spencer Blackett.

Connors, M. E. (1994). Symptom formation: An integrative self psychological perspective. *Psychoanalytic Psychology, 11*(4), 509–523.

Connors, M. E. (2001). Integrative treatment of symptomatic disorders. *Psychoanalytic Psychology, 18*, 74–91.

Cook, W. L., & Douglas, E. M. (1998). The looking-glass self in family context: A social relations analysis. *Journal of Family Psychology, 12*, 299–309.

Cooley, C. H. (1902). *Human nature and the social order*. New York, NY: Charles Scriber's Sons.

Cooper, D. E. (1990). *Existentialism: A reconstruction*. New York, NY: Wiley.

Costa, P. T., Jr., & McCrae, R. R. (1992). *Revised NEO personality inventory (NEO-PI-R) and NEO five-factor inventory (NEO-FFI) professional manual*. Odessa, FL: Psychological Assessment Resources.

Cox, B. J., Enns, M. W., & Clara, I. P. (2004). Psychological dimensions associated with suicidal ideation and attempts in the National Comorbidity Survey. *Suicide and Life-Threatening Behavior, 34*, 209–219.

Cox, B. J., Flett, C., & Stein, M. B. (2004). Self-criticism and social phobia in the US national comorbidity survey. *Journal of Affective Disorders, 82*, 227–234.

Cox, B. J., MacPherson, P. S. R., Enns, M. W., & McWilliams, L. A. (2004). Neuroticism and self-criticism associated with posttraumatic stress disorder in a nationally representative sample. *Behaviour Research and Therapy, 42*, 105–114.

Cox, B. J., McWilliams, L. A., Enns, M. W., & Clara, I. P. (2004). Broad and specific personality dimensions associated with major depression in a nationally representative sample. *Comprehensive Psychiatry, 45*, 246–253.

Coyne, J. C. (1976). Towards an interactional description of depression. *Psychiatry: Interpersonal and Biological Processes, 39*, 28–40.

Coyne, J. C. (1994). Possible contributions of "cognitive science" to the integration of psychotherapy. *Journal of Psychotherapy Integration, 4*, 401–416.

Coyne, J. C., Thompson, R., Klingman, M. S., & Nease, D. E. J. R. (2000). Emotional disorders in primary care. *Journal of Consulting and Clinical Psychology, 70*, 798–809.

Coyne, J. C., & Whiffen, V. E. (1995). Issues in personality as diathesis for depression: The case of sociotropy-dependency and autonomy-self-criticism. *Psychological Bulletin, 118*, 358–378.

Cramer, A. O. J., Waldrop, L. J., van der Maas, H. L. J., & Borsboom, D. (2010). Comorbidity: A network perspective. *Brain and Behavioral Sciences, 33*, 137–193.

Cramer, P. (1995). Identity, narcissism, and defense mechanism in late adolescence. *Journal of Research in Personality, 29*, 341–361.

Cronbach, L. J. (1953). Correlation between persons as a real tool. In O. H. Mowrer (Ed.), *Psychotherapy: Theory and research* (pp. 376–389). New York, NY: Ronald.

Csikszentmihalyi, M. (1990). *Flow: The psychology of optimal experience.* New York, NY: Harper and Row.

Damasio, A. R. (2003). Feelings of emotions and the self. *Annual New York Academy of Science, 1001,* 253–261.

Dasgupta, S. (2007). Multidisciplinary creativity: The case of Herbert A. Simon. *Cognitive Science, 27,* 683–707.

Davidson, L., & McGlashon, T. H. (1997). The varied outcomes of schizophrenia. *Canadian Journal of Psychiatry, 42*(1), 34–43.

Davidson, L., & Shahar, G. (2007). From deficit to desire: A philosophical reconsideration of action models of psychopathology. *Philosophy, Psychiatry, and Psychology, 14,* 215–232.

Davis, J. (1985). *The order of causal logic.* Thousand Oaks, CA: Sage.

Davison, G. C. (1998). Being bolder with the Boulder Model: The challenge of education and training in empirically supported treatments. *Journal of Consulting and Clinical Psychology, 66,* 163–167.

De Oliveira, I. R., Hemmany, C., Powell, V. B., Bonfim, T. D., Duran, E. P., Novais, N., . . . Cesnik, J. A. (2012). Trial-based psychotherapy and the efficacy of trial-based thought record in changing unhelpful core beliefs and reducing self-criticism. *CNS Spectrums, 17,* 16–23.

Deci, E. L., & Ryan, R. M. (1985). *Intrinsic motivation and self determination in human behavior.* New York, NY: Plenum.

Deci, E. L., & Ryan, R. M. (2012a). Motivation, personality, and development within embedded social contexts: An overview of self-determination theory. In R. M. Ryan (Ed.), *Oxford handbook of human motivation* (pp. 85–107). Oxford, England: Oxford University Press.

Deci, E. L., & Ryan, R. M. (2012b). Self-determination theory. In P. A. M. Van Lange, A. W. Kruglanski, & E. T. Higgins (Eds.), *Handbook of theories of social psychology* (Vol. 1, pp. 416–437). Thousand Oaks, CA: Sage.

Deci, E. L., Ryan, R. M., & Guay, F. (2013). Self-determination theory and actualization of human potential. In D. McInerney, H. Marsh, R. Craven, & F. Guay (Eds.), *Theory driving research: New wave perspectives on self-processes and human development* (pp. 109–133). Charlotte, NC: Information Age Press.

Degner, L. F., Hack, T., O'Neil, J., & Kristjanson, L. J. (2003). A new approach to eliciting meaning in the context of breast cancer. *Cancer Nursing, 26,* 169–178.

Depue, R. A., & Monroe, S. M. (1986). Conceptualization and measurement of human disorder in life stress research: The problem of chronic disturbance. *Psychological Bulletin, 99,* 36–51.

Derogatis, L. R., & Spencer, P. M. (1982). *The brief symptom inventory: Administration, scoring, and procedure* (Manual 1). Baltimore, MD: Clinical Psychometric Research.

Desmet, M., Coemans, L., Vanheule, S., & Meganck, R. (2008). Anaclitic and introjective psychopathology and the interpersonal function of perfectionism/self-criticism. *Journal of the American Psychoanalytic Association, 56,* 1337–1342.

Dewsbury, D. A. (2000). The marginalization of academic, non-scientific psychology in the American Psychological Association. *The General Psychologist, 35,* 96–97.

Dewsbury, D. A. (2009). Is psychology losing its foundation? *Review of General Psychology, 13,* 281–189.

Diamond, G. S., Diamond, G. M., & Levy, S. A. (2014). *Attachment-based family therapy for depressed adolescents.* Washington, DC: American Psychological Association Press.

Diesfeld, K. (2008). Interpersonal issues between pain physicians and patients: Strategies to reduce conflict. *Pain Medicine, 9,* 1118–1124.

Dimeff, L., & Linehan, M. M. (2001). Dialectical behavior therapy in a nutshell. *The California Psychologist, 34,* 10–13.

Dimidjian, S., Barrera M., Jr., Martell, C., Munoz, R. F., & Lewinsohn, P. M. (2011). The origins and current status of behavioral activation treatments for depression. *Annual Review of Clinical Psychology, 7,* 1–38.

Dollard, J., & Miller, N. E. (1950). *Personality and psychotherapy.* New York, NY: McGraw-Hill.

Donne, J. (1923). *Donne's devotions.* Cambridge: Cambridge University Press.

Dowrick, C., Dunn, G., Ayuso-Mateos, J. L., Dalgard, O. S., Page, H., & Lehtinen, V. (2000). Problem solving treatment and group psychoeducation for depression: Multicentre randomized controlled trial. Outcomes of Depression International Network (ODIN) Group. *British Medical Journal, 321*, 1450–1454.

DuBois, D. L., Felner, R. D., Brand, S., Adan, A. M., & Evans, E. G. (1992). A prospective study of life stress, social support, and adaptation in early adolescence. *Child Development, 63*, 542–557.

Dubois, D. L., & Tevendale, H. D. (1999). Self-esteem in childhood and adolescence: Vaccine or epiphenomenon? *Applied and Preventive Psychology, 8*, 103–117.

Dunkley, D. M., & Blankstein, K. R. (2000). Self-critical perfectionism, coping, hassles, and current distress: A structural equation modeling approach. *Cognitive Therapy and Research, 24*, 713–730.

Dunkley, D. M., Blankstein, K. R., & Flett, G. L. (1997). Specific cognitive-persona vulnerability styles in depression and the five-factor model of personality. *Personality and Individual Differences, 23*, 1041–1053.

Dunkley, D. M., Blankstein, K. R., Masheb, R. M., & Grilo, C. M. (2003). Personal standards and evaluative concerns dimensions of "clinical" perfectionism: A reply to Shafran et al. (2002, 2003) and Hewitt et al. (2003). *Behaviour Research and Therapy, 44*, 63–84.

Dunkley, D. M., & Grilo, C. M. (2007). Self-criticism, low self-esteem, depressive symptoms, and over-evaluation of shape and weight in binge eating disorder patients. *Behaviour Research and Therapy, 45*, 139–149.

Dunkley, D. M., & Kyparissis, A. (2008). What is the DAS self-critical perfectionism really measuring? Relations with the five-factor model of personality and depressive symptoms. *Personality and Individual Differences, 44*, 1295–1305.

Dunkley, D. M., Masheb, R. M., & Grilo, C. M. (2010). Childhood maltreatment, depressive symptoms, and body dissatisfaction in patients with binge eating disorder: The mediating role of self-criticism. *International Journal of Eating Disorders, 43*, 274–281.

Dunkley, D. M., Sanislow, C. A., Grilo, C. M., & McGlashan, T. H. (2006). Perfectionism and depressive symptoms three years later: Negative social interactions, avoidant coping, and perceived social support as mediators. *Comprehensive Psychiatry, 47*, 106–115.

Dunkley, D. M., Sanislow, C. A., Grilo, C. M., & McGlashan, T. H. (2009). Self-criticism versus neuroticism in predicting depression and psychosocial impairment for 4 years in a clinical sample. *Comprehensive Psychiatry, 50*, 335–346.

Dunkley, D. M., Zuroff, D. C., & Blankstein, K. R. (2003). Self-critical perfectionism and daily affect: Dispositional and situational influences on stress and coping. *Journal of Personality and Social Psychology, 84*, 234–252.

Dunkley, D. M., Zuroff, D. C., & Blankstein, K. R. (2006). Specific perfectionism components versus self-criticism in predicting maladjustment. *Personality and Individual Differences, 40*, 409–420.

Dunning, D., & Fetchenhauer, D. (2013). Behavioral influences in the present tense: On expressive versus instrumental action. *Perspectives in Psychological Science, 8*, 142–145.

Echebarria-Echabe, A., & Fernandez-Guede, E. (2006). Effects of terrorism on attitudes and ideological orientation. *European Journal of Social Psychology, 36*, 259–265.

Egan, S. J., Wade, T. D., & Shafran, R. (2011). Perfectionism as a transdiagnostic process: A clinical review. *Clinical Psychology Review, 31*, 203–212.

Eisner, L. R., Johnson, S. L., & Carver, C. S. (2008). Cognitive responses to failure and success related uniquely bipolar depression versus mania. *Journal of Abnormal Psychology, 117*, 154–163.

Elad-Strenger, J., Fireman, Z., Schiller, M., Besser, A., & Shahar, G. (2013). Vulnerability-resilience dynamics of ideological factors in distress after the evacuation from Gush Katif. *International Journal of Stress Management, 20*, 57–75.

Elad-Strenger, J., & Shahar, G. *The liberal-within-the-conservative and the conservative-within-the-liberal: Effects of political orientation and threats to political worldviews on political radicalization.* Manuscript under review.

Elizur, J., & Minuchin, S. (1989). *Institutionalizing madness: Families, therapy and society.* New York, NY: Basic.

Elkin, I. (1994). The NIMH Treatment of Depression Collaborative Research Program: Where we began and where we are now. In A. E. Bergin & S. L. Garfield (Eds.), *Handbook of psychotherapy and behavior change* (4th ed., pp. 114–135). New York, NY: Wiley.

Emmons, R. A. (1986). Personal striving: An approach to personality and subjective well-being. *Journal of Personality and Social Psychology, 51,* 1058–1068.

English, T., & John, O. P. (2013). Understanding the social effects of emotion regulation: The mediating role of authenticity for individual differences in suppression. *Emotion, 13,* 314–329.

Enns, M. W., Cox, B., & Inayatulla, M. (2003). Personality predictors of outcome for adolescents hospitalized for suicidal ideation. *Journal of the American Academy of Child and Adolescent Psychiatry, 42*(6), 720–727.

Epley, N., Waytz, A., Akalis, S., & Cacioppo, J. T. (2008). When I need a human: Motivational determinants of anthropomorphism. *Social Cognition, 26,* 143–155.

Epley, N., Waytz, A., & Cacioppo, J. T. (2007). On seeing human: A three-factor theory of anthropomorphism. *Psychological Review, 114,* 864–886.

Erikson, E. H. (1959). *Identity and the life cycle.* New York, NY: International Universities Press.

Evans, D. R., Baer, R. A., & Segerstrom, S. C. (2009). The effects of mindfulness and self-consciousness on persistence. *Personality and Individual Differences, 47,* 379–382.

Fadaee, E. (2011). Symbols, metaphors and similes in literature: A case study of "Animal Farm." *Journal of English and Literature, 2,* 19–27.

Farmer, A., Redman, K., Harris, T., Mahmood, A., Sadler, S., Pickering, A., & McGuffin, P. (2002). Neuroticism, extraversion, life events and depression: The Cardiff Depression Study. *British Journal of Psychiatry, 181,* 118–122.

Fazaa, N., & Page, S. (2003). Dependency and self-criticism as predictors of suicidal behavior. *Suicide and Life-Threatening Behavior, 33,* 172–185.

Fennig, S., Hadas, A., Izhakey, L., Roe, D., Apter, A., & Shahar, G. (2008). Self-criticism is a key predictor of eating disorder symptoms among inpatient adolescent girls. *International Journal of Eating Disorders, 41,* 762–765.

Ferrer, E., & McArdle, J. J. (2010). Longitudinal modeling of developmental changes in psychological research. *Current Directions in Psychological Science, 19,* 149–154.

Fichman, L., Koestner, R., & Zuroff, D. C. (1994). Depressive styles in adolescence: Assessment, relation to social functioning and developmental trends. *Journal of Youth and Adolescence, 23,* 315–330.

Firestone, R. W. (1988). *Voice therapy: A psychotherapeutic approach to self-destructive behavior.* Santa Barbara, CA: Glendon Association.

Flood, R. L., & Carson, E. R. (1993). *Dealing with complexity: An introduction to the theory and application of systems science.* New York, NY: Plenum.

Foa, E. B., Rothbaum, B. O., Riggs, D. S., & Murdock, T. B. (1991). Treatment of posttraumatic stress disorder in rape victims: A comparison between cognitive-behavioral procedures and counseling. *Journal of Consulting and Clinical Psychology, 59,* 715–723.

Fodor, I. G. (1992). *Adolescent assertiveness and social skills training: A clinical handbook.* New York, NY: Springer.

Fonagy, P. (2010). The changing shapes of clinical practice: Driven by science or by pragmatics? *Psychoanalytic Psychotherapy, 24,* 22–43.

Fortier, M. S., Duda, J. L., Guerin, E., & Teixeira, P. J. (2012). Promoting physical activity: Development and testing of self-determination theory-based interventions. *International Journal of Behavioral Nutrition and Physical Activity, 9*(1), 20.

Fosha, D. (2000). *The transforming power of affect: A model of accelerated change.* New York, NY: Basic.

Fosha, D. (2013). A heaven in a wild flower: Self, dissociation, and treatment in the context of the neurobiological core self. *Psychoanalytic Inquiry: A Topical Journal for Mental Health Professionals, 33,* 496–523.

Fox, E., Ridgewell, A., & Ashwin, C. (2009). Looking on the bright side: Biased attention and the human serotonin transporter gene. *Proceedings of the Royal Society: Biological Sciences*, *276*, 1747–1751.

Frances, A. (2009). Whither DSM-V? *British Journal of Psychiatry*, *195*, 391–392.

Francis-Raniere, E., Alloy, L. B., & Abramson, L. Y. (2006). Depressive personality styles and bipolar spectrum disorders: Prospective tests of the event congruency hypothesis. *Bipolar Disorders*, *8*, 382–399.

Frank, G. (1984). The Boulder Model: History, rationale, and critique. *Professional Psychology: Research and Practice*, *15*, 417–435.

Frank, K. (1990). Action techniques in psychoanalysis. *Contemporary Psychoanalysis*, *26*, 732–756.

Frankl, V. (1958). On logotherapy and existential analysis. *American Journal of Psychoanalysis*, *18*, 28–37.

Frankl, V. (1966). Logotherapy and existential analysis: A review. *American Journal of Psychotherapy*, *20*, 252–260.

Frankl, V. (1975). Paradoxical intention and dereflection. *Psychotherapy*, *12*, 226–237.

Frantsve, L. M., & Kerns, R. D. (2007). Patient-provider interactions in the management of chronic pain: Current findings within the context of shared medical decision making. *Pain Medicine*, *8*, 25–35.

Fredrickson, B. (2001). The role of positive emotions in positive psychology: The broaden-and-build theory of positive emotions. *American Psychology*, *56*, 218–226.

Freeman, A., Pretzer, J., Fleming, B., & Simon, K. M. (1990). *Clinical applications of cognitive therapy*. New York, NY: Plenum.

Fried, E. I. (2015). Problematic assumptions have slowed down depression research: why symptoms, not syndromes are the way forward. *Frontiers in Psychology*, *6*, 309.

Freud, S. (1917). *Mourning and melancholia*. New York, NY: Vintage. Standard Edition 14, 243–248.

Frost, R. O., Benton, N., & Dowrick, P. W. (1990). Self-evaluation, videotape review, and dysphoria. *Journal of Social and Clinical Psychology*, *9*, 367–374.

Frost, R. O., Heimberg, R. G., Holt, C. S., Mattia, J. I., & Neubauer, A. L. (1993). A comparison of two measures of perfectionism. *Personality and Individual Differences*, *14*, 119–126.

Frost, R. O., & Henderson, K. J. (1991). Perfectionism and reactions to athletic competition. *Journal of Sport and Exercise Psychology*, *13*, 323–335.

Frost, R., Lahart, C., & Rosenblate, R. (1991). The Development of Perfectionism. *Cognitive Therapy and Research*, *15*, 469–490.

Frost, R. O., & Marten, P. A. (1990). Perfectionism and evaluative threat. *Cognitive Therapy and Research*, *14*, 559–572.

Frost, R. O., Marten, P., Lahart, C., & Rosenblate, R. (1990). The dimensions of perfectionism. *Cognitive Therapy and Research*, *14*, 449–468.

Furman, W., & Buhrmeister, D. (1985). Children's perceptions of the personal relationships in their social networks. *Developmental Psychology*, *21*, 1016–1024.

Furman, W., & Buhrmester, D. (1992). Age and sex differences in perceptions of networks of personal relationships. *Child Development*, *63*, 103–115.

Gadamer, H-G. (1989). *Truth and method*. New York, NY: Crossroad.

Gay, P. (1988). *Freud: A life for our time*. New York, NY: Norton.

Geisser, M. E., Robinson, M. E., & Pickern, W. E. (1992). Differences in cognitive coping strategies among pain-sensitive and pain-tolerant individuals on the cold-pressor test. *Behavior Therapy*, *23*, 31–41.

Geller, J. D. (2003). Self-disclosure in psychoanalytic-existential therapy. *Journal of Clinical Psychology*, *59*, 541–554.

Gergen, K. (1991). *The saturated self: Dilemmas of identity in contemporary life*. New York, NY: Basic.

Ghent, E. (1989). Credo: The dialectics of one-person and two-person psychologies. *Contemporary Psychoanalysis*, *25*, 169–211.

Giddens, A. (1991). *Modernity and self-identity: Self and society in late modern age.* Stanford, CA: Stanford University Press.

Gilbert, D., & Wilson, T. D. (2007). Prospection: Experiencing the future. *Science, 317,* 1351–1354.

Gilbert, P. (1989). *Human nature and suffering.* Hove, England: Erlbaum.

Gilbert, P. (1995). Biopsychosocial approaches and evolutionary theory as aids to integration in clinical psychology and psychotherapy. *Clinical Psychology and Psychotherapy, 2,* 135–156.

Gilbert, P. (2000). Social mentalities: Internal "social" conflict and the role of inner warmth and compassion in cognitive therapy. In P. Gilbert & K. G. Bailey (Eds.), *Genes on the couch: Explorations in evolutionary psychotherapy* (pp. 118–150). Philadelphia, PA: Frances and Taylor.

Gilbert, P. (2005a). Social mentalities: A biopsychosocial and evolutionary reflection on social relationships. In M. W. Baldwin (Ed.), *Interpersonal cognition* (pp. 299–335). New York, NY: Guilford.

Gilbert, P. (Ed.). (2005b). *Compassion: Conceptualisations, research and use in psychotherapy.* New York, NY: Routledge.

Gilbert, P. (2009). Introducing compassion-focused therapy. *Advances in Psychiatric Treatment, 15,* 199–208.

Gilbert, P., & Bailey, K. G. (Eds.). (2000). *Genes on the couch: Explorations in evolutionary psychotherapy.* Hove, England: Psychology Press.

Gilbert, P., Baldwin, M. W., Irons, C., Baccus, J. R., & Palmer, M. (2006). Self-criticism and self-warmth: An imagery study exploring their relation to depression. *Journal of Cognitive Psychotherapy: An International Quarterly, 20,* 183–200.

Gilbert, P., Birchwood, M., Gilbert, J., Trower, P., Hay, J., Murray, B., . . . & Miles, J. N. (2001). An exploration of evolved mental mechanisms for dominant and subordinate behaviour in relation to auditory hallucinations in schizophrenia and critical thoughts in depression. *Psychological Medicine, 31,* 117–1127.

Gilbert, P., Clarke, M., Hempel, S., Miles, J. N., & Irons, C. (2004). Criticizing and reassuring oneself: An exploration of forms, styles and reasons in female students. *British Journal of Clinical Psychology, 43,* 31–50.

Gilbert, P., & Irons, C. (2005). Focused therapies and compassionate mind training for shame and self-attacking. In P. Gilbert (Ed.), *Compassion: Conceptualisations, research and use in psychotherapy* (pp. 263–325). New York, NY: Routledge.

Gilbert, P., McEwan, K., Matos, M., & Rivis, A. (2011). Fear of compassion: Development of three self-report measures. *Psychology and Psychotherapy: Theory, Research, and Practice, 84,* 239–255.

Gilbert, P., & Procter, S. (2006). Compassionate mind training for people with high shame and self-criticism: Overview and pilot study of a group therapy approach. *Clinical Psychology and Psychotherapy, 13,* 353–379.

Gilbert, S. J., Spengler, S., Simons, J. S., Steele, J. D., Lawrie, S. M., Frith, C. D., & Burgess, P. W. (2006). Functional specialization within rostral prefrontal cortex (area 10): A meta-analysis. *Journal of Cognitive Neuroscience, 18*(6), 932–948.

Gilboa-Shechtman, E., & Shahar, G. (2006). The sooner—the better: Rates of change as a predictor of functioning in brief treatment for depression. *Psychotherapy Research, 16,* 374–384.

Gill, M. M. (1979). The analysis of transference. *Journal of the American Psychoanalytic Association, 27*(Suppl), 263–288.

Gillath, O., Sesko, A. K., Shaver, P. R., & Chun, D. S. (2010). Attachment, authenticity, and honesty: Dispositional and experimentally induced security can reduce self-and other-deception. *Journal of Personality and Social Psychology, 98,* 841–855.

Glassman, L. H., Weierich, M. R., Hooley, J. M., Deliberto, T. L., & Nock, M. K. (2007). Child maltreatment, non-suicidal self-injury, and the mediating role of self-criticism. *Behaviour Research and Therapy, 45,* 2483–2490.

Gleick, J. (1988). *Chaos: Making a new science.* New York, NY: Penguin.

Gold, J., & Stricker, G. (2001). A relational psychodynamic perspective on assimilative integration. *Journal of Psychotherapy Integration, 11*, 43–58.

Gold, J. R., & Wachtel, P. L. (1993). Cyclical psychodynamics. In G. Stricker & J. R. Gold (Eds.), *Comprehensive handbook of psychotherapy integration* (pp. 59–72). New York, NY: Plenum.

Goldberg, L. R. (1993). The structure of phenotypic personality traits. *American Psychologist, 48*, 26–34.

Goldfried, M. R., Burckell, L. A., & Eubanks-Carter, C. (2003). Therapist self-disclosure in cognitive-behavior therapy. *Journal of Clinical Psychology, 59*, 555–568.

Goldsmith, S. K., Pellmar, T. C., Kleinman, A. M., & Bunny, W. E. (Eds.). (2002). *Reducing suicide: A national imperative.* Washington, DC: National Academy Press.

Gordon, C., & Arian, A. (2001). Threat and decision making. *Journal of Conflict Resolution, 45*, 196–215.

Gottman, J. M. (1993). *What predicts divorce?* Hillsdale, NJ: Erlbaum.

Greenberg, B. G., Li, Q., Lucas, F. R., Hu, S., Sirota, L. A., Benjamin, J., Lesch, K. P., Hamer, D., & Murphy, D. L. (2000). Association between the serotonin transporter promoter polymorphism and personality traits in a primarily female population sample. *American Journal of Medical Genetics (Neuropsychiatric Genetics), 96*, 202–216.

Greenberg, E. P., Kessler, R. C., Birnbaum, G. H., Leong, A. S., Lowe, W. S., & Berglund, P. A. (2003). The economic burden of depression in the United States: How did it change between 1990 and 2000. *Journal of Clinical Psychiatry, 64*, 1465–1475.

Greenberg, L. S., & Watson, J. C. (2006). *Emotion-focused therapy for depression.* Washington, DC: American Psychological Association.

Gretz, S. (2001). *Rabbit food.* Cambridge, MA: Candlewick.

Gross, J. J., & John, O. P. (2003). Individual differences in two emotion regulation processes: Implications for affect, relationships, and well-being. *Journal of Personality and Social Psychology, 83*(2), 348–362.

Gruen, R. J., Silva, R., Ehrlich, J., Schweitzer, J. W., & Friedhoff, A. J. (1997). Vulnerability to stress: Self-criticism and self-induced changes in biochemistry. *Journal of Personality, 65*, 33–47.

Guidano, V. F. (1987). *Complexity of the self: Developmental approach to psychopathology and therapy.* New York, NY: Guilford.

Guisinger, S., & Blatt, S. J. (1994). Individuality and relatedness: Evolution of a fundamental dialectic. *American Psychologist, 49*, 104–111.

Haaga, D. A. F., Dyck, M. J., & Ernst, D. (1991). Empirical status of cognitive theory of depression. *Psychological Bulletin, 110*, 215–236.

Hakamata, Y., Lissek, S., Bar-Haim, Y., Britton, J. C, Fox, N. A., Leibenluft E., . . . & Pine, D. S. (2010). Attention bias modification treatment: A meta-analysis toward the establishment of novel treatment for anxiety. *Biological Psychiatry, 68*, 982–990.

Haley, J. (1969). The art of being a failure as a therapist. *American Journal of Orthopsychiatry, 39*, 691–695.

Hamachek, D. E. (1978). Psychodynamics of normal and neurotic perfectionism. *Psychology, 15*, 27–33.

Hamamura, T., & Heine, S. J. (2008). The role of self-criticism in self-improvement and face maintenance among Japanese. In E. C. Chang (Ed.), *Self-criticism and self-enhancement: Theory, research, and clinical implications* (pp. 105–122). Washington, DC: American Psychological Association Press.

Hammen, C. (1991). The generation of stress in the course of unipolar depression. *Journal of Abnormal Psychology, 100*, 555–561.

Hammen, C. (2006). Stress generation in depression: Reflections on origins, research, and future directions. *Journal of Clinical Psychology, 62*, 1065–1082.

Hammen, C., Marks, T., Mayol, A., & DeMayo, R. (1985). Depressive self-schemes, life stress, and vulnerability to depression. *Journal of Abnormal Psychology, 98*, 154–160.

Han, S., & Northoff, G. (2008). Culture-sensitive neural substrates of human cognition: A transcultural neuroimaging approach. *Nature Reviews Neuroscience, 9*, 646–654.

Hariri, A. R., Drabant, E. M., Munoz, K. E., Kolachana, B. S., Mattay, V. S., Egan, M. F., & Weinberger, D. R. (2005). A susceptibility gene for affective disorders and the response of the human amygdala. *Archives of General Psychiatry, 62,* 146–152.

Hariri, A. R., Mattay, V. S., Tessitore, A., Kolachana, B., Fera, F., Goldman, D., . . . & Weinberger, D. (2002). Serotonin transporter genetic variation and the response of the human amygdala. *Science, 297,* 400–403.

Harlow, R. E., & Cantor, N. (1994). Personality as problem solving: A framework for the analysis of change in daily-life behavior. *Journal of Psychotherapy Integration, 4,* 355–385.

Harter, S. (1993). Causes and consequences of low self-esteem in children and adolescents. In R. F. Baumeister (Ed.), *Self-esteem: The puzzle of low self-regard.* New York, NY: Plenum.

Harter, S. (2002). Authenticity. In C. R. Snyder & S. J. Lopez (Eds.), *Handbook of positive psychology* (pp. 382–394). Oxford, England: Oxford University Press.

Hawley, L. L., Moon-Ho, R. H., Zuroff, D. C., & Blatt, S. J. (2006). The relationship of perfectionism, depression, and therapeutic alliance during treatment for depression: Latent difference score analysis. *Journal of Consulting and Clinical Psychology, 74,* 930–942.

Hayes, S. C., Strosahl, K. D., & Wilson, K. G. (1999). *Acceptance and commitment therapy.* New York, NY: Guilford.

Haynes, S. N., Leisen, M. B., & Blaine, D. D. (1997). Design of individualized behavioral treatment programs using functional analytic clinical case models. *Psychological Assessment, 9,* 334–348.

Heils, A., Teufel, A., Petri, S., Stober, G., Riederer, P., Bengel, D., & Lesch, K. P. (1996). Allelic variation of human serotonin transporter gene expression. *Journal of Neurochemistry, 66,* 2621–2624.

Helgeson, V. S. (1994). Relation of agency and communion to well-being: Evidence and potential explanations. *Psychological Bulletin, 116*(3), 412–428.

Henrich, C. C., Brookmeyer, K. A., & Shahar, G. (2005). Weapon violence in adolescence: Parent and school connectedness as protective factors. *Journal of Adolescent Health, 37,* 306–312.

Herion, R. (2011). Deflection for depression. In H. G. Rosenthal (Ed.), *Favorite counseling and therapy techniques* (pp. 163–164). New York, NY: Routledge.

Hermans, H. J. M. (1988). On the integration of nomothetic and idiographic research methods in the study of personal meaning. *Journal of Personality, 56,* 785–812.

Hermans, H. J. M. (1996). Voicing the self: From information processing to dialogical interchange. *Psychological Bulletin, 119,* 31–50.

Heter, T. S. (2006). *Sartre's ethics of engagement: Authenticity and civic virtue.* London, England: Continuum.

Hewitt, P. L., & Flett, G. L. (1991a). Dimensions of perfectionism in unipolar depression. *Journal of Abnormal Psychology, 100,* 98–101.

Hewitt, P. L., & Flett, G. L. (1991b). Perfectionism in the self and social contexts: Conceptualization, assessment, and association with psychopathology. *Journal of Personality and Social Psychology, 60,* 456–470.

Hewitt, P. L., & Flett, G. L. (1993). Dimensions of perfectionism, daily stress, and depression: A test of the specific vulnerability hypothesis. *Journal of Abnormal Psychology, 102,* 58–65.

Hewitt, P. L., & Flett, G. L. (2002). Perfectionism and stress processes in psychopathology. In G. L. Flett & P. L. Hewitt (Eds.), *Perfectionism: Theory, research, and treatment* (pp. 255–284). Washington, DC: American Psychological Association.

Hewitt, P. L., Flett, G. L., Besser, A., Sherry, S. B., & McGee, B. (2003). Perfectionism is multidimensional: A reply to Shafran, Cooper and Fairburn (2002). *Behaviour Research and Therapy, 41,* 1221–1236.

Hewitt, P. L., Flett, G. L., & Ediger, E. (1996). Perfectionism and depression: Longitudinal assessment of a specific vulnerability hypothesis. *Journal of Abnormal Psychology, 105,* 276–280.

Higgins, E. T. (1987). Self-discrepancy: A theory relating self and affect. *Psychological Review, 94,* 319–340.

Higgins, E. T. (1997). Beyond pleasure and pain. *American Psychologist, 52*, 1280–1300.

Higgins, E. T., Roney, C. J. R., Crowe, E., & Hymes, C. (1994). Ideal versus ought predilections for approach and avoidance: Distinct self-regulatory systems. *Journal of Personality and Social Psychology, 66*, 276–286.

Hilt, L. M., Sander, L. C., Nolen-Hoeksema, S., & Simen, A. A. (2007). The BDNF Val66Met polymorphism predicts rumination and depression differently in young adolescent girls and their mothers. *Neuroscience Letters, 429*, 12–16.

Hirsch, B. Z. (2008). Treating food addiction with logotherapy. *International Forum for Logotherapy, 31*, 3–8.

Hirsch, I. (1994). Dissociation and the interpersonal self. *Contemporary Psychoanalysis, 30*, 777–799.

Hobfoll, S. E., Canetti-Nisim, D., & Johnson, R. J. (2006). Exposure to terrorism, stress-related mental health symptoms, and defensive coping among Jews and Arabs in Israel. *Journal of Consulting and Clinical Psychology, 74*, 207–218.

Hoffman, I. Z. (2009). Doublethinking our way to "scientific" legitimacy: The desiccation of human experience. *Journal of the American Psychoanalytic Association, 57*, 1043–1069.

Holman, H., & Lorig, K. (2004). Patient self-management: A key to effectiveness and efficiency in care of chronic disease. *Public Health Reports, 119*, 239–243.

Hong, S., & Lee, M. (2001). Hierarchical confirmatory factor analysis of the revised Personal Style Inventory: Evidence for the multidimensionality problem of perfectionism. *Educational and Psychological Measurement, 61*, 421–432.

Hooley, J. M., Gruber, S. A., Parker, H. A., Guillaumot, J., Rogowska, J., & Yurgelun-Todd, D. A. (2009). Cortico-limbic response to personally challenging emotional stimuli after complete recovery from depression. *Psychiatry Research: Neuroimaging, 172*, 83–91.

Hooley, J. M., Gruber, S. A., Scott, L. A., Hiller, J. B., & Yurgelun-Todd, D. A. (2005). Activation in dorsolateral prefrontal cortex in response to maternal criticism and praise in recovered depressed and healthy control participants. *Biological Psychiatry, 57*, 809–812.

Horney, K. (1950). *Neurosis and human growth.* New York, NY: W. W. Norton.

Horvath, A. O., & Symonds, B. D. (1991). Relation between working alliance and outcome in psychology: A meta-analysis. *Journal of Counseling Psychology, 38*, 139–149.

Huppert, J. D. (2009). The building blocks of treatment in cognitive-behavioral therapy. *Israel Journal of Psychiatry Related Science, 46*, 245–250.

Huprich, S. K., & Nelson, S. M. (2014). Malignant self-regard: Accounting for communalities in vulnerable narcissistic, depressive, self-defeating, and masochistic personality disorders. *Comprehensive Psychiatry, 55*, 989–998.

Hyler, S. E. (1994). *Personality Disorders Questionnaire, PDQ-4+.* New York, NY: New York State Psychiatric Institute.

Hyman, S. E. (2001). Mood disorders in children and adolescents: An NIMH perspective. *Biological Psychiatry, 49*, 962–969.

Iacoboni, M., Molnar-Szakacs, L., Gallese, V., Buccino, G., Mazziotta, J. C., & Rizzolatti, G. (1999). Cortical mechanisms of human imitation. *Science, 286*, 2526–2528.

Ingram, R. E. (1990). Self-focused attention in clinical disorders: Review and a conceptual modal. *Psychological Bulletin, 107*, 156–176.

Irons, C., Gilbert, P., Baldwin, M. W., Baccus, J. R., & Palmer, M. (2006). Parental recall, attachment relating and self-attacking/self-reassurance: Their relationship with depression. *British Journal of Clinical Psychology, 45*(3), 297–308.

Isometsä, E. T. (2001). Psychological autopsy studies: A review. *European Psychiatry, 16*, 379–385.

Israelashvili, M. (2013). Counseling in Israel. In T. H. Hohenshi & N. E. Amundson (Eds.), *Counseling around the world: An international handbook* (pp. 283–291). Alexandria, VA: American Counseling Association Press.

Itzhakey, L., Shahar, G., Stein, D., & Fennig, S. *Role of self-criticism in non-suicidal self injury (NSSI) among inpatient eating disordered adolescent females.* Manuscript under review.

Jacobs, T. J. (1986). On countertransference enactments. *Journal of the American Psychoanalytic Association, 34*, 289–307.

Jacobson, N. S., Martell, C. R., & Dimidjian, S. (2001). Behavioral activation treatment for depression: Returning to contextual roots. *Clinical Psychology: Science and Practice, 8,* 255–270.

Jarrett, R. B., Minhajuddin, A., Borman, P. D., Dunlap, L., Segal, Z. V., Kidner, C. L., . . . & Thase, M. E. (2012). Cognitive reactivity, dysfunctional attitudes, and depressive relapse and recurrence in cognitive therapy responders. *Behaviour Research and Therapy, 50*(5), 280–286.

Johnson, M. (2003). The vulnerability status of neuroticism: Over-reporting or genuine complaints? *Personality and Individual Differences, 35,* 877–887.

Johnson, M. H., Dziurawiec, S., Ellis, H., & Morton, J. (1991). Newborns' preferential tracking of face-like stimuli and its subsequent decline. *Cognition, 40,* 1–19.

Joiner, T. E., Jr. (1994). Contagious depression: Existence, specificity to depressive symptoms, and the role of reassurance seeking. *Journal of Personality and Social Psychology, 67,* 287–296.

Joiner, T. E., Jr. (2000). Depression's vicious scree: Self-propagating and erosive processes in depression chronicity. *Clinical Psychology: Science and Practice, 7,* 203–218.

Joiner, T. E., Alfano, M. S., & Metalsky, G. I. (1992). When depression breeds contempt: Reassurance-seeking, self-esteem, and rejection of depressed college students by their roommates. *Journal of Abnormal Psychology, 101,* 165–173.

Joiner, T. E., Jr., & Metalsky, G. L. (2001). Excessive reassurance seeking: Delineating a risk factor involved in the development of depressive symptoms. *Psychological Science, 12,* 371–378.

Jokela, M., Batty, G. D., Nyberg, S. T., Virtanen, M., Hermann, N., Singh-Manoux, A., & Kivimäki, M. (2013). Personality and all-cause mortality: Individual-participant meta-analysis of 3,947 deaths in 76,150 adults. *American Journal of Epidemiology, 178,* 667–675.

Joseph, L., & Shimberg, J. (2010). The dynamics of sexual infidelity: Personality style as a reproductive strategy. *Psychoanalytic Psychology, 27,* 273–295.

Judd, L. L., Akiskal, H. S., & Paulus, M. P. (1997). The role and clinical significance of subsyndromal depressive symptoms (SSD) in unipolar major depressive disorder. *Journal of Affective Disorders, 45,* 5–18.

Jung, C. G. (1971). *Collected works of C. G. Jung.* Princeton, NJ: Princeton University Press.

Just, N., & Alloy, L. B. (1997). The response styles theory of depression: Tests and extension of the theory. *Journal of Abnormal Psychology, 106,* 221–229.

Kabat-Zinn, J. (1982). An outpatient program in behavioral medicine for chronic pain patients based on the practice of mindfulness meditation: Theoretical considerations and preliminary results. *General Hospital Psychiatry, 4,* 33–47.

Kabat-Zinn, J. (1990). *Full catastrophe living: Using the wisdom of your body and mind to face stress, pain, and illness.* New York, NY: Random House.

Kabat-Zinn, J. (1994). *Wherever you go, there you are: Mindfulness meditation in everyday life.* New York, NY: Hyperion.

Kandel, E. R. (1998). A new intellectual framework for psychiatry. *American Journal of Psychiatry, 155,* 457–469.

Kannan, D., & Levitt, H. M. (2013). A review of client self-criticism in psychotherapy. *Journal of Psychotherapy Integration, 23,* 166–178.

Kant, I. (1929). *Critique of pure reason* (trans. N. K. Smith). London: Macmillan.

Kasch, K. L., Klein, D. N., & Lara, M. E. (2001). A construct validation study of the Response Style Questionnaire Rumination Scale in participants with a recent-onset major depressive episode. *Psychological Assessment, 13,* 375–383.

Kaufmann, W. (1974). *Nietzsche: Philosopher, psychologist, antichrist.* Princeton, NJ: Princeton University Press.

Kazdin, A., & Blase, S. (2011). Rebooting psychotherapy research and practice to reduce the burden of mental illness. *Perspectives on Psychological Science, 6,* 21–37.

Kazdin, A., & Whitley, M. K. (2006). Comorbidity, case complexity, and effects of evidence-based treatment for children referred for disruptive behaviors. *Journal of Consulting and Clinical Psychology, 74*, 455–467.

Kazdin, A. E. (1992). *Research design in clinical psychology* (2nd ed.). Boston, MA: Allen & Bacon.

Kazdin, A. E. (2007). Evidence-based treatment and practice: New opportunities to bridge clinical research and practice, enhance the knowledge base, and improve patient care. *American Psychologist, 63*, 146–159.

Kellogg, S. (2004). Dialogical encounters: Contemporary perspectives on "chairwork" in psychotherapy. *Psychotherapy: Theory, Research, Practice, Training, 41*, 310–320.

Kelly, A. C., Zuroff, D. C., Foa, C. L., & Gilbert, P. (2010). Who benefits from training in self-compassionate self-regulation? A study of smoking reduction. *Journal of Social and Clinical Psychology, 29*, 727–755.

Kelly, A. C., Zuroff, D. C., & Shahar, G. (2014). Perfectionism. In L. Grossman & S. Walfish (Eds.), *Translating research into practice: A desk reference for practicing mental health professionals* (pp. 233–240). New York: Springer.

Kelly, A. C., Zuroff, D. C., & Shapira, L. B. (2009). Soothing oneself and resisting self-attacks: The treatment of two intrapersonal deficits in depression vulnerability. *Cognitive Therapy and Research, 33*, 301–313.

Kelly, G. A. (1955). *The psychology of personal constructs*. New York, NY: Norton Press.

Kelly, J. B., & Lamb, M. E. (2003). Developmental issues in relocation cases involving young children: When, whether, and how? *Journal of Family Psychology, 17*, 193–205.

Kempe, S., Van Houdenhove, B., Luyten, P., Goossens, L., Bekaert, P., & Van Wambeke, P. (2011). Unraveling the role of perfectionism in chronic fatigue syndrome: Is there a distinction between adaptive and maladaptive perfectionism? *Psychiatry Research, 86*, 373–377.

Kendall, P. C., & Clarkin, J. F. (1992). Introduction to special section: Comorbidity and treatment implications. *Journal of Consulting and Clinical Psychology, 60*, 833–834.

Kenny, D. (1979). *Correlation and causality*. New York, NY: John Wiley & Sons.

Kenrick, D. T., Griskevicius, V., Neuberg, S. L., & Schaller, M. (2010). Renovating the pyramid of needs: Contemporary extensions built upon ancient foundations. *Perspectives in Psychological Science, 5*, 292–314.

Kernis, M. H., & Waschull, S. B. (1995). The interactive roles of stability and level of self-esteem: Research and theory. In M. P. Zanna (Ed.), *Advances in experimental social psychology* (Vol. 27, pp. 93–141). San Diego, CA: Academic Press.

Kim, H. S., Sherman, D. K., Taylor, S. E., Sasaki, J. Y., Chu, T. Q., Ryu, C., . . . & Xu, J. (2010). Culture, serotonin receptor polymorphism and locus of attention. *Social Cognitive and Affective Neuroscience, 5*, 212–218,

King, R. A. (2003). Psychodynamic approaches to youth suicide. In R. A. King & A. Apter (Eds.), *Child and adolescent suicide* (pp. 150–169). Cambridge, England: Cambridge University Press.

Kitayama, S., & Uchida, Y. (2003). Explicit self-criticism and implicit self-regard: Evaluating self and friend in two cultures. *Journal of Experimental Social Psychology, 39*, 476–482.

Kiyoe, L., Yumiko, N., Yumi, N., Sei, O., Yoshihiro, K., Tadashi, F., & Toshiaki, A. F. (2006). Interoceptive hypersensitivity and interoceptive exposure in patients with panic disorder: Specificity and effectiveness. *BMC Psychiatry, 6*, 32.

Klein, S. B. (2012). The self and science: Is it time for a new approach to the study of human experience? *Current Directions in Psychological Science, 21*, 253–257.

Klerman, G. L. (1979). The age of melancholy. *Psychology Today, 10*, 37–88.

Klerman, G. L., & Weissman, M. M. (1989). Increasing rates of depression. *Journal of the American Medical Association, 261*, 2229–2235.

Koechlin, E., & Hyafil, A. (2007). Anterior prefrontal function and the limits of human-decision making. *Science, 318*, 594–598.

Koestner, R., Zuroff, D. C., & Powers, T. A. (1991). Family origins of adolescent self-criticism and its continuity into adulthood. *Journal of Abnormal Psychology, 100*, 191–197.

Kohut, H. (1971). *The analysis of the self*. Chicago, IL: University of Chicago Press.

Kohut, H., & Wolf, E. S. (1978). The disorders of the self and their treatment. *International Journal of Psychoanalysis, 59*, 413–425.

Kolden, G. G., Klein, M. H., Wang, C. C., & Austin, S. B. (2011). Congruence/genuineness. *Psychotherapy, 48*, 65–71.

Kovacs, M. (1992). *Children's Depression Inventory*. New York, NY: Multi-Health Systems.

Kring, A. M., Smith, D. A., & Neale, J. A. (1994). Individual differences in dispositional expressiveness: Development and validation of the Emotional Expressivity Scale. *Journal of Personality and Social Psychology, 66*, 934–949.

Kubie, L. (1934). Relation of the conditioned reflex to psychoanalytic technique. *Archives of Neurology and Psychiatry, 32*, 1137–1142.

Kuperminc, G. P., Blatt, S. J., & Leadbeater, B. J. (1997). Relatedness, self-definition, and early adolescent adjustment. *Cognitive Therapy and Research, 21*, 301–320.

Kuttler, A. F., La Greca, A. M., & Prinstein, M. J. (1999). Friendship qualities and social-emotional functioning of adolescents with close, cross-sex friendships. *Journal of Research on Adolescence, 9*, 339–366.

Kuwabara, H., Sakado, K., Sakado, M., Sato, T., & Someya, T. (2004). The Japanese version of the Depressive Experiences Questionnaire: Its reliability and validity in lifetime depression in a working population. *Comprehensive Psychiatry, 45*, 311–315.

Kwan, V. S. Y., & Fiske, S. T. (2008). Missing links in social cognition: The continuum from nonhuman agents to dehumanized humans. *Social Cognition, 26*, 125–128.

Kwon, P., Campbell, D. G., & Williams, M. G. (2001). Sociotropy and autonomy: Construct validity evidence using TAT narratives. *Journal of Personality Assessment, 77*, 128–138.

Lahey, B. B. (2009). Public health significance of neuroticism. *American Psychologist, 64*, 241–256.

Laing, R. D. (1969). *Self and others* (2nd ed.). New York, NY: Pantheon.

Lambert, M. J., & Ogles, B. M. (2004). The efficacy and effectiveness of psychotherapy. In M. J. Lambert (Ed.), *Bergin and Garfield's handbook of psychotherapy and behavior change* (5th ed., pp. 139–193). New York, NY: Wiley.

Larsen, R. J., & Diener, E. (1987). Affect intensity as an individual difference characteristic: A review. *Journal of Research in Personality, 21*, 1–39.

Larsen, R. J., & Ketelaar, T. (1991). Personality and susceptibility to positive and negative emotional states. *Journal of Personality and Social Psychology, 61*, 132–140.

Lassri, D., & Shahar, G. (2012). Self-criticism mediates the link between childhood emotional maltreatment on young adults' romantic relationships. *Journal of Social and Clinical Psychology, 31*, 618–640.

Layne, J., Porcerelli, J. H., & Shahar, G. (2006). Psychotherapy of self-criticism in a woman with "mixed" anaclitic-introjective depression. *Clinical Case Studies, 5*, 421–436.

Leadbeater, B. J., Kuperminc, G. P., Blatt, S. J., & Herzog, C. (1999). A multivariate model of gender differences in adolescents' internalizing and externalizing problems. *Developmental Psychology, 35*, 1268–1282.

Leahy, R. L. (2008). The therapeutic relationship in cognitive-behavioral therapy. *Behavioural and Cognitive Psychotherapy, 36*, 769–777.

LeDoux, J. (2003). The self, clues from the brain. *Annual New York Academy of Science, 1001*, 295–304

Lerman, S. F., Rudich, Z., Brill, S., & Shahar, G. *Self-criticism interacts with the affective component of pain to predict depressive symptoms in female patients*. Manuscript under review.

Lerman, S. F., Shahar, G., & Rudich, Z. (2012). Self-criticism interacts with the affective component of pain to predict depressive symptoms in female patients. *European Journal of Pain, 16*, 115–122.

Lerner, R. M. (1982). Children and adolescents as producers of their own development. *Developmental Review, 2*, 342–370.

Lesch, K. P., Bengel, D., Heils, A., Sabol, S. Z., Greenberg, B. D., Petri, S., . . . & Levenson, E. (2005). *The fallacy of understanding.* Hillsdale, NJ: Analytic Press.

Levenson, E. A. (1972). *The fallacy of understanding.* New York, NY: Basic.

Levenson, E. A. (1991). *The purloined self.* New York, NY: Contemporary Psychoanalysis Books.

Levy, K. N., Edell, W., Blatt, S. J., Becker, D. R., Kolligan, J., & McGlashan, T. (1994). *The relationship of anaclitic dependency and self-criticism to personality pathology.* Unpublished manuscript, Yale University.

Lewinsohn, P., Rohde, P., Seeley, J., & Fischer, S. (1993). Age-cohort changes in the lifetime occurrence of depression and other mental disorders. *Journal of Abnormal Psychology, 102,* 110–120.

Lewinsohn, P. M., Steinmetz, J. L., Larson, D. W., & Franklin, J. (1981). Depression related cognitions: Antecedents or consequences? *Journal of Abnormal Psychology, 3,* 213–219.

Lieberman, M. D. (2007). Social cognitive neuroscience: A review of core processes. *Annual Review of Psychology, 58,* 259–289.

Linehan, M. M., Goodstein, J. L., Nielsen, S. L., & Chiles, J. A. (1983). Reasons for staying alive when you are thinking of killing yourself: The Reasons for Living Inventory. *Journal of Consulting and Clinical Psychology, 51,* 276–286.

Linville, P. W. (1987). Self-complexity as a cognitive buffer against stress-related illness and depression. *Journal of Personality and Social Psychology, 52,* 663–676.

Little, B. R. (1999). Personal projects and social ecology: Themes and variations across the life span. In J. Brandtstadter & R. M. Lerner (Eds.), *Action and self-development: Theory and research through the life span* (pp. 169–220). Thousand Oaks, CA: Sage.

Longe, O., Maratos, F. A., Gilbert, P., Evans, G., Volker, F., Rockliff, H., & Rippon, G. (2010). Having a word with yourself: Neural correlates of self-criticism and self-reassurance. *NeuroImage, 49,* 1849–1856.

Longmore, R. J., & Worrell, M. (2007). Do we need to challenge thoughts in cognitive behavior therapy? *Clinical Psychology Review, 27,* 173–187.

Luciano, J. V., Sabes-Figuera, R., Cardenosa, E., Penarrubia-María, M. T., Fernandez-Vergel, R., García-Campayo, J., . . . & Serrano-Blanco, A. (2013). Cost-utility of a psychoeducational intervention in fibromyalgia patients compared with usual care: An economic evaluation alongside a 12-month randomized controlled trial. *Clinical Journal of Pain, 29,* 702–711.

Lukas, E. (1981). New ways for dereflection. *International Forum for Logotherapy, 4,* 13–28.

Lukens, E. P., & McFarlane, W. R. (2004). Psychoeducation as evidence-based practice: Considerations for practice, research, and policy. *Brief Treatment and Crisis Intervention, 4,* 205–225.

Luszczynska, A., Benight, C. C., & Cieslak, R. (2009). Self-efficacy and health-related outcomes of collective trauma: A systematic review. *European Psychologist, 14,* 49–60.

Luszczynska, A., Gutiérrez-Doña, B., & Schwarzer, R. (2005). General self-efficacy in various domains of human functioning: Evidence from five countries. *International Journal of Psychology, 40,* 80–89.

Luszczynska, A., Sarkar, Y., & Knoll, N. (2007). Received social support, self-efficacy, and finding benefits in disease as predictors of physical functioning and adherence to antiretroviral therapy. *Patient Education and Counseling, 66,* 37–42.

Luyten, P., & Blatt, S. (2011). Integrating theory-driven and empirically-derived models of personality development and psychopathology: A proposal for DSM V. *Clinical Psychology Review, 31,* 52–68.

Luyten, P., & Blatt, S. J. (2013). Interpersonal relatedness and self-definition in normal and disrupted personality development. *American Psychologist, 68,* 172–183.

Luyten, P., Kempe, S., Van Wambeke, P., Cales, S., Blatt, S. J., & Van Houdenhove, B. (2011). Self-critical perfectionism, stress generation, and stress sensitivity in patients with chronic fatigue syndrome: Relationships with severity of depression. *Psychiatry: Interpersonal and Biological Processes, 74,* 21–30.

Lynch, F. L., & Clarke, G. N. (2006). Estimating the economic burden of depression in children and adolescents. *American Journal of Preventive Medicine, 31,* 143–151.

Lysaker, P. H., & Hermans, H. J. M. (2007). The dialogical self in psychotherapy for persons with schizophrenia: A case study. *Journal of Clinical Psychology, 63*, 129–139.

Ma, Y., Li, B., Wang, C., Shi, Z., Sun, Y., Sheng, F., . . . & Han, S. (2013). HTTLPR polymorphism modulates neural mechanisms of negative self-reflection. *Cerebral Cortex.* doi:10.1093/scan/nss103

MacLeod, C. M. (1979). Individual differences in learning and memory: A unitary information processing approach. *Journal of Research in Personality, 13*, 530–545.

Maltby, J., & Day, L. (2000). Depressive symptoms and religious orientation: Examining the relationship between religiosity and depression within the context of other correlates of depression. *Personality and Individual Differences, 28*, 383–393.

Manickaraj, A. K., & Mital, S. (2012). Personalized medicine in pediatric cardiology: Do little changes make a big difference? *Current Opinion in Pediatrics, 24*, 584–591.

Mann, J. (1973). *Time-limited psychotherapy.* Cambridge, MA: Harvard University Press.

Marcia, J. E. (1966). Development and validation of ego identity status. *Journal of Personality and Social Psychology, 3*, 551–558.

Markus, H. R., & Kitayama, S. (1991). Culture and the self: Implications for cognition, emotion, and motivation. *Psychological Review, 98*, 224–253.

Markus, H. R., & Nurius, P. (1986). Possible selves. *American Psychologist, 41*, 954–969.

Marshall, M. B., Zuroff, D. C., McBride, C., & Bagby, R. M. (2008). Self-criticism predicts differential response to treatment for major depression? *Journal of Clinical Psychology, 64*, 231–244.

Martin, Y., Gilbert, P., McEwan, K., & Irons, C. (2006). The relation of entrapment, shame, and guilt to depression in carers of people with dementia. *Aging and Mental Health, 10*, 101–106.

Marx, B. P., Heidt, J. M., & Gold, S. D. (2005). Perceived uncontrollability and unpredictability, self-regulation, and sexual revictimization. *Review of General Psychology, 9*, 67–90.

Maser, J. D., & Cloninger, R. C. (Eds.) (1990). *Comorbidity of mood and anxiety disorders.* Washington, DC: American Psychiatric Press.

Maslach, C., Schaufeli, W. B., & Leiter, M. P. (2001). Job burnout. *Annual Review of Psychology, 52*, 397–422.

Maslow, A. (1968). *Toward a psychology of being* (2nd ed.). Princeton, NJ: Van Nostrand.

Masten, A. S. (2014). *Ordinary magic: Resilience in development.* New York, NY: Guilford.

Masten, A. S., & Tellegen, A. (2012). Resilience in developmental psychopathology: Contributions of the Project Competence Longitudinal Study. *Development and Psychopathology, 24*, 345–361.

Masten, A. S., & Wright, M. O'D. (2009). Resilience over the lifespan: Developmental perspectives on resistance, recovery, and transformation. In J. W. Reich, A. J. Zautra, & J. S. Hall (Eds.), *Handbook of adult resilience* (pp. 213–237). New York, NY: Guilford.

Mathews, A., & MacLeod, C. (2005). Cognitive vulnerability to emotional disorders. *Annual Review in Clinical Psychology, 1*, 167–195.

Matsuda, A., Yamaoka, K., Tango, T., Matsuda, T., & Nishimoto, H. (2014). Effectiveness of psychoeducational support on quality of life in early-stage breast cancer patients: A systematic review and meta-analysis of randomized controlled trials. *Quality of Life Research, 23*, 21–30.

Matto, H., & Realo, A. (2001). The Estonian Self-Concept Clarity Scale: Psychometric properties and personality correlates. *Personality and Individual Differences, 30*, 59–70.

May, R. (1958). *Existence: A new dimension in psychiatry and psychology.* New York, NY: Basic.

McAdams, D. P. (2013). The psychological self as actor, agent, and author. *Perspectives in Psychological Science, 8*, 272–295.

McBridge, C., Zuroff, D. C., Bacchiochi, J., & Bagby, R. M. (2006). Depressive Experiences Questionnaire: Does it measure maladaptive and adaptive forms of dependency? *Social Behavior and Personality, 34*, 1–16.

McConnell, A. R. (2011). The multiple self-aspects framework: Self-concept representation and its implications. *Personality and Social Psychology Review, 15*, 3–27.

McCormick, M. P., O'Connor, E. E., Cappella, E., & McClowry, S. G. (2013). Teacher-child relationships and academic achievement: A multilevel propensity score model approach. *Journal of School Psychology, 51*, 611–624.

McCrae, R. R., & John, O. P. (1992). An introduction to the Five-Factor Model and its applications. *Journal of Personality, 60*, 175–215.

McCranie, E. W., & Bass, J. D. (1984). Childhood family antecedents of dependency and self-criticism: Implications for depression. *Journal of Abnormal Psychology, 93*, 3–8.

McCullough, J. P., Klein, D. N., Keller, M., Holzer, C. E., III., Davis, S. M., Kornstein, S. G., . . . & Harrison, W. M. (2000). Comparison of DSM-III-R chronic depression and major depression superimposed on dysthymia (double depression): Validity of the distinction. *Journal of Abnormal Psychology, 109*, 419–427.

McCullough, L. (1997). *Changing character: Short-term anxiety regulating psychotherapy for restructuring defenses, affect, and attachment.* New York, NY: Basic.

McEwen, W. S. (1998). Stress, adaptation and disease. *Annual New York Academy of Science, 840*, 33–44.

McFarland, L., Barlow, J., & Turner, A. (2009). Understanding metaphor to facilitate emotional expression during a chronic disease self-management course. *Patient Education and Counseling, 77*, 255–259.

McFarlane, W. R., Dixon, L., Lukens, E., & Lucksted, A. (2003). Family psychoeducation and schizophrenia: A review of the literature. *Journal of Marital and Family Therapy, 29*, 223–245.

McGregor, H., Lieberman, J. D., Solomon, S., Greenberg, J., Arndt, J., Simon, L., & Pyszczynski, T. (1998). Terror management and aggression: Evidence that mortality salience motivates aggression against worldview threatening others. *Journal of Personality and Social Psychology, 74*, 590–605.

McLachlan, S., & Hagger, M. S. (2010). Effects of an autonomy-supportive intervention on tutor behaviors in a higher education context. *Teaching and Teacher Education, 26*, 1205–1211.

McLaughlin, K. A., & Nolen-Hoeksema, S. (2011). Rumination as a transdiagnostic factor in depression and anxiety. *Behaviour Research and Therapy, 49*, 186–193.

Mead, G. H. (1934). *Mind, self, and society.* Chicago, IL: University of Chicago Press.

Meichenbaum, D. H. (1977). *Cognitive behavior modification: An integrative approach.* New York, NY: Plenum.

Miranda, R., & Nolen-Hoeksema, S. (2007). Brooding and reflection: Rumination predicts suicidal ideation at 1-year follow-up in a community sample. *Behaviour Research and Therapy, 45*, 3088–3095.

Mitchell, S. A. (1988). *Relational concepts in psychoanalysis.* Cambridge, MA: Harvard University Press.

Mitchell, S. A. (1990). *Hope and dread in psychoanalysis.* New York, NY: Basic.

Mitchell, S. A. (1995). Interaction in the Kleinian and interpersonal traditions. *Contemporary Psychoanalysis, 59*, 65–91.

Mitchell, S. A., & Black, M. J. (1995). *Freud and beyond: A history of modern psychoanalytic thought.* New York, NY: Basic.

Mittelstaedt, W., & Tasca, G. (1988). Contraindications in clinical psychology training: A trainee's perspective of the Boulder Model. *Professional Psychology: Research and Practice, 19*, 353–355.

Mongrain, M. (1998). Parental representations and support-seeking behaviors related to dependency and self-criticism. *Journal of Personality, 66*, 151–173.

Mongrain, M. (2014). Compassion, happiness and self-esteem. In A. C. Michalos (Ed.), *Encyclopedia of quality of life research* (pp. 1129–1133). Dordrecht, The Netherlands: Springer.

Mongrain, M., & Blackburn, S. (2006). Cognitive vulnerability, lifetime risk, and recurrence of major depression in graduate students. *Cognitive Therapy and Research, 29*, 747–768.

Mongrain, M., & Leather, F. (2006). Immature dependency and self-criticism predict the recurrence of major depression. *Journal of Clinical Psychology, 62*, 705–713.

Mongrain, M., Vettese, L. C., Shuster, B., & Kendal, N. (1998). Perceptual biases, affect, and behavior in the relationships of dependents and self-critics. *Journal of Personality and Social Psychology, 75,* 230–241.

Monroe, S. M., & Reid, M. W. (2009). Life stress and major depression. *Current Directions in Psychological Science, 18,* 68–72.

Monroe, S. M., & Simons, A. D. (1991). Diathesis-stress theories in the context of life stress research: Implications for the depressive disorders. *Psychological Bulletin, 110,* 406–425.

Monsell, S. (2003). Task switching. *Trends on Cognitive Sciences, 7,* 134–140.

Moos, R. H. (1990). Depressed outpatients' life context, amount of treatment, and treatment outcome. *Journal of Nervous and Mental Disease, 178,* 105–112.

Mor, N., & Winquist, J. (2002). Self-focused attention and negative affect: A meta-analysis. *Psychological Bulletin, 128,* 638–662.

Morse, J. Q., Robins, C. J., & Gittes-Fox, M. (2002). Sociotropy, autonomy, and personality disorder criteria in psychiatric patients. *Journal of Personality Disorders, 16,* 549–560.

Moussavi, S., Chatterji, S., Verdes, E., Tandon, A., Patel, V., & Ustun, B. (2007). Depression, chronic diseases and decrements in health: Results from the World Health Surveys. *Lancet, 370,* 851–858.

Muller, J. P. (1999). Consultation from the position of the third. *American Journal of Psychoanalysis, 59,* 113–118.

Murray, S. L., Holmes, J. G., Dolderman, D., & Griffin, D. W. (2000). What the motivated mind sees: Comparing friends' perspectives to married partners' views of each other. *Journal of Experimental Social Psychology, 36,* 600–620.

Nathan, P. E. (2000). The Boulder Model: A dream deferred or lost? *American Psychologist, 55,* 250–252.

Needles, D., & Abramson, L. Y. (1990). Positive life events, attributional style, and hopefulness: Testing a model of recovery from depression. *Journal of Abnormal Psychology, 99,* 156–165.

Newton, I. (1959). *The correspondence of Isaac Newton: Vol. 1:1661-1675.* Ed. H. W. Turnbull. Cambridge: Cambridge University Press.

Nietzel, M. T., & Harris, M. J. (1990). Relationship of dependency and achievement/autonomy to depression. *Clinical Psychology Review, 10,* 279–297.

Nisbett, R. E., Peng, K., Choi, I., & Norenzayan, A. (2001). Culture and systems of thought: Holistic versus analytic cognition. *Psychological Review, 108,* 291–310.

Nolen-Hoeksema, S. (1990). *Sex differences in depression.* Stanford, CA: Stanford University Press.

Nolen-Hoeksema, S. (1991). Responses to depression and their effects on the duration of depressive episodes. *Journal of Abnormal Psychology, 100,* 569–582.

Nolen-Hoeksema, S. (2000). The role of rumination in depressive disorders and mixed anxiety/depressive symptoms. *Journal of Abnormal Psychology, 109,* 504–511.

Nolen-Hoeksema, S., & Davis, C. G. (1999). Thanks for sharing that: Ruminators and their social support networks. *Journal of Personality and Social Psychology, 77,* 801–814.

Nolen-Hoeksema, S., Larson, J., & Grayson, C. (1999). Explaining the gender difference in depressive symptoms. *Journal of Personality and Social Psychology, 77,* 1061–1072.

Nolen-Hoeksema, S., & Morrow, J. (1991). A prospective study of depression and posttraumatic stress symptoms after a natural disaster: The 1989 Loma Prieta earthquake. *Journal of Personality & Social Psychology, 61*(1), 115–121.

Nolen-Hoeksema, S., Morrow, J., & Fredrickson, B. L. (1993). Response styles and the duration of episodes of depressed mood. *Journal of Abnormal Psychology, 102,* 20–28.

Nolen-Hoeksema, S., Parker, L. E., & Larson, J. (1994). Ruminative coping with depressed mood following loss. *Journal of Personality and Social Psychology, 67,* 92–104.

Nolen-Hoeksema, S., Stice, E., Wade, E., & Bohon, C. (2007). Reciprocal relations between rumination and bulimic, substance abuse, and depressive symptoms in female adolescents. *Journal of Abnormal Psychology, 116,* 198–207.

Noll, J. G. (2005). Does childhood sexual abuse set in motion a cycle of violence against women? What we know and what we need to learn. *Journal of Interpersonal Violence, 20,* 455–462.

Norcross, J. C., & Goldfried, M. R. (Eds.). (2005). *Handbook of psychotherapy integration* (2nd ed.). New York, NY: Oxford University Press.

Northoff, G. (2007). Psychopathology and pathophysiology of the self in depression: Neuropsychiatric hypothesis. *Journal of Affective Disorders, 204*, 1–14.

Northoff, G., & Bermpohl, F. (2004). Cortical midline structures and the self. *Trends in Cognitive Sciences, 8*, 102–107.

Northoff, G., Heinzel, A., de Greck, M., Bermpohl, F., Dobrowolny, H., & Panksepp, J. (2006). Self-referential processing in our brain—A meta-analysis of imaging studies on the self. *NeuroImage, 31*(1), 440–457.

Noyman-Veksler, G., Weinberg, D., Fennig, S., Davidson, L., & Shahar, G. (2013). Perceived stigma exposure in schizophrenia: The key role of self-concept clarity. *Self and Identity, 12*, 663–674.

O'Connor, E. E., Dearing, E., & Collins, B. A. (2011). Teacher-child relationship and behavior problem trajectories in elementary school. *American Educational Research Journal, 48*, 120–162.

O'Connor, R., & Noyce, R. (2008). Personality and cognitive processes: Self-criticism and different types of rumination as predictors of suicide ideation. *Behaviour Research and Therapy, 46*, 392–401.

Ogden, P., Minton, K., & Pain, C. (2006). *Trauma and the body: A sensorimotor approach to psychotherapy.* New York, NY: Norton.

Ogden, T. H. (1994). The analytic third: Working with intersubjective clinical facts. *International Journal of Psycho-Analysis, 75*, 3–20.

Ogden, T. H. (1997). Reverie and metaphor: Some thoughts on how I work as a psychoanalyst. *International Journal of Psychoanalysis, 78*, 719–732.

Ogden, T. H. (1999). "The music of what happens" in poetry and psychoanalysis. *International Journal of Psychoanalysis, 80*, 979–994.

Oman, D., Thoresen, C. E., & McMahon, K. (1999). Volunteerism and mortality among the community-dwelling elderly. *Journal of Health Psychology, 4*, 301–316.

Orth, U., & Robins, R. W. (2014). Understanding the link between low self-esteem and depression. *Current Directions in Psychological Science, 22*, 455–460.

Orth, U., Robins, R. W., & Meier, L. L. (2009). Disentangling the effects of low self-esteem and stressful events on depression: Findings from three longitudinal studies. *Journal of Personality and Social Psychology, 97*, 307–321.

Orth, U., Robins, R. W., & Roberts, B. W. (2008). Low self-esteem prospectively predicts depression in adolescence and young adulthood. *Journal of Personality and Social Psychology, 95*, 695–708.

Ostry, A., & Nathoo, T. (2009). *The one best way? Breastfeeding history, politics, and policy in Canada.* Waterloo, Canada: Wilfrid Laurier University Press.

O'Sullivan, J. J., & Quevillon, R. P. (1992). 40 years later: Is the Boulder Model still alive? *American Psychologist, 47*, 67–70.

Ouimette, P. C., Klein, D. N., Anderson, R., Riso, L. P., & Lizardi, H. (1994). Relationship of sociotropy/autonomy and dependency/self-criticism to *DSM-III-R* personality disorders. *Journal of Abnormal Psychology, 103*, 743–749.

Pagura, J., Cox, B. J., Sareen, J., & Enns, M. W. (2006). Childhood adversities associated with self-criticism in a nationally representative sample. *Personality and Individual Differences, 41*, 1287–1298.

Panksepp, J. (1998). Attention deficit hyperactivity disorders, psychostimulants, and intolerance of childhood playfulness: A tragedy in the making? *Current Directions in Psychological Science, 7*, 91–98.

Panksepp, J. (2007). Can play diminish ADHD and facilitate the construction of the social brain? *Journal of the Canadian Academy of Child and Adolescent Psychiatry, 16*, 57–66.

Panksepp, J., & Watt, D. (2011). Why does depression hurt? Ancestral primary-process separation-distress (PAnIc/GRIef) and diminished brain reward (SeeKInG) processes in the genesis of depressive affect. *Psychiatry, 74*, 5–13,

Paris, B. J. (1999). Karen Horney's vision of the self. *American Journal of Psychoanalysis, 59,* 157–166.

Parker, L. E., & Detterman, D. K. (1988). The balance between clinical and research interests among Boulder Model graduate students. *Professional Psychology: Research and Practice, 19,* 243–344.

Pearl, J. (2000). *Causality: Models, reasoning, and inference.* Cambridge, England: Cambridge University Press.

Persons, J. B. (2012). *The case formulation approach to cognitive-behavioral therapy.* New York, NY: Guilford.

Persons, J. B., & Miranda, J. (1992). Cognitive theories of vulnerability to depression: Reconciling negative evidence. *Cognitive Therapy and Research, 16,* 482–502.

Pettit, J. W., & Joiner, T. E. (2006). *Chronic depression: Interpersonal sources, therapeutic solutions.* Washington, DC: American Psychological Association.

Pezawas, L., Meyer-Lindenberg, A., Drabant, E. M., Verchinski, B. A., Munoz, K. E., Kolachana, B. S., ... & Weinberger, D. R. (2005). 5-HTTLPR polymorphism impacts human cingulate-amygdala interactions: A genetic susceptibility mechanism for depression. *Nature Neuroscience, 8,* 828–834.

Piaget, J. (1956). *The origins of intelligence in children* (trans. M. Cook). New York, NY: International University Press.

Post, S. G. (Ed.). (2007). *Altruism and health: Perspectives from empirical research.* New York, NY: Oxford University Press.

Poulin, M. J. (2014). Volunteering predicts health among those who value others: Two national studies. *Health Psychology, 33,* 120–129.

Powers, T. A., Koestner, R., Zuroff, D. C., Milyavskaya, M., & Gorin, A. A. (2011). The effects of self-criticism and self-oriented perfectionism on goal pursuit. *Personality and Social Psychology Bulletin, 37,* 964–975.

Priel, B., & Besser, A. (1999). Vulnerability to postpartum depressive symptomatology: Dependency, self-criticism, and the moderating role of antenatal attachment. *Journal of Social and Clinical Psychology, 18,* 240–253.

Priel, B., & Besser, A. (2000). Dependency and self-criticism among first-time mothers: The roles of global and specific support. *Journal of Social and Clinical Psychology, 19,* 437–450.

Priel, B., & Shahar, G. (2000). Dependency, self-criticism, social context and distress: Comparing moderating and mediating models. *Personality and Individual Differences, 28,* 515–525.

Pyszczynski, T., & Greenberg, J. (1986). Evidence for a depressive self-focusing style. *Journal of Research in Personality, 20,* 95–106.

Radloff, L. S. (1977). A self-reported depression scale for research in the general population. *Applied Psychological Measures, 1,* 385–401.

Rafaeli, E., Bernstein, D. P., & Young, J. (2010). *Schema therapy: Distinctive features.* New York, NY: Taylor & Francis.

Rafaeli-Mor, E., & Steinberg, J. (2002). Self-complexity and well-being: A review and research synthesis. *Personality and Social Psychology Review, 6*(1), 31–58.

Rameson, L. T., Satpute, A. B., & Lieberman, M. D. (2010). The neural correlates of implicit and explicit self-relevant processing, *NeuroImage, 50,* 701–708.

Rank, O. (1968). *Will therapy and truth and reality.* New York, NY: Alfred Knopf.

Rector, N. A., Bagby, R. M., Segal, Z. V., Joffe, R. T., & Levitt, A. (2000). Self-criticism and dependency in depressed patients treated with cognitive therapy or pharmacotherapy. *Cognitive Therapy and Research, 24,* 571–584.

Reeve, J. (1998). Autonomy support as an interpersonal motivating style: Is it teachable? *Contemporary Educational Psychology, 23,* 312–330.

Rege, M., Telle, K., & Votruba, M. (2011). Parental job loss and children's school performance. *Review of Economic Studies, 78,* 1462–1489.

Regev, R., Shahar, G., & Lipsitz, J. (2012). Is social self-criticism a unique dimension of vulnerability to social anxiety and depressive symptoms? *International Journal of Cognitive Psychotherapy, 5,* 211–218.

Reich, A. (1960). Pathologic forms of self-esteem regulation. *Psychoanalytic Study of the Child, 15,* 214–232.

Reisman, J. M. (1976). *A history of clinical psychology.* New York, NY: Irvington.

Reiss, D., Plomin, R., Neiderhiser, J. M., & Hetherington, E. M. (2003). *The relationship code: Deciphering genetic and social influences on adolescent development.* Cambridge, MA: Harvard University Press.

Risch, N., Herrell, R., Lehner, T., Liang, K. Y., Eaves, L., Hoh, J., ... & Merikangas, K. R. (2009). Interaction between the serotonin transporter gene (5-HTTLPR), stressful life events, and risk of depression: a meta-analysis. *Journal of the American Medical Association, 301,* 2462–2471.

Riskind, J. H., Rector, N. A., & Taylor, S. (2012). Looming cognitive vulnerability to anxiety and its reduction in psychotherapy. *Journal of Psychotherapy Integration, 22,* 137–162.

Roberts, B. W., Kuncel, N. R., Shiner, R., Caspi, A., & Goldberg, L. R. (2007). The power of personality: The competitive validity of personality traits, socioeconomic status, and cognitive ability for predicting important life outcomes. *Perspectives on Psychological Science, 2,* 313–345.

Roberts, J. E., & Monroe, S. E. (1998). Vulnerable self-esteem and social processes in depression: Toward an interpersonal model of self-esteem regulation. In T. E. Joiner, Jr., & J. C. Coyne (Eds.), *The interactional nature of depression* (pp. 149–187). Washington, DC: American Psychological Association.

Robins, C. J. (1995). Personality-event interaction models of depression. *European Journal of Personality, 9,* 367–378.

Robins, C. J., Ladd, J. S., Welkowitz, J., Blaney, P. H., Diaz, R., & Kutcher, G. (1994). The Personal Style Inventory: Preliminary validation studies of a new measure of sociotropy and autonomy. *Journal of Psychopathology and Behavioral Assessment, 16,* 277–300.

Rogers, C. (1951). *Client-centered therapy: Its current practice, implications and theory.* London, England: Constable.

Rogers, C. (1959). A theory of therapy, personality and interpersonal relationships as developed in the client-centered framework. In S. Koch (Ed.), *Psychology: A study of a science. Vol. 3: Formulations of the person and the social context.* New York, NY: McGraw Hill.

Rogers, C. (1961). *On becoming a person: A therapist's view of psychotherapy.* London, England: Constable.

Rogers, C. (1962). Toward becoming a fully functioning person. In A. B. Comb (Ed.), *Perceiving, behaving, and becoming: A new focus for education.* Washington, DC: Association for Supervision and Curriculum Development.

Rogers, C. (1963). The actualizing tendency in relation to "motives" and to consciousness. In M. Jones (Ed.), *Nebraska symposium on motivation* (Vol. 2, pp. 1–24). Lincoln, NE: University of Nebraska Press.

Rogers, C. (1967). The conditions of change from a client-centered viewpoint. In B. Berenson & R. Carkhuff (Eds.), *Sources of gain in counseling and psychotherapy* (pp. 71–85). New York, NY: Holt, Rinehart, & Winston.

Roiser, J. P., Elliott, R., & Sahakian, B. J. (2012). Cognitive mechanisms of treatment in depression. *Neuropsychopharmacology Reviews, 37,* 117–136.

Rollins, J. (2002). AIDS, law and the rhetoric of sexuality. *Law and Society Review, 36,* 161–191.

Rosenberg, M. (1959). *Conceiving the self.* New York, NY: Basic.

Rosenberg, M. (1965). *Society and the adolescent self-image.* Princeton, NJ: Princeton University Press.

Rosenman, S. (2008). Metaphor, meaning and psychiatry. *Australasian Psychiatry, 16,* 391–396.

Rothbart, M. K. (2011). *Becoming who we are: Temperament and personality in development.* New York, NY: Guilford.

Rothbart, M. K., & Bates, J. E. (1998). Temperament. In W. Damon & N. Eisenberg (Eds.), *Handbook of child psychology: Vol. 3. Social, emotional and personality development* (5th ed., pp. 105–176). New York, NY: Wiley.

Rubin, Z. (1975). Disclosing oneself to a stranger: Reciprocity and its limits. *Journal of Experimental Social Psychology, 11*, 233–260.

Rudd, M. D., & Joiner, T. (1997). Countertransference and the therapeutic relationship: A cognitive perspective. *Journal of Cognitive Psychotherapy: An International Quarterly, 11*, 231–250.

Rudd, M. D., Joiner, T., & Rajab, M. H. (1999). The relationship between suicide ideators, attempters, and multiple attempters in a young adults sample. *Journal of Abnormal Psychology, 105*(4), 541–550.

Rudd, M. D., Joiner, T., & Rajab, M. H. (2001). *Treating suicidal behavior: An effective, time-limited approach.* New York, NY: Guilford.

Rude, S. S., & Burnham, B. L. (1993). Do interpersonal and achievement vulnerabilities interact with congruent events to predict depression? Comparison of DEQ, SAS, DAS, and combined scales. *Cognitive Therapy and Research, 17*, 531–548.

Rudich, Z., Lerman, S. F., Gurevich, B., & Shahar, G. (2010). Pain specialists' evaluation of patients' prognosis during the first visit predicts subsequent depression and the affective pain dimension. *Pain Medicine, 11*, 446–452.

Rudich, Z., Lerman, S. F., Wexler, N., Gurevitch, B., & Shahar, G. (2008). Self-criticism is a stronger predictor of physician's evaluation of prognosis than pain severity and diagnosis. *Journal of Pain, 9*, 210–216.

Rushworth, M. F., Noonan, M. P., Boorman, E. D., Walton, M. E., & Behrens, T. E. (2011). Frontal cortex and reward-guided learning and decision-making. *Neuron, 70*, 1054–1069.

Russell, J. A., Bachorowski, J. A., & Fernández-Dols, J. M. (2003). Facial and vocal expressions of emotion. *Annual Review of Psychology, 54*, 329–349.

Ryan, R. M., & Deci, E. L. (2000a). Intrinsic and extrinsic motivations: Classic definitions and new directions. *Contemporary Educational Psychology, 25*, 24–67. doi:10.1006/ceps.1999.1020, available online at http://www.idealibrary.com

Ryan, R. M., & Deci, E. L. (2000b). Self-determination theory and the facilitation of intrinsic motivation, social development, and well-being. *American Psychologist, 55*, 68–78.

Rychlak, J. (1977). *The psychology of rigorous humanism.* New York, NY: Wiley.

Ryder, A. G., McBride, C., & Bagby, R. M. (2008). The association of affiliation and achievement personality styles to DSM-IV personality disorders. *Journal of Personality Disorders, 22*, 208–216.

Ryff, C. D. (1989). Happiness is everything, or is it? Explorations on the meaning of psychological well-being. *Journal of Personality and Social Psychology, 57*, 1069–1081.

Ryff, C. D., & Singer, B. H. (2008). Know thyself and become what you are: A eudaimonic approach to psychological well-being. *Journal of Happiness Studies, 9*, 13–39.

Sachs-Ericsson, N., Verona, E., Joiner, T., & Preacher, K. J. (2006). Parental verbal abuse and the mediating role of self-criticism in adult internalizing disorders. *Journal of Affective Disorders, 93*, 71–78.

Safran, J. D. (1995). *Psychoanalysis and Buddhism: An unfolding dialogue.* Somerville, MA: Wisdom Publications.

Safran, J. D., & Muran, J. C. (2000). *Negotiating the therapeutic alliance: A relational treatment guide.* New York, NY: Guilford.

Salovey, P. (1992). Mood-induced self-focused attention. *Journal of Personality and Social Psychology, 62*, 699–707.

Sameroff, A. J. (Ed.). (2009). *The transactional model of development: How children and contexts shape each other.* Washington, DC: American Psychological Association.

Samuelson, P. A. (1948). Consumption theory in terms of revealed preference. *Economica, 15*, 243–253.

Sartre, J-P. (1939). *Intentionality: A fundamental idea of Husserl's phenomenology* (trans. Joseph Fell). Retrieved from http://www.mccoyspace.com/nyu/12_s/anarchy/texts/03-Jean-Paul_Sartre-Intentionality.pdf.

Sartre, J-P. (1944). *No exit.* http://www.vanderbilt.edu/olli/class-materials/Jean-Paul_Sartre.pdf.

Satir, V. (1978). *Your many faces.* Berkeley, CA: Celestrial Arts.

Schafer, R. (1968). *Aspects of internalization.* Madison, CT: International Universities Press.

Schanche, E. (2013). The transdiagnostic phenomenon of self-criticism. *Psychotherapy, 50,* 316–321.

Schiller, M., Hammen, C., & Shahar, G. *Self, stress, and symptoms in young adulthood: Strong support for psychopathological scarring in Israeli freshmen.* Manuscript in preparation.

Schneider, K. J. (2007). *Existential-integrative psychotherapy: Guidepost to the core of practice.* London, England: Routledge.

Schutte, N. S., Malouff, J. M., & Thorsteinsson, E. B. (2013). Increasing emotional intelligence through training: Current status and future directions. *International Journal of Emotional Education, 5,* 56–72.

Schwarzer, R., & Jerusalem, M. (1995). Generalized self-efficacy scale. In J. Weinman, S. Wright, & M. Johnston (Eds.), *Measures in health psychology: A user's portfolio. Causal and control beliefs* (pp. 35–37). Windsor, England: NFER-Nelson.

Segal, Z. V., & Ingram, R. E. (1994). Mood priming and construct activation in tests of cognitive vulnerability to unipolar depression. *Clinical Psychology Review, 14,* 663–695.

Seligman, M. E. P. (1990). Why is there so much depression today? The waxing of the individual and the waning of the commons. In R. E. Ingram (Ed.), *Contemporary psychological approaches to depression: Theory, research, and treatment* (pp. 1–9). New York, NY: Plenum.

Seligman, M. E. P., Railton, P., Baumeister, R. F., & Sripada, C. (2013). Navigating into the future or driven by the past. *Perspectives in Psychological Science, 8,* 119–141.

Sen, S., Burmeister, M., & Ghosh, D. (2004). Meta-analysis of the association between a serotonin transporter promoter polymorphism (5-HTTLPR) and anxiety-related personality traits. *American Journal of Medical Genetics, 127,* 85–89.

Sengstock, M. C., McFarland, M., & Hwalek, M. A. (1990). Identification of elder abuse in institutional settings: Required changes in existing protocols. *Journal of Elder Abuse and Neglect, 2,* 31–50.

Shahar, B., Carlin, E. R., Engle, D. E., Hegde, J., Szepsenwol, O., & Arkowitz, H. (2012). A pilot investigation of emotion-focused two-chair dialogue intervention for self-criticism. *Clinical Psychology and Psychotherapy, 19,* 496–507.

Shahar, B., Szsepsenwol, O., Zilcha-Mano, S., Haim, N., Zamir, O., Levi-Yeshuvi, S., & Levit-Binnun, N. (2014). A wait-list randomized controlled trial of Loving-Kindness Meditation programme for self-criticism. *Clinical Psychology and Psychotherapy.* doi:10.1002/cpp.1893 [Epub ahead of print].

Shahar, G. (2001). Personality, shame, and the breakdown of social ties: The voice of quantitative depression research. *Psychiatry: Interpersonal and Biological Processes, 64,* 229–238.

Shahar, G. (2004). Transference-countertransference: Where the (political) action is. *Journal of Psychotherapy Integration, 14,* 371–396.

Shahar, G. (2006a). Clinical action: Introduction to the special section on the action perspective in clinical psychology. *Journal of Clinical Psychology, 29,* 1053–1064.

Shahar, G. (2006b). An investigation of the perfectionism/self-criticism dimension of the Personal Styles Inventory. *Cognitive Therapy and Research, 30,* 185–200.

Shahar, G. (2008). What measure of interpersonal dependency predicts changes in social support? *Journal of Personality Assessment, 90,* 61–65.

Shahar, G. (2010). Poetics, pragmatics, schematics, and the psychoanalysis-research dialogue (rift). *Psychoanalytic Psychotherapy, 24,* 315–328.

Shahar, G. (2011). Projectuality vs. eventuality: Sullivan, the ambivalent intentionalist. *Journal of Psychotherapy Integration, 21,* 211–220.

Shahar, G. (2012). "I don't want to be here": Projectuality and eventuality in Ms. T's case. *Journal of Psychotherapy Integration, 22,* 27–32.

Shahar, G. (2013a). The heroic self: Conceptualization, measurement, and role in distress. *International Journal of Cognitive Psychotherapy, 6,* 248–264.

Shahar, G. (2013b). An integrative psychotherapist's account of his focus in the treatment of self-critical patients. *Psychotherapy, 50,* 322–325.

Shahar, G. (2015). Object relations theory. In R. Cautin & S. Lillinfeld (Eds.), *Encyclopedia of clinical psychology.* New York, NY: Wiley.

Shahar, G., Bar-Hamburger, R., & Meyer, T. D. *Role of depressive personality style and substance use among Israeli young adults.* Manuscript in preparation.

Shahar, G., & Blatt, S. J. (2005). Benevolent interpersonal schemas facilitate therapeutic change: Further analysis of the Menninger Psychotherapy Research Project. *Psychotherapy Research, 15,* 345–349.

Shahar, G., Blatt, S. J., & Ford, R. Q. (2003). Mixed anaclitic-introjective psychopathology in treatment-resistant inpatients undergoing psychoanalytic psychotherapy. *Psychoanalytic Psychology, 20,* 84–102.

Shahar, G., Blatt, S. J., & Zuroff, D. C. (2007). Satisfaction with social relationships buffers against the adverse effect of (mid-level) self-critical perfectionism on outcome in brief treatment for depression. *Journal of Social and Clinical Psychology, 26,* 540–555.

Shahar, G., Blatt, S. J., Zuroff, D. C., Krupnick, J., & Sotsky, S. M. (2004). Perfectionism impedes social relations and response to brief treatment for depression. *Journal of Social and Clinical Psychology, 23,* 140–154.

Shahar, G., Blatt, S. J., Zuroff, D. C., Kuperminck, G. P., & Leadbeater, B. J. (2004). Reciprocal relations between depressive symptoms and self-criticism (but not dependency) among early adolescent girls (but not boys). *Cognitive Therapy and Research, 28,* 85–103.

Shahar, G., Blatt, S. J., Zuroff, D. C., & Pilkonis, P. A. (2003). Role of perfectionism and personality disorder features in patients' responses to brief treatment for depression. *Journal of Consulting and Clinical Psychology, 71,* 229–233.

Shahar, G., Chinman, M., Sells, D., & Davidson, L. (2003). An action model of socially disruptive behavior among patients with severe mental illness: The role of self-reported child abuse and suspiciousness-hostility. *Psychiatry: Interpersonal and Biological Processes, 66,* 42–52.

Shahar, G., Cross, L. W., & Henrich, C. C. (2004). Representations in action (Or: action models of development meet psychoanalytic conceptualizations of mental representations). *Psychoanalytic Study of the Child, 59,* 261–293.

Shahar, G., & Davidson, L. (2009). Participation-engagement: A philosophically based heuristic for prioritizing clinical interventions in the treatment of comorbid, complex, and chronic psychiatric conditions. *Psychiatry: Interpersonal and Biological Processes, 72,* 154–176.

Shahar, G., Elad-Strenger, J., & Henrich, C. C. (2012). Risky resilience and resilient risk: The key role of intentionality in an emerging dialectic. *Journal of Social and Clinical Psychology, 31,* 618–640.

Shahar, G., Gallagher, L. F., Blatt, S. J., Kuperminc, G. P., & Leadbeater, B. J. (2004). An interactive-synergetic approach to the assessment of personality vulnerability to depression: Illustration with the adolescent version of the Depressive Experiences Questionnaire. *Journal of Clinical Psychology, 60,* 605–625.

Shahar, G., & Gilboa-Shechtman, E. (2007). Depressive personality styles and social anxiety in young adults. *Journal of Cognitive Psychotherapy, 27,* 273–282.

Shahar, G., & Henrich, C. C. (2010). Do depressive symptoms erode self-esteem in early adolescence? *Self and Identity, 9,* 403–415.

Shahar, G., & Henrich, C. C. (2013). Axis of Criticism Model (ACRIM): An integrative conceptualization of person-context exchanges in vulnerability to adolescent psychopathology. *Journal of Psychotherapy Integration, 23,* 236–249.

Shahar, G., & Henrich, C. C. Further evidence for a reciprocal relationship between adolescent self-criticism and depression, this time in participants exposed to terrorism. Manuscript in preparation.

Shahar, G., Henrich, C. C., Blatt, S. J., Ryan, R., & Little, T. D. (2003). Interpersonal relatedness, self-definition, and their motivational orientation during adolescence: A theoretical and empirical integration. *Developmental Psychology, 39,* 470–483.

Shahar, G., Henrich, C. C., Winokur, A., Blatt, S. J., Kuperminc, G. P., & Leadbeater, B. J. (2006). Self-criticism and depressive symptoms interact to predict middle school academic achievement. *Journal of Clinical Psychology, 62,* 147–155.

Shahar, G., Horesh, N., & Cohen, G. (2008). Helping them get their act together: An Action Theory approach to treatment termination in personality disorders. In W. O'Donohue and M. Cucciare (Eds.), *A clinician's guide to the termination of psychotherapy* (pp. 363–381).New York: Taylor and Francis.

Shahar, G., Joiner, T. E., Jr., Zuroff, D. C., & Blatt, S. J. (2004). Personality, interpersonal behavior, and depression: Co-existence of stress-specific moderating and mediating effects. *Personality and Individual Differences, 36,* 1583–1596.

Shahar, G., Kalnitzki, E., Shulman, S., & Blatt, S. J. (2006). Personality, motivation, and the construction of goals during the transition to adulthood. *Personality and Individual Differences, 40,* 53–63.

Shahar, G., Lassri, D., & Luyten, P. (2014). Depression in chronic illness: A behavioral medicine approach. In D. Mostofsky (Ed.), *Handbook of behavioral medicine* (pp. 3–22). New York, NY: Wiley.

Shahar, G., & Lerman, S. F. (2013). The personification of chronic physical illness: Its role in adjustment and implications for psychotherapy integration. *Journal of Psychotherapy Integration, 23,* 49–58.

Shahar, G., & Porcerelli, J. H. (2006). The Action Formulation (TAF): A heuristic for clinical case formulation. *Journal of Clinical Psychology, 29,* 1115–1127.

Shahar, G., & Priel, B. (2002). Positive life events and adolescent emotional distress: In search for protective-interactive processes. *Journal of Social and Clinical Psychology, 21,* 645–668.

Shahar, G., & Priel, B. (2003). Active vulnerability, adolescent distress, and the mediating/suppressing role of life events. *Personality and Individual Differences, 35,* 199–218.

Shahar, G., & Schiller, M. (in press). Pushing further the psychotherapy integration envelope. *PsycCRITIQUES.*

Shahar, G., Soffer, N., & Gilboa-Shechtman, E. (2008). Sociotropy, autonomy, and self-criticism are three distinguishable dimensions of cognitive-personality vulnerability. *International Journal of Cognitive Psychotherapy, 22,* 219–227.

Shahar, G., Zohar, A., & Apter, A. (2007). Personality matters: A special issue in honor of Sidney J. Blatt. *Israel Journal of Psychiatry, 44,* 251–254.

Shea, M. T., Pilkonis, P. A., Beckham, E., Collins, J. F., Elkin, I., Slotsky, S. M., & Docherty, J. P. (1990). Personality disorders and treatment outcome in the NIMH Treatment of Depression Collaborative Research Program. *American Journal of Psychiatry, 147,* 711–718.

Shefler, G. (2001). *Time-limited psychotherapy in practice.* New York, NY: Brunner-Routledge.

Sheldon, K. M., Ryan, R. M., Rawsthorne, L. J., & Illardi, B. (1997). Trait self and true self: Cross-role variation in the Big-Five personality traits and its relations with psychological authenticity and subjective well-being. *Journal of Personality and Social Psychology, 73,* 1380–1393.

Shelton, S. H. (1990). Developing the construct of general self-efficacy. *Psychological Reports, 66,* 987–994.

Sheppes, G., Meiran, N., Gilboa-Shechtman, E., & Shahar, G. (2008). Cognitive mechanisms underlying implicit negative self-concept in dysphoria. *Emotion, 8,* 386–394.

Sheppes, G., Meiran, N., Spivak, O., & Shahar, G. (2010). Implicit self-concept predicts depressive symptoms under failure: A longitudinal, stress-diathesis approach. *Journal of Research in Personality, 44,* 602–609.

Sherwin, S. (2001). Feminist ethics and the metaphor of AIDS. *Journal of Medicine and Philosophy, 26*(4), 343–364.

Shoham, V., Butler, E. A., Rohrbaugh, M. J., & Trost, S. E. (2007). System-symptom fit in couples: Emotion regulation when one or both partners smoke. *Journal of Abnormal Psychology, 116*, 848–853.

Shoham, V., & Rohrbaugh, M. J. (1997). Interrupting ironic processes. *Psychological Science, 8*, 151–153.

Shoham, V., Rohrbaugh, M. J., Onken, L. S., Cuthbert, B. N., Beveridge, R. M., & Fowles, T. R. (2014). Redefining clinical science training: Purpose and products of the Delaware project. *Clinical Psychological Science, 2*, 8–21.

Shulman, S., Kalnitzki, E., & Shahar, G. (2009). Meeting developmental challenges during emerging adulthood: The role of personality and social resources. *Journal of Adolescent Research, 24*, 242–267.

Shumaker, D. (2012). An existential-integrative treatment of anxious and depressed adolescents. *Journal of Humanistic Psychology, 52*, 375–400.

Sikora, K. (2007). Personalized medicine for cancer: From molecular signature to therapeutic choice. *Advances in Cancer Research, 96*, 345–369.

Siviy, S. M., & Panksepp, J. (2011). In search of the neurobiological substrates for social playfulness in mammalian brains. *Neuroscience and Biobehavioral Reviews, 35*, 1821–1830.

Skitka, L. J., Bauman, C. W., Aramovich, N. P., & Scott Morgan, G. (2006). Confrontational and preventative policy responses to terrorism: Anger wants a fight and fear wants "them" to go away. *Basic and Applied Social Psychology, 28*, 375–384.

Sloman, L., & Price, J. S. (1987). Losing behavior (yielding subroutine) and human depression: Proximate and selective mechanisms. *Ethology and Sociobiology, 8*, 99S–109S.

Sloman, L., Price, J. S., Gilbert, P., & Gardner, R. (1994). Adaptive function of depression: Psychotherapeutic implications. *American Journal of Psychotherapy, 48*, 401–417.

Smith, J. (1999). Life planning: Anticipating future life goals and managing personal development. In J. Brandstädter & R. M. Lerner (Eds.), *Action and self-development: Theory and research through the life span* (pp. 223–255). Thousand Oaks, CA: Sage.

Snyder, M., & Swann, W. B., Jr. (1978). Hypothesis testing processes in social interaction. *Journal of Personality and Social Psychology, 36*, 1202–1212.

Soenens, B., Vansteenkiste, M., & Luyten, P. (2010). Towards a domain-specific approach to the study of parental psychological control: Distinguishing between dependency-oriented and achievement-oriented psychological control. *Journal of Personality, 78*, 217–256.

Soffer, N., Gilboa-Shechtman, E., & Shahar, G. (2008). The relationships of childhood emotional abuse and neglect to depressive vulnerability and low self-efficacy. *International Journal of Cognitive Psychotherapy, 1*, 151–162.

Soffer, N., & Shahar, G. (2007). Evidence-based mental health practice? Long live the (individual) difference. *Israel Journal of Psychiatry, 44*, 301–308.

Solberg Nes, L., Roach, A. R., & Segerstrom, S. C. (2009). Executive functions, self-regulation, and chronic pain: A review. *Annals of Behavioral Medicine, 37*, 173–183.

Solomon, Z., & Dekel, R. (2005). Posttraumatic stress disorder among Israeli exprisoners of war 18 and 30 years after release. *Journal of Clinical Psychiatry, 66*, 1031–1037.

Sontag, S. (1978). *Illness as metaphor and AIDS and its metaphors.* New York, NY: Farrar, Straus & Giroux.

Soucy-Chartier, I., & Provencher, M. D. (2013). Behavioural activation for depression: Efficacy, effectiveness and dissemination. *Journal of Affective Disorders, 145*, 292–299.

Sowislo, J. F., & Orth, U. (2013). Does low self-esteem predict depression and anxiety? A meta-analysis of longitudinal studies. *Psychological Bulletin, 139*, 213–240.

Spasojevic, J., & Alloy, L. (2001). Rumination as a common mechanism relating depressive risk factors to depression. *Emotion, 1*, 25–37.

Spence, D. P. (1982). *Narrative truth and historical truth.* New York, NY: Norton.

Starr, L. R., Hammen, C., Brennan, P. A., & Najman, J. M. (2012). Serotonin transporter gene as a predictor of stress generation in depression. *Journal of Abnormal Psychology, 121*, 810–818.

Steenbarger, B. N., Smith, H. B., & Budman, S. H. (1996). Integrating science and practice in outcomes assessment: A Boulder Model for a managed care era. *Psychotherapy, 33,* 246–253.

Sternberg, R. J. (2005). *Unity in psychology: Possibility or pipedream?* Washington, DC: American Psychological Association.

Stice, E., Shaw, H., Bohon, C., Marti, C. N., & Rohde, P. (2009). A meta-analytic review of depression prevention programs for children and adolescents: Factors that predict magnitude of intervention effects. *Journal of Consultant and Clinical Psychology, 77,* 486–503.

Stolorow, R. D., & Atwood, G. E. (1992). *Contexts of being: The intersubjective foundations of psychological life.* New York, NY: Routledge.

Stolorow, R. D., Brandshaft, B., & Atwood, G. E. (1987). *Psychoanalytic treatment: An intersubjective approach.* Hillsdale, NJ: Analytic Press.

Story, A. L. (2004). Self-esteem and self-certainty: A mediational analysis. *European Journal of Personality, 18,* 115–125.

Strenger, C. (2002). *Individuality, the impossible project.* New York, NY: Others Press.

Strenger, C. (2011). *The fear of insignificance: Searching for meaning in the twenty-first century.* New York, NY: Palgrave-Macmillan.

Stricker, G. (2000). The scientist-practitioner model: Gandhi was right again. *American Psychologist, 55,* 253–254.

Stricker, G., & Gold, J. R. (Eds.). (1993). *Comprehensive handbook of psychotherapy integration.* New York, NY: Plenum.

Stricker, G., & Trierweiler, S. J. (1995). The local clinical scientist. A bridge between science and practice. *American Psychology, 50*(12), 995–1002.

Strober, M. (2004). Managing the chronic, treatment-resistant patient with anorexia nervosa. *International Journal of Eating Disorders, 36,* 245–255.

Sturman, E. D., & Mongrain, M. (2005). Self-criticism and major depression: An evolutionary perspective. *British Journal of Clinical Psychology, 44,* 505–519.

Sturman, E. D., & Mongrain, M. (2008). The role of personality in defeat: A revised social rank model. *European Journal of Personality, 22,* 55–79.

Sullivan, H. S. (1924). *Schizophrenia as a human process.* New York, NY: Norton

Sullivan, H. S. (1953). *The interpersonal theory of psychiatry.* New York, NY: Norton.

Summers, F. (2003). The future as intrinsic to the psyche and psychoanalytic therapy. *Contemporary Psychoanalysis, 39,* 135–153.

Sussman, M. B. (1995). *A perilous calling: The hazards of psychotherapy practice.* New York, NY: Wiley.

Swann, W. B., Jr. (1983). Self-verification: Bringing social reality into harmony with the self. In J. Suls & A. G. Greenwald (Eds.), *Social psychological perspectives on the self* (Vol. 2, pp. 33–66). Hillsdale, NJ: Erlbaum.

Swann, W. B., Jr. (1987). Identity negotiation: Where two roads meet. *Journal of Personality and Social Psychology, 53,* 1038–1051.

Swann, W. B., Jr. (1990). To be adored or to be known: The interplay of self-enhancement and self-verification. In R. M. Sorrentino & E. T. Higgins (Eds.), *Motivation & cognition* (Vol. 2, pp. 408–448). New York, NY: Guilford.

Swann, W. B., Jr., Pelham, B. W., & Krull, D. S. (1989). Agreeable fancy or disagreeable truth? Reconciling self-enhancement and self-verification. *Journal of Personality and Social Psychology, 57,* 782–791.

Swann, W. B., Jr., & Read, S. J. (1981). Acquiring self-knowledge: The search for feedback that fits. *Journal of Personality and Social Psychology, 41,* 1119–1128.

Swann, W. B., Jr., Rentfrow, P. J., & Guinn, J. (2003). Self-verification: The search for coherence. In M. Leary & J. Tagney (Eds.), *Handbook of self and identity* (pp. 367–383). New York, NY: Guilford.

Symington, N. (1983). The analyst's act of freedom as agent of therapeutic change. *International Review of Psychoanalysis, 10,* 282–292.

Tang, Q., Zhou, Z., Liao, S., & Zhu, X. (2011). A study on relationships between dependency, self-criticism, and depressive symptoms. *Journal of Social and Clinical Psychology, 19,* 385–387.

Tanzer, M., Avidan, G., & Shahar, G. (2013). Does social support protect against recognition of angry facial expressions following failure? *Cognition and Emotion, 27,* 1335–1344.

Tanzer, M., Shahar, G., & Avidan, G. (2013). A smile worthy of your cognition: General self-efficacious individuals recognize and remember happy faces. *Journal of Social and Clinical Psychology, 32,* 1–16.

Tanzer, M., Shahar, G., & Avidan, G. *Social support is associated with a weak recognition of angry facial expressions.* Manuscript in preparation.

Taranis, L., & Meyer, C. (2010). Perfectionism and compulsive exercise among female exercisers: High personal standards or self-criticism? *Personality and Individual Differences, 49,* 3–7.

Teasdale, J. D. (1983). Negative thinking in depression: Cause, affect, or reciprocal relation? *Advances in Behavior Research and Therapy, 5,* 3–25.

Tepper, B. (2007). Abusive supervision in work organizations: Review, synthesis, and research agenda. *Journal of Management, 33,* 261–289.

Thelen, E., & Smith, L. B. (2006). Dynamic systems theories. In W. Damon & R. M. Lerner (Eds.), *Theoretical models of human development: Vol. 1, Handbook of child psychology* (6th ed., pp. 258–312). New York, NY: Wiley.

Thompson, M. G. (1994). The fidelity to experience in existential psychoanalysis. In K. Schneider & R. May (Eds.), *The psychology of existence: An integrative, clinical perspective* (pp. 233–247). New York, NY: McGraw-Hill.

Thompson, R., & Zuroff, D. C. (2004). The Levels of Self-Criticism Scale: Comparative self-criticism and internalized self-criticism. *Personality and Individual Differences, 36,* 419–430.

Tillich, P. (1952). *The courage to be.* New Haven, CT: Yale University Press.

Tiskoff, S. A., & Verrelli, B. C. (2003). Patterns of human genetic diversity: Implications for human evolutionary history and disease. *Annual Review of Genomics and Human Genetics, 4,* 293–240.

Treynor, W., Gonzales, R., & Nolen-Hoeksema, S. (2003). Rumination reconsidered: A psychometric analysis. *Cognitive Therapy and Research, 27,* 247–259.

Turner, R. H. (1976). The true self: From institution to impulse. *American Journal of Sociology, 81,* 989–1016.

Tursi, M. F., Baes, C. V., Camacho, F. R., Tofoli, S. M., & Juruena, M. F. (2013). Effectiveness of psychoeducation for depression: A systematic review. *Australian and New Zealand Journal of Psychiatry, 47,* 1019–1031.

Ullman, C. (2006). Bearing witness: Across the barriers in society and in the clinic. *Psychoanalytic Dialogues, 16,* 181–198.

Vallejo, J., Gasto, C., Catalan, R., Bulbena, A., & Menchon, J. M. (1991). Predictors of antidepressant treatment outcome in melancholia: Psychosocial, clinical and biological indicators. *Journal of Affective Disorders, 21,* 151–162.

Vansteenkiste, M., Simons, J., Lens, W., Sheldon, K. M., & Deci, E. L. (2004). Motivation learning, performance and persistence: The synergistic effects of intrinsic goal contents and autonomy-supportive contexts. *Journal of Personality and Social Psychology, 87,* 246–260.

Vartanian, L. R. (2009). When the body defines the self: Self-concept clarity, internalization and body image. *Journal of Social and Clinical Psychology, 28,* 94–126.

Vliegen, N., Casalin, S., & Luyten, P. (2014). The course of postpartum depression: A review of longitudinal studies. *Harvard Review of Psychiatry, 22,* 1–22

Vliegen, N., & Luyten, P. (2009). Dependency and self-criticism in post-partum depression and anxiety: A case control study. *Clinical Psychology and Psychotherapy, 16,* 22–32.

Wachtel, E. F., & Wachtel, P. L. (1986). *Family dynamics in individual psychotherapy: A guide to clinical strategies.* New York, NY: Guilford Press.

Wachtel, P. L. (1977). *Psychoanalysis and behavior therapy: Toward an integration*. New York, NY: Basic.

Wachtel, P. L. (1994). Cyclical processes in personality and psychopathology. *Journal of Abnormal Psychology, 103*, 51–66.

Wachtel, P. L. (1997). *Psychoanalysis, behavior therapy, and the relational world*. Washington, DC: American Psychological Association.

Wachtel, P. L. (2011). *Therapeutic communication: Knowing what to say when* (2nd ed.). New York, NY: Guilford.

Wachtel, P. L. (2014). *Cyclical psychodynamics and the contextual self: The inner world, the intimate world, and the world of culture and society*. New York: Routledge

Walker-Andrews, A. S. (1997). Infants' perception of expressive behaviors: Differentiation of multimodal information. *Psychological Bulletin, 121*, 437–456

Wark, L., Thomas, M., & Peterson, S. (2001). Internal family systems therapy for children in family therapy. *Journal of Marital and Family Therapy, 27*, 189–200.

Watson, D. (2005). Rethinking the mood and anxiety disorders: A quantitative hierarchical model for DSM-V. *Journal of Abnormal Psychology, 114*, 522–536.

Watson, J. C., Goldman, R., & Greenberg, L. S. (2007). Evoking and exploring emotion. In J. C. Watson, R. Goldman, & L. S. Greenberg (Eds.), *Case studies in emotion-focused treatment of depression: A comparison of good and poor outcome* (pp. 27–51). Washington, DC: American Psychological Association Press.

Watzlawick, P., Weakland, J., & Fish, R. (1974). *Change: Principles of problem formation and resolution*. New York, NY: Norton.

Waytz, A., Cacioppo, J., & Epley, N. (2010). Who sees human? The stability and importance of individual differences in anthropomorphism. *Perspectives in Psychological Science, 5*, 219–232.

Wearden, A. J., Tarrier, N., Barrowclough, C., Zastowny, T. R., & Rahill, A. A. (2000). A review of expressed emotion research in health care. *Clinical Psychology Review, 20*, 633–666.

Wedig, M. M., & Nock, M. K. (2007). Parental expressed emotion and adolescent self-injury. *Journal of the American Academy of Child and Adolescent Psychiatry, 46*, 1171–1178.

Weinberg, D., Shahar, G., Noyman, G., Davidson, L., McGlashan, T. H., & Fennig, S. (2012). Role of the self in schizophrenia: A multidimensional examination of short-term outcomes. *Psychiatry: Biological and Interpersonal Processes, 75*(3), 285–297.

Weissman, A. N., & Beck, A. T. (1978). *Development and validation of the dysfunctional attitudes scale*. Paper presented at the American Educational Research Association Annual Convention, Toronto, Canada.

Weisz, J. R., Chorpita, B. F., Palinkas, L. A., Schoenwald, S. K., Miranda, J., Bearman, S. K., . . . & Gibbons, R. D. (2012). Testing standard and modular designs for psychotherapy with youth depression, anxiety, and conduct problems: A randomized effectiveness trial. *Archives of General Psychiatry, 69*, 274–282.

Welch, C. A., Czerwinski, D., Ghimire, B., & Bertsimas, D. (2009). Depression and costs of health care. *Psychosomatics, 50*, 392–401.

Werner, H. (1948). *Comparative psychology of mental development* (2nd ed.). Chicago, IL: Follett.

Werner, H. (1957). The concept of development from a comparative and organismic point of view. In D. B. Harris (Ed.), *The concept of development* (pp. 125–147). Minneapolis, MN: University of Minnesota Press.

Westen, D. (1996). A model and a method for uncovering the nomothetic from the idiographic: An alternative for the Five-Factor Model? *Journal of Research in Personality, 30*, 400–413.

Westen, D., Novotny, C. M., & Thompson-Brenner, H. (2004). The empirical status of empirically supported psychotherapies: Assumptions, findings, and reporting in controlled clinical trials. *Psychological Bulletin, 130*, 631–663.

Wetherell, J. L., Ayers, C. R., Sorell, J. T., Thorp, S. R., Nuevo, R., Belding, W., . . . & Patterson, T. L. (2009). Modular psychotherapy for anxiety in older primary care patients. *American Journal of Geriatric Psychiatry, 17*, 483–492.

Whelton, W. J., & Greenberg, L. S. (2005). Emotion in self-criticism. *Personality and Individual Differences, 38,* 1583–1595.

Whelton, W. J., Paulson, B., & Marusiak, C. W. (2007). Self-criticism and the therapeutic relationship. *Counselling Psychology Quarterly, 20,* 135–148.

Whiffen, V. E., & Aube, J. A. (1999). Personality, interpersonal context, and depression in couples. *Journal of Social and Personnel Relationships, 16,* 369–383.

Whiffen, V. E., Parker, G. B., Wilhelm, K., Mitchell, P. B., & Malhi, G. (2003). Parental care and personality in nonmelancholic and melancholic depression. *Journal of Nervous and Mental Disease, 191,* 358–364.

Wiggins, J. S. (1996). *The Five-Factor Model of personality: Theoretical perspectives.* New York, NY: Guilford.

Williams, M. H. (1997). Boundary violations: Do some contended standards of care fail to encompass commonplace procedures of humanistic, behavioral, and eclectic psychotherapies? *Psychotherapy, 34,* 238–249.

Williams, S. B., O'Connor, E. A., Eder, M., & Whitlock, E. P. (2009). Screening for child and adolescent depression in primary care settings: A systematic evidence review for the US Preventive Services Task Force. *Pediatrics, 123,* 716–735.

Wilson, T. D., & Dunn, E. W. (2004). Self-knowledge: Its limits, value, and potential for improvement. *Annual Review of Psychology, 55,* 493–518.

Winnicott, D. W. (1949). Hate in the countertransference. *International Journal of Psychoanalysis, 30,* 69–74.

Winnicott, D. W. (1960). The theory of parent-infant relationship. *International Journal of Psychoanalysis, 41,* 585–595.

Winnicott, D. W. (1965). Ego distortion in terms of true and false self. In *The maturational processes and the facilitating environment* (pp. 140–152). London, England: Hogarth and the Institute of Psycho-Analysis.

Winnicott, D. W. (1969). The use of an object. *International Journal of Psychoanalysis, 50,* 711–716.

Winnicott, D. W. (1971). *Playing and reality.* London, England: Routledge.

Winnicott, D. W. (1987). *The spontaneous gesture: Selected papers.* Cambridge, MA: Harvard University Press.

Witkin, H. A. (1950). Individual differences in ease of perception of embedded figures. *Journal of Personality, 19,* 1–15.

Wood, A. M., Linley, P. A., Maltby, J., Baliousis, M., & Joseph, S. (2008). The authentic personality: A theoretical and empirical conceptualization and the development of the authentic self. *Journal of Counseling Psychology, 55,* 385–399.

World Health Organization. (1992). *International statistical classification of diseases and related health problems (ICD-10).* Geneva, Switzerland: Author.

Wylie, G., Hungin, A. P., & Neely, J. (2002). Impaired glucose tolerance: Qualitative and quantitative study of general practitioners' knowledge and perceptions. *British Medical Journal, 324,* 1190.

Yalom, I. D. (1980). *Existential psychotherapy.* New York: Basic.

Yao, S., Fang, J., Zhu, X., & Zuroff, D. C. (2009). The Depressive Experiences Questionnaire: Construct validity and prediction of depressive symptoms in a sample of Chinese undergraduates. *Depression and Anxiety, 26,* 930–937.

Yeung, K-T., & Martin, J. (2003). The looking glass self: An empirical test and elaboration. *Social Forces, 81*(3), 843–879.

Yiend, J. (2010). The effects of emotion on attention: A review of attentional processing of emotional information. *Cognition and Emotion, 24,* 3–47.

Young, J. E., Klosko, J. S., & Weishaar, M. (2003). *Schema therapy: A practitioner's guide.* New York, NY: Guilford.

Yu, J. J., & Gample, W. C. (2009). Adolescent relations with their mothers, siblings, and peers: An exploration of the roles of maternal and adolescent self-criticism. *Journal of Clinical Child and Adolescent Psychology, 38,* 672–683.

Zachar, P., & Leong, F. T. (2000). A 1-year longitudinal study of scientists and practitioner interest in psychology: Assessing the Boulder Model. *Professional Psychology: Research and Practice, 31,* 575–580.

Ziv-Beiman, S. (2013). Therapist self-disclosure as an integrative intervention. *Journal of Psychotherapy Integration, 23,* 59–74.

Ziv-Beiman, S., & Shahar, G. (2015). Psychotherapy integration. In R. Cautin & S. Lilinfeld (Eds.), *The encyclopedia of clinical psychology.* New York, NY: Wiley.

Zlotnick, C., Shea, T. M., Pilkonis, P. A., Elkin, I., & Ryan, C. (1996). Gender, type of treatment, dysfunctional attitudes, social support, life events, and depressive symptoms over naturalistic follow-up. *American Journal of Psychiatry, 153,* 1021–1027.

Zuroff, D. C. (1992). New directions for cognitive models of depression. *Psychological Inquiry, 3,* 274–277.

Zuroff, D. C., Blatt, S. J., Sotsky, S. M., Krupnick, J. L., Martin, D. J., Sanislow, C. A., & Simmens, S. (2000). Relation of therapeutic alliance and perfectionism to outcome in brief outpatient treatment of depression. *Journal of Consulting and Clinical Psychology, 68,* 114–124.

Zuroff, D. C., & Duncan, N. (1999). Self-criticism and conflict resolution in romantic couples. *Canadian Journal of Behavioural Science, 31,* 1137–1149.

Zuroff, D. C., Fournier, M. A., Patall, E. A., & Leybman, M. J. (2010). Steps toward an evolutionary personality psychology: Individual differences in the social rank domain. *Canadian Psychology, 51,* 58–66.

Zuroff, D. C., & Mongrain, M. (1987). Dependency and self-criticism: Vulnerability factors for depressive affective states. *Journal of Abnormal Psychology, 96,* 14–22.

Zuroff, D. C., Mongrain, M., & Santor, D. A. (2004a). Conceptualizing and measuring personality vulnerability to depression: Comment on Coyne and Whiffen (1995). *Psychological Bulletin, 130,* 489–511.

Zuroff, D. C., Mongrain, M., & Santor, D. A. (2004b). Investing in the personality vulnerability research program—Current dividends and future growth: Rejoinder to Coyne, Thompson, and Whiffen (2004). *Psychological Bulletin, 130,* 518–522.

Zuroff, D. C., Moskowitz, D. S., Wielgus, M. S., Powers, T. A., & Franko, D. L. (1983). Construct validation of the dependency and self-criticism scales of the Depressive Experiences Questionnaire. *Journal of Research in Personality, 17,* 226–241.

Zuroff, D. C., Santor, D. A., & Mongrain, M. (2005). Dependency, self-criticism, and maladjustment. In J. S. Auerbach, K. J. Levy, & C. E. Schaffer (Eds.), *Relatedness, self-definition and mental representation: Essays in honor of Sidney J. Blatt* (pp. 75–90). London, England: Brunner-Routledge.

ABOUT THE AUTHOR AND STREALTH

Golan Shahar, PhD, is Professor of Clinical-Health and Developmental-Health Psychology at Ben-Gurion University of the Negev, Israel, where he directs the Stress, Self, and Health Lab (STREALTH) and serves as the founding director of the Center for the Advancement of Research on Stress and related mood disorders (CARES). He is also a visiting professor of Psychiatry at Yale University School of Medicine.

Prof. Shahar is the author of over 130 publications/book chapters in the fields of stress, psychopathology, psychosomatics, personality and the self-concept, and psychotherapy. He is currently chief editor of the *Journal of Psychotherapy Integration,* the official journal of the Society for the Exploration of Psychotherapy Integration, published by the American Psychological Association. He practices clinical-health psychology in Israel and is the author of a book of poems entitled *Psycho-Al-Na-Liza.* This is his first scholarly book.

Based at the Department of Psychology of Ben-Gurion University of the Negev in Israel, STREALTH (http://golanshahar.wix.com/strealth#!lab-members/c1jm9) is a multidisciplinary research laboratory whose work focuses on disentangling the complex relationships between stressful situations, subjective (self-related) processes, and a myriad of health-related outcomes (e.g., psychopathology, physical illness, violence, health behaviors).

INDEX

abandonment, 12
absence principle, 18, 22
absenteeism, 91
acceptance and commitment therapy, 111, 133
achievement, 12, 13, 34, 57, 88, 89, 93, 98, 158
  academic, 9, 28, 85, 161
  goal, 35
action formulation (TAF), 103
action theory, 13, 15, 115
activation, 49
  behavioral, 89, 123, 134, 135, 143, 160
  brain, 75–76, 159
  self-critical, 89, 125
AD(H)D, 79, 116
Adam, 24–25, 152–153
adolescents, xiii, 13, 18, 20, 22, 24, 28, 67, 73, 82, 84, 85, 86, 88, 90, 97, 105, 113, 116, 117, 118, 123, 125, 128, 130, 140, 153, 167
  boys, 11, 19, 25, 28, 33
  early, 85, 116, 161
  girls, 11, 19, 25
adulthood, 20, 24, 67, 90, 116, 130, 164. See also young adulthood, young adults
affect regulation, 30, 157
affective disorders, 159
age of melancholy (Klerman), 88
agency, x, 151
agents in relations (AIR), 76, 82, 168
aggression, 11, 22, 33, 49, 148, 158
agreeableness, 30
AIDS, 131
allele, 74, 164. See also L allele, S allele
amotivation, 23–25, 78
amygdala, 75, 76, 159, 164
anaclitic personality (Blatt), 42–45, 54, 93. See also autonomy, introjective, sociotropy; introjective personality
  anaclitic-introjective distinction, 12, 44, 50, 53, 93

depression, 6, 43
disorders, 25–26, 43
anger, 20, 46, 78, 114, 121
anhedonia, 135
anorexia nervosa, 9, 151
anthropomorphism/personification, 131
anxiety, 8, 9, 11, 20, 30, 31, 33, 36, 37, 49, 53, 69, 121, 124, 129, 131, 135, 144
  child, 70, 83
  disorder, 9, 104
  maternal, 70
  regulating therapy (McCullough), 163
  social, 9, 103, 104, 163
apathy, 23
Aristotle, 61
attachment-based family therapy, 167
attachment themes, 61, 167
attention, present-moment, 61, 64–65
attentional style, 62
Attitude Toward the Self Scale, 99
authenticity, xiii, 57–80, 82–84, 85, 88, 90, 92–94, 98, 107–108, 112, 123, 133, 134, 138, 148, 156, 164, 165, 169
  child's, 82–83
  dispositional, 61
  future-oriented, 61, 64, 70
  oppressed, 82
  patient, 117, 132, 154
  self-reported, 121
  therapist, 149
Authenticity and Self-Knowledge (ASK), 57–80, 90, 92–94, 107, 115, 147, 157, 165, 169
autonomy, 12, 13, 45–47, 100, 160. See also sociotropy
avoidant coping style, 20, 35
  personality disorder, 26, 43, 121
Axis of Criticism model (ACRIM), xiii, 81–94, 107, 108, 157–158

Bad Me (Sullivan), 140
Bad Mother, 140
Bandura, 13, 32, 47–48, 49, 54, 56, 93, 94, 110,
    113, 135, 142, 151
basal ganglia, 75
BDI-II, 11, 22, 28, 29
BDNF, 75
    Val66Met polymorphism, 75
Beck, 7, 45–47, 54, 56, 94, 100
Beck Depression Inventory (BDI), 22, 24, 160
    BDI-II, 11, 22, 29
behavioral genetics, 63
being in-the-world (Heidegger), 65, 134
Besser, Avi, xvii
Big Five Model, 29, 156. See also Five
    Factor Model
binging, 9
bio-evolutionary tendencies, 55
bio-psychological force, 52
Bion, 124, 166, 167
bipolar spectrum, 9, 105, 116
Blatt, Sidney, x, 11, 12, 15, 18, 19, 22, 27, 31,
    42–45, 53, 56, 82, 93, 94, 99, 105, 135,
    139, 158
borderline personality, 26, 43
Boulder Model, x, xi
Brief Symptoms Inventory (BSI), 23
Brodmann area, 65, 164
Bronfenbrenner, Urie, xiii, 87–89, 109, 156, 165
brooding, 36. See also reflective pondering,
    rumination
Buber, Martin 166
buffering, 104, 128, 136
bulimia, 36

camaraderie, 126
care-giving, 48–50, 55, 63, 92, 151, 165
caregivers, 48, 62–63, 92
careers, 35, 127, 134, 139
cascade, self-critical, 19–21, 47, 48, 50, 54–55,
    56, 92, 105, 122, 124, 136, 170
case complexity, 105
case formulation, 99–104, 116
causality, 10, 51
Center for Epidemiological Studies, 11
    Depression Scale, 160
Chang, Edward, xvii
chaos theories, 164
Child Depression Inventory (CDI),
    22–23, 50, 51
chronic fatigue syndrome, 40, 158
chronic illness, xviii, ix, xvi, xvii, 70, 124, 132,
    137, 138, 150–151, 158, 166. See also pain
chronicity, 105
chronosystem, 88, 90, 156
chumship (Sullivan), 85

Churchill, 130
circadian rhythms, 62
cluster of schemas, 46
cognitive-affective evaluation, 16
    schemas, 43, 91, 94, 119
cognitive behavioral therapy, 15, 41, 43, 57, 106,
    119, 120, 132, 152, 153
cognitive-evolutionary theory, 41, 48–51
cognitive restructuring, 120, 142–145
cognitive schemas, maladaptive, 119
cognitive therapy, 119, 120, 143, 166
collaborative empiricism, 120
common (non-specific) factors, 107–108, 166
comorbidity, xii, 32, 104, 105, 118, 134, 166
compass, poorly-calibrated, 79–80
compassionate, self-critics as, 50, 121, 138
compassionate mind training (CMT), 49,
    120, 133
compassion-based treatment, 51, 55, 123, 160
competition, 49, 80
computer tasks, 102
conduct disorder, 36, 98
conflict processing, 76
congruency hypothesis, 12–13
conscientiousness, 30
construct validity of the cause (CVC), 21, 163
containing (Bion), 148, 150, 166, 167
coping strategies, 17–19, 103, 125, 157
    maladaptive, 17–19
corrective emotional experience, 107, 113
cortical regions, 75–76, 159
countertransference, 123, 145–149, 166. See also
    transference
Cox, Brian, xvii, 32
Cronbach, 166
culture, Arab-Bedouin, 45, 89
    and genes, 75. See also genes
    collectivist, 45, 75, 89
    East Asian, 75
    expectations of, 88
    individualistic, 75, 89
    Western, 44, 45, 75, 79, 88, 90, 138
curiosity, 62, 67, 78, 124, 125, 128, 130
cyclical interactions, 86
cyclical psychodynamic model (Wachtel), xiii,
    14, 110, 111

daily activities, 47, 76, 123, 138
    negative, 17–120
Davidson, Larry, xv, 66, 105, 134, 138
Dead Poets Society, 83–84, 88
death, 8, 117, 144, 152
defense attorney, 120, 143–145
degeneration, 20, 91
delinquency, 11, 33, 158
dependency, 6, 12, 13–15, 54, 93, 100, 157, 167

DEQ, 46
needs, 6
tendencies, 12
interpersonal, 50
depression, ix, xiii, iii, v, vi, viii-xvii, 18, 19, 20,
22, 23, 24, 25, 30, 31, 32, 33, 34, 35, 36,
37, 41, 43, 44, 45–47, 49, 57, 73, 74, 75,
76, 79, 92, 98, 100, 104, 105, 119, 120,
123, 124, 126, 127, 131, 135, 137, 148,
152, 158, 159, 160, 163, 167
adolescent, 22, 24
anaclitic, 6, 12, 43
double, 57, 105, 131
episodes of, 57
gender differences in, 36
hysterical, 43
introjective, 6, 12, 43
major, 3, 15, 22, 31, 32, 37, 105
manualized, treatment for, xii, 43–44
new onset of, 8, 36
pain-related, 17
personologic, 26
postpartum, 92
suicidal, 57, 97, 148
symptoms, 3, 6, 11, 16, 19, 22, 23, 25, 27, 28,
29, 30, 31, 36, 72, 92, 102, 105, 121,
136, 160
unipolar, 6, 8, 9, 76, 88, 104, 135, 158,
160, 161
depressive disorders, 26, 31
Depressive Experiences Questionnaire
(DEQ), 6–8, 17, 28, 32, 33, 34, 35,
45–46, 99–103
DEQ dependency, 46
DEQ efficacy, 33
DEQ-SC6, 7, 100
depressive personality disorder (DPD), 26, 27
features, 27–29, 37–38
depressive vulnerability, 12
anaclitic, 6
cognitive theory of, 6
introjective, 6
psychodynamic theory of, 12
dereflection, 123, 137–138
devaluation of self/others, 26
developmental psychology, 116
developmental problems, 9, 52, 156
*Diagnostic and Statistical Manual for Mental
Disorders*, 22, 29, 156
dialectic developmental process, 43
dialectical behavioral therapy (DBT), 111
dialogue, 5, 19, 143
inner, 19, 143
in self-criticism, 5, 19, 121, 130, 143
differential treatment response, 105
disclosure, 113
patient, 113

therapist, ix, 113, 130, 152–153
distress, xi, xiii, 11, 14, 16, 17, 20, 30, 36, 49, 72,
80, 87, 99, 113, 114, 120, 121, 122, 124,
128, 131, 136, 158, 170, 177
cancer-related, 124
depressive, 153
parental, 88
DNA, 164
dorsal anterior cingulate cortex, 76
dorsal lateral prefrontal cortex, 76
Dunkley, xvii, 11, 17
dynamic systems, 164
Dysfunctional Attitudes Scale, 7, 99, 100
dysthymic disorder, 24, 134

eating disorders, 9, 20, 28, 73
ecological/ethological research, 10
ecological development theory, xiii, 87, 109
efficacy, 6, 23, 100, 104, 157
elderly, 92, 118
abuse of, 92
Elizur, Joel, 164
emotional
complexity, 62
facial expressions/perception, 71, 72, 74, 159
intelligence, 161
processing, 71–72
styles, 62, 69
stimuli, 71–72, 159
emotion-focused therapy, 233, 234, 237, 247
empathy, 68, 120, 167
for self, 120, 127
therapeutic stance, x, 127
empirical evidence/research, xii, xvii, 5, 7, 19,
20, 21, 29, 34, 37, 41, 44, 45, 50, 52, 53,
55, 56, 65, 72, 83, 93, 101, 103, 109, 110,
137, 142, 147, 155, 157, 158, 163, 170
empirical psychology, 58
em-presentation, 123, 149–152, 169
enactment, 167
engagement, 76, 123, 134–136
Enns, Murray, xvii, 30, 32
environment, 4, 47, 63, 67, 69, 71, 77, 82, 93, 103,
109, 112, 156
competitive, 80, 88
contextual, 75, 109
critical, 115
holding, 71, 148
nurturing, 64, 112
parental, 68
physical, 124
school, 88
social, 4, 13, 14, 17, 20, 22, 63, 64, 67, 80, 87,
93, 103, 122, 153, 156
supportive, 49, 91
therapeutic, 140

environmental selection, 80
epidemiology/public health approach (E/PH), 7
equifinality, 81
error monitoring, 76
evaluation, xii, 5, 16, 26, 49, 71, 80, 100, 109, 165
    global self, 31
    self, 88, 93, 120
eventuality, 66, 70, 169. *See also* stress
evolution, 48, 50, 77, 82, 94, 157, 170
    prerequisites, 77
evolutionary psychology, 157
existentialism, 41, 64, 67, 76, 89, 111, 112, 123,
    133, 135, 137, 151, 152, 157
exosystem, 87–88, 89
exploratory factor analysis, 30
expressed emotion (EE), 84
    critical expressed emotion (CEE), 85, 91, 92,
    124–126, 127, 169
external validity, 163
externalizing symptoms, 33, 36
extroversion, 30

fMRI, 76, 159
5-HTR1A polymorphism, 74, 159, 164
family relationships, 47, 85
family-systems therapy, 69, 151, 153, 157
fear of object loss, 19
Five Factor Model, 29, 156. *See also* Big
    Five Model
forensic psychology, 63, 158
Forms of Self-Criticizing/Attacking and
    Self-Reassuring scale (FSCRS), 49, 99, 101
Frederikson, Barbara, 79
Freud, 41, 82, 83, 108, 210
Fromm, Erich, 267
Fromm-Reichmann, Frieda, 267
frontal lobe, 79
Frost Multidimensional Perfectionism Scale,
    34, 163
fully-functioning person (Rogers), 60, 65, 68
future, 13, 24, 46, 54, 64–67, 70, 77, 84, 91, 107,
    112, 120, 122, 125, 132, 145, 169, 170
    future-oriented, 61, 64, 70, 84, 111, 112, 132,
    147, 167

gay community, 138, 141
genes, 75, 81, 90, 159
    depressive, 81
    self-focus, 90
genetics, 8, 63, 75, 109
    molecular, 75
Giddens, Anthony, 88–89
Gilbert, Paul, xvii, 6, 41, 48–51, 56, 92, 94, 99,
    120, 121, 160
Gill, Morton, 145

globalization, 89
goals, 7, 18, 23, 24, 65, 70, 74, 89, 134, 145, 169
    career, 127
    personal, 35
    relational, 167
    therapeutic, 106
goal attainment, 24, 35, 154
goal constructs, 23, 65, 147
goal pursuit, 35
goal-directed action, 4, 46, 48, 61, 64, 84, 111,
    147, 167, 169, 170
going-on-being (Winnicott), 65, 68, 71, 77
Good Me (Sullivan), 140
grade point average, 25
grandiosity, 26
guilt, 6, 12, 22, 53, 114, 152–153

Harry Potter, 113
hate, 118, 148
health psychology, 158
Heidegger, 64, 65, 66, 134
Henrich, Christopher, xv, 18, 25, 89
Heraclitus, 155
Higgins, Tory, 53
histrionic personality disorder, 43
hopelessness, 32, 51
humanistic perspective, 41, 51–56, 151, 152, 164
humanistic-existential perspective, 41, 112,
    153, 157
humanistic-existential-phenomenological
    school of thought, 67
humanistic-psychodynamic perspective, 153
humor, 3, 116, 123, 125
Huprich, Stephen, 29
hypomanic symptoms, 9

idealization, 26
identified patient, 84, 167
identity, 59, 63, 70, 73, 78, 117, 146, 169
    authentic, 52, 84, 93
    confusion, 25, 26, 33
    diffusion, 73
    self, 12, 89, 170
    sexual, 70
identity theory (Erikson), 72–73
idiographic, 104
Ilan, 57–58, 105, 114
impingement (Winnicott), 71, 82
impulse control, 26
inadequacy, 26, 89
independence, 45, 90
individuality, 44, 104, 105
    in Western world, 45, 90
    patient, 104, 105, 106, 107
    therapist, 107

individuation, 167
information craze, 89
information processing, 50, 74
inhibition, 26, 41, 49, 76, 159
inner voice, 13, 125, 128, 133
inquisitive action, 84, 107, 116, 123, 139–142,
    164, 169, 170
insight (Wachtel), 110–111
internal validity, 163
internalization (Schafer), 33, 36, 49, 56, 94, 113
International Classification of Diseases (ICD), 22, 165
interoceptive exposure, 106
interpersonal
    relations, 12, 42, 43, 49, 51, 93, 103, 107,
        122, 123, 124, 145, 146, 154, 169. *See also*
        object relations
    behavior, 71, 110
    circumstances, xii, 19, 21, 94, 113
    cycles, vicious, 83, 103, 107, 110, 112, 115,
        116. *See also* vicious cycles
    dependency, 50
    domains, 27, 28, 103
    environment, 20
    events, 12, 13
    factors, 14, 72
    functioning, 9, 26
    inquiry, 123, 135, 139–142
    loss, 50
    psychoanalytic school, 139, 140
    strategies, 49
    stress, 13, 86
    strife, 54, 56, 103
    ruptures, 142
    therapy, 15, 43, 123, 153
    variables, 16
    vulnerability, 17
interpersonal therapy for depression
    (IPT), 123
intersubjective matrix, 112–116
interventions, 13, 51, 98, 106, 107, 112, 117,
    118–154, 160–161, 164, 165, 166
    prescriptive, 106, 134
intrapsychic processes, 110
introjective personality, 6, 12, 42, 43, 44, 45, 46,
    50, 53, 54, 89, 93
    disorders, 43,
    patients, 43, 44
ironic cycles, 83, 110. *See also* vicious cycles

Jennifer, 131
Jonathan, 134

Kant, 18, 66
Kierkegaard, 129
Kohut, 114, 127, 166

L allele, 74–75
language, 4, 88, 124. *See also* metaphor, narrative
    lay, 5, 34
latent difference (change) scores, 11
Leonard, 141–142
life-events, 12, 13, 14,
    negative, 14, 15, 18, 20, 23, 74–75
    positive, 14, 18, 20, 22, 23, 157
    prediction of, 23, 24
life-span, 13, 88, 90–92, 93, 116, 156
life-stress, 4, 12, 13, 70, 73, 111, 136, 158, 165.
        See also stress
    generation of, 4, 103
limbic structures, 159, 164
local clinical scientist (Stricker &
        Trierweiler), 109
logotherapy (Frankl), 137
loving kindness meditation, 121, 122, 160

McAdams, Dan, 67
macrosystem, 87, 88, 90
maladjustment, 23, 34, 87
malignant self-regard, 29
maltreatment, 67, 91
masochistic personality, 29, 140
    sadomasochism, 150
maternal antisocial behavior, 32
May, Rollo, 135
medial prefrontal cortex, 75
medicine, 104, 110
    behavioral, 158
    personalized, 104, 109, 110
melancholia, 41
    age of (Klerman), 88
memory, 62, 72, 74, 132, 164
menopause, 116
mental activity, 69
    content, 42,
    disorders, 8, 9, 10, 22, 165
    health, 42, 43, 59, 85, 135–136, 137, 153, 155,
        161, 169
        reform, 165
    hygiene, 133
    illness, x, xii, 8, 98
    mechanisms, 48
    representations/constructs, 42, 51, 73, 94
    resources, 70
    social mentalities, 48, 49
    state, 111, 124, 133
    system, 143
mesosystem, 87, 88
metaphor, 76, 109, 111, 120, 131–132, 143
metaphorization of illness, 131–132
Michael, 144
microsystem, 87, 88, 90
midline structures, 75–76, 159, 164

mindfulness, 111, 123, 132–134, 143, 154. *See also* self-regulation
-based therapy, 123, 136
mindfulness-based stress reduction (Kabat-Zinn), 133
mirroring, 71
Mitchell, Stephen, 147–148
modes (Beck), 45–47, 54, 94
modular psychotherapy, 109, 110
modus tollens, 10, 21
mothers
  criticism by, 76, 159
  faces of, 71,
  good, 140
  good enough, 71, 92, 153
  pressure to breastfeed, 92
motivation, 17–18, 23, 24, 32, 48, 52, 59
  autonomous/intrinsic, 17–20, 22, 23, 52
  controlled/extrinsic, 18, 23
motivational mechanisms, 22
  processes, 46, 54
  systems, 22
  style, 18
multifinality, 81
Multiple Selves Analysis, 25, 123, 128–132. *See also* Personal Projects Analysis

narcissism, 26, 43
narcissistic personality disorder, 26, 29
narrative, xii, 67, 78, 103, 112, 132, 164
National Comorbidity Survey, 32
neediness, maladaptive, 44
needs, 60, 167
  anaclitic-dependent, 6, 44
  authentic self's, 68
  individual patient's, 106, 115
  therapist's, 115
negative affect, 35
negativity aversion, 102
neglect, maternal, 32, 52, 57, 141
neurocognitive science, 50, 111
neuroscience, xii, 65, 75
  affective (Panksepp), 79
  cognitive-affective, 111
neurosis, 59
neuroticism, xiii, 21, 29–30, 32, 34, 37, 73, 74, 82, 163
Nietzsche, 52, 164
nomothetic, 104
non-specific factors. *See* common factors
nonsuicidal self-injury (NSSI), xvi, 28, 165. *See also* self-injury
Not Me (Sullivan), 140

object relations, 42, 142, 151
object relations theory (ORT), 42, 151

Object Relations Inventory (Blatt), 99
obsessive compulsive disorder, 26, 43, 118, 121
odd-eccentric personality disorder, 27–28
ontogeny, 58
openness to experience, 30, 120
ordinary magic (Masten), 68, 70
organismic experience (Rogers), 51–53, 55, 68
  valuing, 52–53, 55, 56, 60, 68
out-group hostility, 158

Personality Assessment Form (PAF), 27
pain, 9, 16, 17, 59, 82, 113, 127, 136, 142, 148
  chronic, 9, 16, 124, 158
  clinics, 16
  developmental, 52
  emotional, 122, 148
  guilt and, 152
  pain-related depression, 17
  physical, 16, 62, 78
  physician, 16
  sensory/affective, 16, 17, 113, 166, 167
pain-pleasure thresholds, 62
pairs of roles (Gilbert), 48
panic attack, 106
panic disorder, 118, 134
paradoxical intention (Frankl), 137
paranoid disorder, 43
parents, 24, 25, 49, 52, 54, 55, 62, 68, 70, 71, 82, 83, 84, 85, 86, 89, 92, 94, 123, 125, 126, 127, 164, 167
  and therapy, 124–127
  child relationship, 13, 42, 43, 53–55, 56, 59, 82, 83, 85, 94, 127, 140
  critical, 82–83, 86, 88, 92
  early parenthood, 84
  first-time, 92
  good enough, 92
  judgmental, 53, 56
  not-yet parents, 153
  of depressed children, 126
  permissive, 25
  punitive, 53
  standards of, 24. *See also* standards
participation (Tillich), 135, 137
participation-engagement (PAREN), 123, 134–136
Particularized Mode of Adaptation (PMA), 77, 170
pathological personality, 25
patient-physician relationship, 16–17
peers, 13, 22, 25, 63, 70, 85–86, 87, 88, 90
perfectionism, xiii, 15, 21, 26, 34, 35, 37, 100, 106
  adaptive, 72
  critical, 17, 18
  excessive-evaluative-concerns, 26, 34
  multidimensional, 34

neurotic, 72
other-oriented, 34
positive, 163
pretreatment, 27
self-critical/maladaptive, 33–35
self-oriented, 35
socially-prescribed, 72
performance, 5, 6, 89, 100, 170
person-context transactions, 47, 142
Personal Projects Analysis (PPA), 65, 128–132, 169. *See also* Multiple Selves Analysis
Personal Style Inventory (PSI), 7, 45, 99–100
personality, 8, 30, 46, 55, 58, 59, 60, 64, 69, 73, 93, 97, 98
adolescent, 86
and depression, 23
and self-criticism, 25–29
borderline, 26, 43
configurations, 42, 54
constructs, 13,
development, xv, 6, 54, 85
two-polarities model, 93
disorders, ix, xiii, 9, 11, 14, 15, 21, 25–29, 31, 43, 103, 105, 115, 118, 121–122, 134, 156
duality, 50
factors, 22–23, 32, 37
functioning, 27
normotic, 59
pathology, 115
pretreatment, 15
proclivities, 112
psychology, 30, 34, 65, 104, 156
resilience, 13
self-concept, 18, 31
traits, 4, 12, 18, 30, 32, 156–157
variables, 66, 79
vulnerability, 6, 10, 13, 14, 22, 50, 100, 105,
Personality Disorders Questionnaire-4 (PDQ-4), 28
personality construct theory (G. Kelly), 72–73
personification, 130–132
phobias, 108
physiological-affective-cognitive proclivities, 13, 61–63, 65, 67, 69, 76–79, 82, 84, 93, 117, 169
Piaget, 42, 94, 101
plasma homovanillic acid, 46
Plato, 41
play, 79, 125, 143
sanctuaries, 79
pleasure, 18, 33, 62, 130
political science, 158
politics, 130, 135, 147
two-person, 147
Porcerelli, John, 103
positive regard, 52
postmodernism, 56, 69, 89, 165

poverty, 105, 126
pragmatism, 76, 139
precuneus, 149
prefrontal cortex, 65, 75, 76
Particularized Mode of Adaptation, 82, 94
primes, 163
prognosis, 16–17
projective identification, 166
projectuality, 66, 70, 84, 138, 147, 155, 170
prosecutor, 120, 143–145, 120, 143–145
protective processes, 18
psychoanalysis, xii, 41, 43, 47, 67, 151, 152, 166
existential, 135
relational, 145, 147, 152
psychodynamic object-relations theory, 151
psychoeducation, 123, 124–128
in schools, 125–126
psychometric research, 44
psychopathology, ix, x, xv, 12, 15, 16, 17, 18, 21, 23, 24, 30, 31, 35, 37, 41, 44, 45, 46, 48, 53, 54–55, 59, 72, 73, 74, 86, 93, 104, 109, 110, 148, 151, 156, 158, 163
and face stimuli, 72
and rumination, 35
and self-criticism, 45, 53
BSI, 23, 24
developmental, 18, 81, 116
prediction of, 37, 45
risk factor for, 30
self-concept, 37
theories, 47–48, 121–122
vulnerability to, 21, 37
Western conceptualization of, 44–45
psychosis, xv, 118
psychosomatic disorders, 9, 12, 117, 137
psychotherapy, xii, xv, 54, 57, 61, 72, 105, 107, 114, 115, 119, 126, 127, 128, 132, 139, 145, 148, 149, 167
child, 167
cognitive, 45, 143
dynamic, 166
evidence-based, 128
existential, 135, 137
integration, xv, 14, 108–112, 117, 142, 145
outcome, 122, 166
psychoanalytically-oriented, 43, 151
psychodynamic, 146
PTSD, 9, 32, 98, 104, 158
puberty, 116

radical intentionalism, 111
Reason for Living Scale, 153
reassurance, 6
self, 49, 121
recentering, 123, 132–134, 143

reciprocal determinism (Bandura), 47–48,
        54, 110
reflective pondering, 36. *See also* brooding,
        rumination
reflexivity, 89
rejection, 3, 12, 50, 83, 85, 86, 103, 169
relational reframe (RR) technique, 167
resilience, 13, 15, 33, 44, 50, 72, 73, 79, 103, 157,
        158, 165
revictimization, 67
reward and punishment, 47, 49, 52, 69, 135, 158
rigidity, 60, 73, 112, 143
Rina, 3–5, 19, 35, 50, 131, 136, 141
Ripley, Tom, 63–67
risk, 15, 18, 19, 20, 30, 33, 44, 73, 99, 103, 105,
        115, 117, 131, 158, 160
    resilience dialectic, 33
Rogers, Carl, xiii, 41, 51–56, 68, 81–82, 93, 94,
        120, 164
romantic dissatisfaction, 92
romantic relationships, 92
    and victimizing, 92
Rosenberg Self-Esteem Scale, 32
routine analysis, 123, 134–135, 138–139
rumination, xiii, 21, 35–37, 73, 75, 136. *See also*
        brooding, reflective pondering
rupture
    criticism-based, 107
    interpersonal, 85–86, 142, 167
    therapeutic, 107, 114–115, 117, 123, 124,
        145–149, 170

S allele, 74–76, 159
Salovey, Peter, 80
Sartre, 71, 76, 134, 135
scarring hypothesis, 18–19
Schafer, Roy, 113
Schanche, Elizabeth, 121
Schema Therapy (Young), 69, 128, 166
schizophrenia, 73, 84
schizotypic disorder, 53
school, 11, 22, 25, 70, 83–84, 86–88, 90, 108,
        125–126, 131, 150, 151, 156,
    staff/personnel, 13, 85–86, 90, 125–126, 150
SCRINTERVIEW, 165
self
    actualization, 52, 59, 65, 68, 84, 120, 153
    affirmation, 61, 77, 80, 135
    as actor, 67
    as agent, x, 5, 6, 67
    as author, 67
    authentic, 58, 61, 64–72, 80, 83, 84,
        90, 93, 98, 112, 138, 156, 169. *See*
        authenticity
    disgust-inducing, 49
    false, 6, 60, 82

hated (Gilbert), 49–50, 101
hostility toward, 5–6, 170
ideal, 51–53, 55
inadequate (Gilbert), 49–50, 77, 101
mental representations of, 42, 51
multiple selves/self-aspects, 5, 25, 49, 68–69,
        104, 122, 123, 128–133, 136, 140,
        153–154, 169
nuclear self (Kohut), 59
ought-self, 53
real self (Turner), 60
relationship with the self, 5, 170
self-bashing, 6, 26, 35, 46, 124, 143
self-censure, 48, 54, 93
self-compassion, 50, 120, 121, 138
self-critical vulnerability (SCV), xiii, 12, 15,
        19, 45, 87, 90, 153
self-deception, 59
self-derogation, 57, 114, 120, 128, 143
self-disclosure, therapist, ix, 113, 125, 130,
        152–153
self-efficacy, 74, 157
    dimension-based tendency, 32
    generalized, 31–33, 37, 38, 72
    self-regulatory, 32
self-esteem, xiii, 21, 26, 31–33, 37, 61, 67,
        73, 137
self-evaluation, 88, 120
self-focused attention, 36, 74, 76, 81, 132,
        137, 159
self-fulfilling prophecy, 17
self-guides, 53
self-injury/mutilation, 28, 61, 116, 165, 166.
        See also Nonsuicidal Self-Injury
self-hatred, 3
self-image, 26, 53, 146
self-preservation, 77
self-processing, 76
self-punitiveness, 158
self-reassurance, 49, 121
self-reference task, 102
self-regard, 29, 41, 68
self-regulation, 47, 74, 133, 154. *See also*
        mindfulness
self-reliance, 44
self-report questionnaires, 159
self-reproach, 41, 47, 48, 54, 93, 94
self-scrutiny, 78
self-self relationship, 49, 55
self-standards, 93, 158. *See also* standards
self-verification theory (Swann), 72–73
self-worth, 6, 31, 43, 47
    sense of, 4, 24, 26, 43, 53, 71, 73
    true, 55, 57, 58–68, 70, 82, 120, 167, 169
self-critical voices, 80, 128, 129, 131, 132, 136,
        140, 143
variables, 66

self-concept, xvi, 5, 18, 31, 37, 50–53, 55, 69–73, 75, 102, 128, 132, 143, 153, 169
   clarity, 72–73, 157
self-determination theory (SDT) (Deci & Ryan), 18, 22, 41, 58, 83
self-discrepancy theory (Higgins), 41, 53, 55
self-knowledge (SK), 13, 55, 56, 57–80, 81, 88, 90, 92–94, 107, 112, 123, 128, 165, 169
sense of coherence (Antonovsky), 73
serotonergic system, 164
serotonin, 74, 159, 164
Shahar, Ben, 121, 128, 160
shame, 16, 49, 53, 78, 89, 92, 113, 121, 153
significant others, 5, 50, 52, 101, 170
signs, self-critical, 159–160
silence, 123–124
Skinner, 47, 135
social adjustment, 85
social anxiety, 9, 103, 104, 163
social ecology, 86
social functioning, 61
social inhibition, 26
social institutions, 90, 94
social mentalities (Gilbert), 48–49
social networks, 27–28, 86, 104
social rank, 48–50
social relationships, 15, 16, 86, 106, 110
social roles, 60, 67
social support, 14–15, 19, 50, 72, 85–86, 87, 92, 103, 111, 157
social cognitive theory (Bandura), 93, 136
social-environmental systems, 156
sociotropy, 45–46, 100. See also autonomy
Sociotropy-Autonomy Scale (SAS), 45, 46
   SAS/PSI autonomy, 46
somatoform disorders, 97, 118
Sontag, Susan, 131
standards, 5, 6, 7, 35, 48, 54, 74, 78, 82, 93, 101, 152, 158
   parental, 34, 78, 82
   personal, 5, 6, 7, 34, 35, 48, 54, 74, 93, 101, 152, 158, 163
   self, 93, 158
   social, 73
statistical interaction, 64
stepping out, 150–151
stranger on the train, 113
STREALTH, xvi-xvii, 100, 102, 155, 158, 160, 161, 207
Strenger, Carlo, 89
stress 4, 5, 8, 12, 13, 46, 70, 71, 73, 74–75, 79, 82, 85, 86, 87, 102, 103, 105, 111, 125, 136, 144, 158, 165, 169. See also eventuality, life-stress, PTSD
   achievement-related, 13
   as binding criticism-based relationships, 87
   buffering by self-complexity, 128

diathesis model, 12, 86
   external, 43, 98
   failure-related, 13
   generation, 48, 87, 104, 159
   interpersonal, 13
   minimization, 48
   social, 86
stress-inoculators, 124
stressors, 66, 76, 83, 165
subcortical regions, 79
subgenual cingulate gyrus, 75, 164
subjective inadequacy, 26
subjectivity, 60
   therapist, 112–116, 117, 145, 149–153, 166, 169
submissiveness, 51, 55
substance (ab)use, 8, 9, 11, 36
suicidality, 8, 9, 37, 75, 110, 116, 117, 151, 160
suicide, 31, 83, 91, 153
   attempts, ix, 32, 74, 138
   causes of, 91,
   completed, 165
   ideation, 11, 32, 36
   parental, 153
Sullivan, Harry Stack, 65, 70, 85, 129, 139, 140
supervision
   parental, 90
   therapist, 91, 148–149
symbolic interaction school of thought, 5
symptoms/symptomatic, 97–99, 117

taking a stand, 149–150
TDCRP, 11, 12, 15, 16, 27, 29, 35, 51, 100, 102, 105, 106
teacher-child relationships, 85
temperament, 30, 62, 169, 170
terrorism, 158
therapeutic alliance, 15, 16, 27, 28, 105, 106, 113, 119, 122, 125, 153
therapeutic belief system (TBS) (Rudd & Joiner), 166
therapists, 27, 51, 94, 103, 104, 106, 107, 108, 109, 112, 116, 117, 120, 121, 122, 123, 125, 126, 130, 134, 137, 141, 142, 143, 145, 147, 148, 150, 151, 152, 153, 154, 166, 167, 169, 170
   and parents, 126–127
   authentic self of, 149
   good enough, 58, 114
   life-narrative of, 112
   master, 148
   personality of, 112
   proclivities of, 112
   self-disclosure, 113, 125, 130, 152–153
   subjectivity of, 112–116, 117, 149, 166
   supervision of, 148–149

therapy, xii, 3, 27, 50, 57, 61, 80, 97, 103, 105,
        106, 109, 110, 113, 120, 123, 126, 127,
        128, 129, 131, 133, 141, 144, 145, 146,
        149, 150, 153, 164, 166
    child, 167
    family, 164, 167
    multisessions, 151
    personal, 149
    termination of, 4, 15, 27, 115–116, 136,
        141, 146
Thompson, Clara, 139
thrownness (Heidegger), 64
Tillich, 135, 137
transference, 123, 145–149, 166. *See also*
        countertransference
traumatic events, 32
trial-based cognitive restructuring (de
        Oliveira), 143
trial-based thought record (TBTR), 120
truth, 4, 21, 78
Turning Ruptures into Questions (TRIQ),
        147, 170
two-person psychology, 145, 147
tyranny, 130, 167

Val66Me gene, 75
ventral striatum, 75
ventromedial prefrontal cortex, 149
vicious cycles, 5, 84–86, 88, 90, 92, 93, 107,
        108, 115, 127, 129, 141, 145, 156. *See also*
        ironic cycles
Vico, 165
victimization, 67, 86, 92
voice therapy (Firestone), 119
violence, 9, 105, 126, 150, 158
volunteering, 137–138
vulnerability, xii-xiii, 6, 10, 13, 21, 37, 44, 45,
        50, 54, 56, 74, 76, 85, 86, 89, 93, 100,
        103, 153,

self-critical, xii-xiii, 15, 19, 20, 45, 87, 91, 105,
        110, 121, 153, 157, 158, 163
    active, xii, 47
    and critically-expressed emotion, 85
    depressive, 12
    dimensions of, 21, 53, 124, 155,
    in maladaptive neediness, 44
    internal, 12
    personality, xii, 6, 10, 13, 105
    resilience, 157
    to psychopathology, xii

Wachtel, Paul, xiii, xv, 14, 110, 111, 142, 145
wedge, xiii, 63, 76–78, 80, 90, 92, 93, 107,
        108, 112, 115, 138, 148, 156, 160,
        161, 169
well-baby clinic, 92
well-being, 18, 47, 61, 83, 91, 128
Werner, Heinz, 42, 94
Western culture, 44–45, 75, 79, 88, 90, 138
White, William Alanson, 140
Winnicott, 6, 57, 70, 71, 80, 82, 94, 118, 125, 143,
        147, 166
witnessing, 151
Woolf, Virginia, 139
workplace, 90, 91, 116, 156
worthlessness, 22, 26

Yalom, Irvin, 132
Yoni, 149–150
young adults/adulthood, xiii, 3, 23, 24,
        25, 28, 57, 67, 90, 91, 97, 102, 103,
        105, 113, 116, 117, 128, 130, 131,
        133, 140, 150, 151, 153, 169. *See also*
        adolescents

Zuroff, 11, 13, 15, 22, 27, 29, 34, 102, 160

Ingram Content Group UK Ltd.
Milton Keynes UK
UKHW022327120423
420094UK00003B/129